W9-AEE-847

A GILSON READER

A GILSON READER

SELECTED WRITINGS OF ETIENNE GILSON

Edited, with an Introduction,
by
ANTON C. PEGIS, LL.D., F.R.S.C.
Professor of the History of Philosophy
Pontifical Institute of Mediaeval Studies,
Toronto

HANOVER HOUSE
GARDEN CITY, NEW YORK

Nihil obstat: Rev. T. J. Muckle, C.S.B.,
Censor Deputatis

Imprimatur: ✠ Charles Cardinal McGuigan, D.D.,
Archbishop of Toronto
May 24, 1957

Library of Congress Catalog Card Number 57–11313

Printed in the United States of America

CONTENTS

INTRODUCTION

There is considerable daring, if not presumption, in trying to reduce a living person to a book, and even more daring in turning a writer of over thirty-five books into the neatly arranged contents of a single volume. If it has taken Etienne Gilson so many books to say what he had to say and to discuss what has interested him, how can anyone present him in a book? The "essence" of Gilson, or of any other writer, is not thus caught and embalmed for posterity. Persons are not essences, even concentrated essences, and those who fancy that they have put a man between two covers have not measured the difference between a person, living or dead, and the abstractions he has embodied in words.

I must therefore begin my Introduction by recognizing that its subject lies safely beyond the reach of my pen. And this is as it should be. While publishing his many books in both French and English, and commuting as a teacher between Paris and Toronto, Gilson the scholar has come to stand for three things in the contemporary world: a humble and tenacious pursuit of truth, a zealous and even fierce defense of intellectual freedom, and an enormous erudition. To be sure, anyone who knows anything about the world of philosophy has for many decades been aware of Gilson as a scholar of worldwide reputation, dispassionate and well-nigh impeccable. But non-Catholic readers have seen in him a "liberal" Catholic scholar, which is a remarkable tribute, whereas some Catholic readers have found him too much a Thomist, while still others have been both puzzled and irritated by his effort to discover, beyond the traditions of Thomistic commentators, the personal thought of St. Thomas himself.

What is true in all these reactions is that Gilson has no easily recognizable predecessors with whom to be compared. Both as a historian and as a philosopher, he has been much like a laboratory scientist, examining every problem from the beginning at the moment it presented itself to him. As a consequence, by bringing to his research, his teaching, and his writing an open mind guided by a disciplined judgment, he has achieved results that are landmarks both in history and philosophy. He has been "liberal" because he has looked for philosophical truth without prejudice. This is also why he has come to be a Thomist. But it is only fair to add that Gilson's Thomism is something unique. He has broken Thomistic traditions to reach that Thomism, among them (for example) some long-standing misconceptions on the role of Cardinal Cajetan in the interpretation of the metaphysics of St. Thomas Aquinas. He has given absolutely no comfort to those Thomists who have thought to modernize Thomism by detaching it from the theology of the Angelic Doctor. He has refused to separate in the name of St. Thomas what St. Thomas himself not only did not separate but even offered positive evidence against separating. In the notion of "Christian Philosophy" Gilson has achieved, and is still developing, the culminating moment in a long effort to formulate a philosophy that answers to the nature and the conditions of the Christian man; which is to say a philosophy that is: *rational*, because he is by nature rational; *Christian*, because through faith his reason is living in a state of promotion by revelation; *engaged*, and therefore open and living in its own day, so that it may serve the needs of Catholic education and learning in the modern world.

This is Etienne Gilson, Catholic scholar, historian and philosopher, dedicated to his vocation as a Christian teacher, and seeking in that teaching to be faithful to the light with which God has endowed man in order to serve best as a teacher the light with which God has saved man.

A

Etienne Gilson was born in Paris on June 13, 1884. He was educated at the Petit Seminaire de Notre-Dame-des-Champs and the Sorbonne (1895–1906). After some years spent in high school teaching, he received his Doctorat-ès-Lettres in 1913. His major dissertation was *La liberté chez Descartes et la théologie*. He served in the French army in World War I, was captured at the battle of Verdun, and spent his years of captivity (1915–18) in studying, among other things, the philosophy of St. Bonaventure and the Russian language. In 1919 he was a professor at the University of Strasbourg. In 1921 he was appointed Professor of the History of Philosophy at the Sorbonne, where he had studied with Lucien Lévy-Bruhl and Victor Delbos. During the next ten years he achieved world-wide acclaim as a medievalist and as a writer. In 1932 he inaugurated the first Chair of the History of Medieval Philosophy at the Collège de France. Fifteen years later (1947) he became one of the French immortals: he was received into the small and august body of the Académie Française.

Meantime, Gilson received recognition from the outstanding universities of the world. He was invited to give many well-known lecture series, among them the Gifford Lectures at the University of Aberdeen (1930–31), the William James Lectures at Harvard University (1935), the Richards Lectures at the University of Virginia (1938), the Mahlon Powell Lectures at Indiana University (1940), the Mellon Lectures at the National Gallery, Washington, D.C. (1955). In 1927, while at Harvard University, Gilson was invited by the Congregation of St. Basil to go to Toronto and there carry out his plan of establishing an Institute of Mediaeval Studies. Since its establishment in 1929 in connection with St. Michael's College, in the University of Toronto, the Institute has achieved an international reputation as a graduate school of medieval studies under Gilson's direction. In 1939 the Institute was honored with a Pontifical Charter by Pope Pius XII. The second World War interrupted Gilson's work in Toronto. On January 1, 1951, however, he resigned from his chair at the Collège de France, devoting all his time to the direction of research at the Toronto Institute.

The titles of Gilson's books indicate his productiveness as a scholar and the variety of his interests as a writer. Apart from his work on the seventeenth century, he has written major studies on all the outstanding medieval theologians and philosophers, from St. Augustine to Ockham. What is extraordinary about this writing is the objectivity and sympathetic understanding that he has brought to the interpretation of such diverse personalities. For one historian to have written classical expositions of St. Augustine, St. Bonaventure, St.

Thomas Aquinas, and Duns Scotus is a unique achievement. But perhaps the most important part of that achievement, remarkable as it is in its own right, lies in Gilson himself rather than in his books.

B

Gilson came to the study of medieval philosophy in the middle twenties under the advice of his teacher, Lévy-Bruhl. When he did so, he already had an acknowledged reputation as a student of modern philosophy, and especially of Descartes and the rationalist tradition after him. He brought to medieval studies, therefore, not only the training of the Sorbonne but also a deep knowledge of the Cartesian philosophical reform and revolution. That finished scholar, Lévy-Bruhl, could not have known the consequences of sending a Gilson so prepared into the world of medieval scholasticism. His training enabled Gilson to study medieval thought in a fresh and original way, and to discover within it, not the petrified philosophy stored in the manuals of the early modern schoolmen, but the living and highly individual speculations of medieval thinkers themselves. His knowledge of Descartes, moreover, impelled Gilson to carry on within his own mind a sort of dialogue between medieval and modern thought. Out of this dialogue has grown his distinctive signature as a philosophical historian, a historian who has studied ideas in the laboratory of history and who has come out of that study as a philosophical purist.

Two distinct but closely related aspects of Gilson's work illustrate the point under discussion. When Gilson entered the field of medieval philosophy, there was a commonly received view that the philosophy of the middle ages formed a homogeneous body of ideas that could be called "scholastic philosophy" or "scholasticism." This view was accepted by both the proponents and the opponents of medieval philosophy. Even more, it was accepted by both the Catholic historians of medieval philosophy and the modern scholastic philosophers as well, who looked upon the philosophy of St. Thomas as somehow forming the peak and the model of scholasticism. But when Gilson took up the study of this supposed homogeneous scholasticism, he found that it was neither homogeneous nor common among such medieval thinkers as St.

Anselm, St. Bonaventure, St. Albert the Great, St. Thomas Aquinas, and Duns Scotus, to mention no others. These men were all theologians, and this they certainly had in common; but the philosophical ideas they used in their theologies were far from common. They were often formed in opposition to one another, no less often they were drawn from conflicting philosophical traditions, and when they came from one and the same tradition (for example, the Aristotelian) they traveled over diverse channels and carried divergent doctrinal meanings and intentions.

Such a result led Gilson to an inevitable conclusion. There were several medieval philosophies; there was no common philosophical doctrine called "scholasticism." In the same way, there is no common modern scholastic philosophical doctrine, since these are as many as their medieval predecessors. More than any other historian, Gilson brought to an end the notion of a scholastic synthesis, medieval or modern. This supposed synthesis was, in reality, a syncretism of incompatible philosophical notions unknown to thirteenth-century theologians themselves. At this decisive point began Gilson's comparative study of the philosophical doctrines of the great medieval theologians. The results were likewise decisive. As Gilson discovered, St. Bonaventure never intended to be another St. Thomas; he followed his own and highly devotional road as a Christian thinker. St. Albert, while loyal to the memory of his great pupil, did not agree with the giant from Aquino before or after the latter's death. Duns Scotus did not follow St. Thomas, even to improve upon him. From the beginning he set out on a different philosophical course, opposing St. Thomas for granting too much to nature and St. Bonaventure for granting too little.

But there is more. For the differences among medieval thinkers that Gilson has recorded in his histories and monographs were differences in ideas. Now just as divergent ideas could not be mixed together, so they could not be held together by one and the same mind. One would have to entertain little or no respect for ideas to think otherwise. As a historian, Gilson could be faithful to all sorts of ideas, and he could follow them much in the manner of a scientist following the progress of an experiment. But this very fidelity was preparing

Gilson for a personal philosophical decision in the presence of ideas of a different intellectual texture. The expression of that decision grew slowly, although its direction was evident long before Gilson called himself a Thomist. A Thomist Gilson did become, but one whose Thomism has been a sign of contradiction to his contemporaries. To modern philosophers Gilson is a Thomist and even a scholastic. To scholastic philosophers he seems to be a sort of intransigent Thomist. To other Thomists he appears as an inflexible Thomist who opposes any effort to modernize or develop Thomism as a philosophy in the modern world.

The purism of Gilson appears in all its distinctiveness when the question of the modernization of Thomism is raised. Why should not Thomism establish itself as a philosophy in the modern world, deal with modern problems, put on modern dress, and speak as a modern philosophy among other philosophies? In the presence of this question, Gilson has raised two issues that go to the heart of the matter. Can Thomism become so modern as to answer questions whose existence is *incompatible* with its own point of view? Descartes and Kant are modern philosophers, and they are both distinguished by beginning philosophy with an effort to save the human mind from skepticism. Descartes in his *Meditations* and Kant in his *Critique* diagnosed the human mind, prescribed a method whereby it could avoid skepticism, and then embarked on their philosophies, using minds rendered safe from skepticism by the apparatus of a methodic critique. Moreover, it is a matter of history that Descartes and Kant, instead of saving the certitude of human knowledge, were the founders of idealisms. Descartes never thought himself out of his mind, and Kant never reached (and never could reach) things in themselves. Having set out to establish realism on a sure foundation, both Descartes and Kant established, not realism, but the beginnings of idealism. Nor were Descartes and Kant untrue to themselves in reaching such results: their starting points could lead nowhere else. Now, not only did St. Thomas Aquinas not know the problems of Descartes and Kant, but his philosophical outlook could not be directed toward their problems. Why not? Because he thought that knowledge was naturally evident and naturally realistic. This point is part and parcel of the Thomistic outlook. How, then, can there be a Thomistic answer to the Cartesian problem of knowledge? If this problem is an authentic one, Thomism as a philosophy is worse than out of date; it is dead. If the problem is not an authentic one, no one gains by proceeding as though it is. To Gilson, Descartes's problem is not an authentic one. In this instance, then, for Thomism to become modern cannot consist in answering an unreal philosophical problem; it rather consists in stating and explaining the nature of human knowledge in all its realistic character.

The point of this conclusion can be generalized to apply to the whole question of the modernizing of the philosophy of St. Thomas Aquinas. Here Gilson has been occupied with a fact that is so simple and at the same time so large as to be almost too visible. The philosophy of St. Thomas was the philosophy of a theologian. It is to be found in his theological writings, it is there used for theological purposes, and it has the order and the development necessary to such purposes. What is more, the philosophy of St. Thomas is at its creative best in the service of faith. There is therefore a historical reason for not separating the personal philosophy of St. Thomas from his theology. He never did it. But we can go farther with Gilson and ask: Is there any necessity to do with Thomism what St. Thomas himself did not do? In other words, does Thomism as a philosophy need "to set up shop" outside theology? Does the rational nature of philosophy require this? An affirmative answer to the question would imply that, in order to be properly itself, philosophy must come out of the world of faith and establish itself as the work of reason without the guidance or the direction of revelation. In other words, philosophy cannot be philosophy and Christian at the same time. This position would agree with the view that there have been philosophers in the Western world only before the Christian era and only after Descartes set aside his Catholic faith as one of the conditions of philosophizing properly.

Here is a far-reaching issue to which Gilson has devoted two celebrated books: *The Spirit of Mediaeval Philosophy* and *Christianity and Philosophy*. The historical study of ancient and medieval philosophy has convinced him of what may be called the philosophically creative character of the Christian religion. Plato and Aristotle were philosophical masters for centuries of Christian thinkers, but on any number of crucial questions Christian thinkers created their own ideas to express features of their own Christian world that the Greeks did not know and never voiced. The freedom of God, His love and His generosity, creation, the nature of time and history, the nature of man as a composite of soul and body, human freedom and moral responsibility, human beatitude—all these and similar notions Christian thinkers created in answer to the rational exigencies of their world; they did not find them in any pagan philosopher.

The point hardly needs proving at this date, if only because Gilson proved it decisively twenty-five years ago. Indeed, following the teaching of St. Thomas, Gilson's attention has gone from the question of fact to what may be called the question of principle. It is a fact that St. Augustine transformed Plotinus and an even larger fact that St. Thomas transformed Aristotle. But according to St. Thomas, the Christian faith did not simply come after or replace Greek philosophy. Nor did it even merely correct the errors of Greek reason by the authority of revealed truth. On the contrary, the appeal of the *Summa Contra Gentiles* was ultimately an appeal to the rationality of reason. Christianity could contain all of Greek philosophy and more; the only thing it could not contain was philosophical error. Not only, therefore, could it receive all the philosophy of Aristotle that was true, it could also correct that philosophy where it was not true, and add to it philosophical notions that it never knew. In other words, St. Thomas has taught Gilson that Christianity both respects and promotes the rationality of philosophy, and this it does on religious grounds. Whatever truth there is in the world and whatever rationality there is in man come from the same God Who is the author of the Christian revelation. In principle, reason is at home within revelation, which exists both to fulfill it within itself and to teach it truths about God that are beyond its grasp. How could it be otherwise? As grace perfects nature, so revelation perfects reason. Living within the world of revelation, therefore, the human reason finds itself in an irreversible historical state of rationality unknown to the

Greeks, and it can describe within the world of revelation a rational order of knowledge and of truth that is no less rational in its structure for being the work of a believing reason.

Like other philosophers, Gilson knows that philosophy must be rational in order to be at all. In this sense, philosophy can be only the work of reason, just as it can be only philosophy. Yet this is not the problem. Under the influence of revelation, medieval theologians transformed Greek philosophy in its very rationality. To repeat, this is a historical fact. But in the process of achieving such a transformation of philosophical notions under the teaching of revelation, St. Thomas Aquinas recognized and insisted upon an inherent appropriateness in the situation. The truths that the ancient philosophers were trying to reach, and reached either badly or partly or sporadically or even not at all, were truths that all men needed for the proper direction of their lives. In revealing such truths to men, God was also placing at their disposal notions which, if they so chose, they could use to correct, deepen, and set on the right road the philosophical efforts of the ancient Greeks.

In short, Christian philosophy is more than a fact of history. In becoming Christian, philosophy has discovered (among other things) its own true nature. Far from losing that nature within the world of revelation, philosophy has purified and developed it under the positive influence of faith. Wherever St. Thomas the theologian walked ahead of St. Thomas the philosopher, philosophy gained in truth and in depth. That is why Gilson, reflecting on the teaching and accomplishments of the Angelic Doctor, is resolutely opposed to the Cartesian separation of philosophy from theology that so many scholastics have practiced. On questions of interest to the salvation of man, philosophy has learned from revelation truths that are decisive conquests, and it has learned to follow an order that maximizes the influence of the most basic notion of all; namely, the notion of God as the pure act of being. Under the influence of revelation, philosophy has become, not less, but more rational. Such is the conclusion of Gilson as a historian of philosophy, such is his conviction as a philosopher. Moreover, in reaching this position, Gilson has done nothing more than to join in his own way the views on St. Thomas and Christian philosophy to which Pope Leo XIII gave a lasting expression in the encyclical *Aeterni Patris* in 1879.

The transition from Gilson the philosopher to Gilson the educator is as natural as the transition from the scholar to the philosopher. The comparative study of medieval doctrines brought Gilson to the door of St. Thomas Aquinas. To Gilson the historian of ideas, St. Thomas appeared as the man who successfully met the challenge of Greek intellectualism, and especially the intellectualism of Aristotle and his commentators. In the presence of Aristotelian reason and the philosophical world created by that reason, St. Thomas neither bowed nor fled; he created a philosophical world that was native to Christianity, truly rational in its structure, and one in which Aristotelianism was genuinely alive as a philosophy for the profound and astonishing reason that St. Thomas undertook to say for Aristotle what Aristotle would have said for himself under the same circumstances. No thinker has paid Aristotle a higher compliment than this.

To Gilson the philosopher, moreover, the Thomistic philosophical revolution was a work of pure intelligence. It was the work of a Christian theologian who set out to be a thinker in the service of revealed truth and the measure of whose dedication was his fidelity to intelligence and the purity of its work. Thomistic intellectualism has impressed Gilson both on religious grounds and on its own merits. Like St. Thomas, Gilson is an intellectual missionary, a student and a teacher of Christian truth. Again like St. Thomas, he does not teach his zeal as a Christian; he rather teaches zealously, that is to say, with a total dedication to employing his human reason according to its internal demands as an intellectual power. Only such an employment of reason is defensible in Christian philosophy, since the aim of such a philosophy is to think the truth about God and man with openness and freedom. Indeed, Christian philosophy itself can exist only if the human reason is open both to the truths of faith and to its own light, and if that same reason follows, unreservedly and without fear, both the truth above it and the light within it.

Gilson's educational ideas stem from this equilibrium in his thought. The prime function of education is to teach truth to man as an intellectual being. This does not deny other important objectives in education, but it does insist that unless this objective is achieved, the teaching function of the school is not being achieved at all. To teach is to teach truth to an intellect, the intellect of the student. Today this is an unpopular view with those educators, both Catholic and non-Catholic, who have forgotten or who deny the intellectual nature of man and who use moral and social substitutes for intellectual formation. To Gilson, at least, such substitutes can lead only to intellectual barbarism in education. This barbarism is particularly offensive to the Christian view of civilization and culture, and to the Christian monuments of that civilization and culture. It is even more offensive to one of the most cherished of Christian notions, the notion that the intellectual light in man constitutes in a special way the presence of something divine within him. To educate man is to take part in the growth of something within man of which only God is the master. For man as man is living in a world of truth, a world of which God alone is the author and teacher, of which human teachers are but servants, and in which all men are apprentices to their own rational adulthood so that they may grow to walk in it as free men under their own judgment.

C

On December 28, 1946, the Parisian weekly, *Le Littéraire*, published on its front page an interview with Etienne Gilson by Paul Guth. The subject of the interview was: Is the world going toward a new middle ages? The interview followed a lecture by Gilson at the Collège de France on "Metaphysical Knowledge according to Duns Scotus." Behind this subject lay an important theme: the transition from the Greek age of reason to the Christian age of revelation. Could Aristotle, guided only by the natural reason, prove that the contemplation of God was the last end of man? Could he prove that man will be raised on the last day and enjoy for all eternity the vision of God? He could not, and neither could any other pagan. That is why, according to Duns, the era of the philosophers was over, having given way to the era of the theologians. Here was Gilson, therefore, treating once more the theme of Christian philosophy.

How is it, he was asked by Guth after the lecture, that you chose to study the middle ages? To this Gilson replied: "I owe my interest in letters to the priests of the Petit Séminaire de Notre-Dame-des-Champs. But the man who gave me St. Thomas, the master of my life, was Lévy-Bruhl—the disciple of Auguste Comte, a mind foreign to all religion and all metaphysics. 'You should study the relations of Descartes and scholasticism,' he told me. 'Read St. Thomas.' He sent me on a tour of medieval philosophy before turning to modern philosophy. He did not think that I would stay there." Why did Gilson stay in the middle ages? "Because I found that what was best in the great metaphysical systems of the seventeenth century was no more than some fragmentary remains of a much deeper metaphysics, that of the middle ages. A source is always better than a tributary. Today, medieval ideas are returning to us through German and Danish philosophers. That is why it is better to go back to their beginnings." Then: "One must be ultra-modern to devote one's life to the middle ages." Why? "Idealistic philosophy is dead. Today all philosophies are philosophies of the concrete and of evil: existentialism and Marxism. In the middle ages, Thomism was such a philosophy—a complete philosophy of human destiny." But is Thomism modern? "Thomism is bursting with life; it is the philosophy of the future. It will engage in a philosophical dialogue with existentialism and Marxism, because these are serious philosophies." What will Thomism have to say in the presence of existentialism and Marxism? This:

"Thomism, which is an existentialism in its own right, since I was able to rediscover the importance of *existence* for St. Thomas, sets out from the notion of the human person. It shows that man, as an individual, is part of a group, but as a person endowed with intelligence he transcends the group. One may subordinate the individual to society in material problems; but one must respect the autonomy of man in his intelligence and his soul. According to Aristotle, only a beast or a god can withdraw himself from society. Man is neither the one nor the other. According to Christian Thomism, he is at once a living being forming a part of society and a rational being that transcends society and is the son of God."

Whether these prospects for Thomism will be realized in

the future remains to be seen. But for Gilson we are living *after* what has been called the era of modern philosophy. In this new age, full of historical pressures and conflicts, of new and unexplored philosophical horizons, Thomism is for Gilson a philosophy equipped to deal with man in all the concreteness of his life and in all the existential dimensions of his thought. Gilson came out of the middle ages, therefore, not to rejoin modern philosophy, but to help build a new philosophy in the wake of the death of rationalism and idealism. If the pupil of Lévy-Bruhl names this philosophy Thomism, it is only to recognize its source and to express his gratitude to the Angelic Doctor. Let us simply call this new philosophy Christian philosophy and say of it that it will be open to revelation, existential, and concrete. Let us add that it will owe to Gilson more than one foundation, as well as more than one liberating vision and lesson drawn from the past.

D

The selections that I have included in this volume will enable the reader to see something of the work of Gilson the scholar, the historian and student of Christian philosophy, the Thomist, the educator. In following this thread across his writings, I have had to ignore many subjects that have formed an intimate part of his life. I have given no selections from his writings on art and music, which began in the trenches in the first World War. Nor have I included any of his writings on politics and education in France. I have followed a theme rather than any systematic organization of Gilson's writings. I have tried to show Gilson as a philosophical historian at three distinct phases of his development: the historian of medieval thinkers, the student of Christian philosophy, the disciple of St. Thomas Aquinas. This is the "main" Gilson, the intellectual scholar, the Catholic teacher whose disciplined intellect has served Christianity with a selfless respect for truth, for the intellect itself, and for man.

Of the selections I have chosen, five have not appeared in English before; and, of these, two have never been printed before. I must thank the Reverend L. K. Shook, C.S.B., President of St. Michael's College, Toronto, for allowing me to print "Education and Higher Learning" in this volume. I must also thank the various publishers who permitted me to reprint the other selections from Gilson's publications. Most of all, I must thank Professor Gilson himself for answering many questions and especially for writing "What Is Christian Philosophy?" specifically for this volume. My original selection on this point was the second chapter of *The Spirit of Mediaeval Philosophy*. It was a happy accident that made it impossible for me to use this original selection. As a result, I can include an exposition of Christian philosophy by Gilson that has been written in the light of some twenty-five years of discussion on the subject and summarizes the essential features of a complex and controversial problem as it appears to him today.

Needless to say, Professor Gilson is not responsible for my selections or for my views. As a teacher and a friend, he knows how much I owe him. Yet in expressing my gratitude to him, I would like to acknowledge what I really cannot repay. No one can repay a teacher for what he has received, and I am old enough to realize that teachers do not wish to be repaid. In this spirit, let me add the hope that the present volume may be both a token of friendship and a reasonably faithful approach to its subject.

Yonkers, New York
6 February 1957

ANTON C. PEGIS

A Gilson Reader: Sources

PART ONE: *The Signature of the Man*

1. "The Ethics of Higher Studies," *Harvard Alumni Bulletin*, 30, October 27, 1927, pp. 127–130.
2. "The Intelligence in the Service of Christ the King," *Christianity and Philosophy*, Eng. tr. R. M. McDonald, C.S.B. (New York: Sheed and Ward, 1939), pp. 103–125.
3. "The Distinctiveness of the Philosophic Order," *Philosophy and History*, Essays Presented to Ernest Cassirer, ed. Raymond Klibansky (Oxford: University Press, 1936), pp. 61–76. Eng. tr. D. A. Patton.

PART TWO: *The Historian of Medieval Philosophy*

4. "The Idea of Philosophy in St. Augustine and in St. Thomas Aquinas," *Vie intellectuelle*, 8, 1930, pp. 46–62; also *Acta Hebdomadae Augustinianae-Thomisticae* (Rome-Turin, 1931), pp. 57–87, Eng. tr. A. C. Pegis.
5. "The Future of Augustinian Metaphysics," *A Monument to Saint Augustine* (London: Sheed and Ward, 1930), pp. 278–315.
6. "The Spirit of Saint Bonaventure," *The Philosophy of Saint Bonaventure*, Eng. tr. Dom I. Trethowan and F. J. Sheed (New York: Sheed and Ward, 1938), pp. 470–495.
7. "John Duns Scotus," *History of Christian Philosophy in the Middle Ages* (New York: Random House, 1956), pp. 454–464.
8. "Theology and the Unity of Knowledge," *The Unity of Knowledge*, ed. Lewis Leary (New York: Doubleday & Company, Inc., 1956), pp. 35–46.
9. "Historical Research and the Future of Scholasticism," *The Modern Schoolman*, vol. XXIX, 1, November 1, 1951, pp. 1–10.

PART THREE: *The Disciple of Christian Philosophy*

10. "Greek Philosophy and Christianity," *History of Christian Philosophy*, pp. 540–545.
11. What Is Christian Philosophy? Previously unpublished.
12. "God and Christian Philosophy," *God and Philosophy* (New Haven: Yale University Press, 1941), pp. 38–73.
13. "Science, Philosophy and Religious Wisdom," *Proceedings of the American Catholic Philosophical Association*, vol. XXVI, 1952, pp. 5–13.

PART FOUR: *The Student of Saint Thomas Aquinas*

14. "The Christian Teacher," *The Christian Philosophy of Saint Thomas Aquinas* (New York: Random House, 1956), pp. 3–7.
15. "Haec Sublimis Veritas," *The Christian Philosophy of Saint Thomas Aquinas*, pp. 84–95.
16. "The Spirit of Thomism," *The Christian Philosophy of Saint Thomas Aquinas*, pp. 357–378.

PART FIVE: *The Christian Teacher*

17. *St. Thomas Aquinas and Our Colleagues* (Princeton: The Aquinas Foundation, 1953), 26 pp.
18. "The Eminence of Teaching," *Disputed Questions in Education*, II (New York: Doubleday & Company, Inc., 1954).
19. *Education and Higher Learning*. Printed with the kind permission of the Rev. L. K. Shook, C.S.B., President, St. Michael's College, in the University of Toronto, where the paper was presented as a lecture on the occasion of the centenary of St. Michael's College (1953).

PART SIX: *Summing Up*

20. "Wisdom and Time," *Lumière et Vie*, I, 1951, pp. 77–92, Eng. tr. A. C. Pegis.
21. "Where Is Christendom?", *Temoignage*, January 1, 1956, pp. 29–30, Eng. tr. A. C. Pegis.

PART SEVEN: *The Writings of Etienne Gilson*

PART ONE

The Signature of the Man

An unswerving and open commitment to the truth wherever it is to be found: this is the core of Etienne Gilson the erudite scholar and historian, the philosopher, the man, the Catholic. As a teacher, he has put his scholarship in the service of Truth and not of any prejudice, not even his own. As a Catholic, he has urged theologians and philosophers to know and to respect the nature of intelligence as the prime condition of using it properly at any time, and especially in the service of Christ. As a historian, with a remarkable respect for ideas, he has insisted on the distinctive character of philosophical knowledge in the presence of the conquests of modern science.

1. The Ethics of Higher Studies

Members of the Graduate School of Arts and Sciences: From the very moment I knew I was to address you today, I searched for a subject that would prove of some interest to every one of you. We are here, students as well as professors, representative of the most diverse branches of studies—so diverse, indeed, that in critical moments we sometimes wonder what can possibly be the use of certain extraordinary disciplines that are represented in the catalogues of our universities: the deciphering of hieroglyphics, or the teaching of medieval metaphysics, for instance. At the same time, and apart from any other consideration, we feel that underlying this extreme diversity of interests there is a sort of common denominator, an aim and purpose, that is common to every discipline represented in a university—namely, scholarship. Take branches of studies as widely divergent as you please—sciences, history, literature, or the fine arts—in so far as they are considered as the subject matter of higher studies, they must, all of them, aim toward a certain ideal that is designated by this word "scholarship." This is so evident that universities are more or less entitled to that denomination according as their standards of scholarship are more or less high. I take it for granted that, so far, we all agree. The trouble begins when we try to pass beyond that point and to get a definition of what scholarship is.

I am well aware of the fact that definitions are not always necessary, and perhaps not even possible. But since the old days of Socrates we know that even where they are not necessary they are useful; and we may add that even where they are not possible it is still a profitable thing to attempt them. The more profitable here, as it is not a rare experience for professors to meet young people, especially among the best of their students, who live in sad despair of ever achieving for themselves the wonderful ideal of which some of their teachers are to them the very embodiment. They cannot realize that slow and patient effort can and will lead a mind that knows very little to know very much, and so in their despair of getting immediately what they want, they give it up entirely. Now this is precisely the error I should like to remove from your minds; namely, the false assumption that scholarship is something rare in itself, reserved for a few specially selected persons, which is attained by these few persons only in their old age, and with which we most of us are therefore in no way concerned.

Such an error originates first in the popular misconception that a scholar is a man who knows everything. The more ignorant people are, the more inclined they are to believe that there are men in possession of universal knowledge. Of course it is enough to enter the Widener Library and to glance at its catalogue in order to be radically cured of that disease, so I need not press the matter any more.

I should like to insist, however, on a more refined form of the same error that is common enough among students. While in southern France a few weeks ago, already thoughtful of what I should say to you, I was suddenly arrested by the following advertisement on the door of a shop: "If it is anything concerning motorcars, ask us. We know it." I fell then to thinking that some young people entertain an idea of the scholar which would make him very much like that shopkeeper. I really cannot speak for other branches of learning, but I am at least bound to say that, if scholarship be anything like that, there is no scholarship possible in my own line. If I were invited to nail at my door such a notice: "If it is anything concerning medieval philosophy, ask me. I know it," I should feel obliged to decline so flattering an invitation. The only thing I might possibly venture to add is this piece of advice: Whenever you meet such a notice, don't enter the shop, or you will be sorry for it.

Just as a scholar is not a man who knows everything in general, so he is not a man who knows everything even in his own line. He is a man who knows practically all that can at the present time be known in his line, who realizes his own ignorance and is working very hard to reduce it. Scholarship, therefore, does not consist primarily in the quantity of knowledge a man possesses, but in the way he possesses it;

and as I want to leave you with that idea, I shall tell you immediately that a true scholar is essentially a man whose intellectual life is part and parcel of his moral life; in other words, a scholar is a man who has decided, once for all, to carry all the requirements of his moral consciousness into his intellectual life. If you do it immediately, if you take this pledge and stick to it, you have already begun to be true scholars. If you do it more thoroughly than your teacher does, you have already begun to be a better scholar than he is, and you are on the only road that leads to broad and deep scholarship.

The first virtue you will impose on yourselves by taking such a step will be intellectual honesty. We know perfectly well what moral honesty is, and we would never for the world allow ourselves to sin against it; intellectual honesty is a much less known virtue, and higher studies will precisely teach you what it is. Moral honesty is, at the bottom, a scrupulous respect for the rules of justice; intellectual honesty is a scrupulous respect for truth. This statement may appear, at first sight, as an abstract and verbal parallelism, but try seriously to follow it down to its last consequences, and you will realize what it means. Let us take an example.

It is a frequently and broadly discussed issue, what form higher teaching should assume, and how it should be given out to students; whether, I mean, higher teaching should present itself with its technical difficulties, expressed in a sometimes obscure language and surrounded with all the facts and reasons that can possibly justify its assertions; or if higher teaching is free to express itself in a more popular way, through giving only the more universal and more easily intelligible of its results. Now, there is not the slightest doubt that professors have to teach results; but the higher you rise in the scale of university teaching, the more convinced you feel that if we are here to teach and to learn results, we are here still more to teach and to learn how to get them. A place where men would meet daily for a certain number of months every year with a view merely to absorbing knowledge would be neither a real university nor a place for higher teaching. Before absorbing knowledge, one has to produce it; and to those who reach that point no doubt is left as to what our studies must be. All that heavy and pedantic display of erudition that so much displeases us in many books then receives its own justification.

Of course there is useless and therefore ridiculous erudition. There is, too, and more often than is commonly suspected, sham erudition, which is very speedily detected by the true scholar and is to real learning what hypocrisy is to real virtue. But take a really honest book, a really honest lecture, a really honest dissertation, and you will see that all this display of quotations, references, facts, documents, and observations are there only because it was morally impossible to omit them. The true scholar who gives you a bibliography will certainly give you the titles of all the books he has read concerning the question, and only those titles. He is not the man to quote a book he has never used, or to use a book he never quotes. He would not do it, because he thinks his reader has a right to know whence he derived his information and where one has to look for more. The true scholar never says that a man wrote such and such a sentence without saying at the same time where he wrote it, not because it looks well to make quotations and to give references, but because we have a right to verify his quotation and to see whether, in its original context, the sentence has that very meaning which it seems to have when cut loose from it. If you are a true scholar and write down that quotation for me, you will not write it from memory at the risk of changing a word or two in it, because through changing its words you might change its meaning, impose on a man what he never said, and impose on me the false conviction that this man said what he really had not. There are no negligible details for intellectual honesty any more than for moral honesty.

There are, of course, possible objections to what I have said, and some of them deeply rooted in very old prejudices. It is difficult not to think of a learned man, as of a rather old one, who has had plenty of time to accumulate the quantity of knowledge which makes the difference between the merely cultivated man and the learned one. I do not overlook the difference between the young man who is just beginning his course of studies and the man already rich with the fruits of long labor. My only contention is that quantity can be considered as negligible. For, give me quality, and quantity will follow necessarily, exactly as you start or you strengthen a moral habit every time you act in a righteous way. By and by, through the repetition of the same effort, you achieve an accumulation of knowledge that may be considered as the necessary result of your perseverance in intellectual honesty. Just apply to higher studies the practical remarks of Bain concerning the acquisition of moral habits, namely: "Launch yourselves with as strong and decided an initiative as possible"; and "Never suffer an exception to occur till the new habit is securely rooted in your life." With these two maxims, if you steadily stick to them during your college years, you are bound to acquire an indestructible habit of learning the right things in the right way. I remember having read, in a French translation of William James' *Briefer Course* of psychology, a sentence that has stood before my mind ever since, and is there still as a happy promise: "Let no youth have any anxiety about the upshot of his education. Whatever the line of it may be, if he keep faithfully busy each hour of the working day, he may safely leave the result to itself. He can with perfect certainty count on waking up some fine morning to find himself one of the competent ones of his generation, in whatever pursuit he may have singled out" (p. 150). I was a very young student when I read it, and have never failed to remember it every time discouragement has loomed on my horizon as a dark menace. Let it be to you what it has been to me, the more so as, by bringing to Harvard what Harvard has long ago given to me, I am but returning to its students their own possession.

I have nearly finished, but that which is most difficult to say has not been said. As in painful surgical operations, I shall try to be very short and to get through as quickly as possible. There is a sure recipe for holding the attention and winning the hearts of modern young people; namely, to invite them to the wrecking of old codes and of ancient idols. If you tell them they are perfectly free minds before a perfectly new world, and add, if you choose, that they have a right—nay, a duty—to trample down all the old standards of conduct and knowledge and to lay down the bases for new ones, you are very likely to win their approval. Unfortunately, if adulterated goods may sometimes turn out to be good sellers, buyers, as a rule, are sooner or later sorry they bought them. What I shall preach to you, on the contrary, is a much-neglected, despised, and unpopular virtue; namely, humility. Let us clothe it in a more modern garment and call it submission to truth or, if you care for technical terms, "objectivity." I commend it to you at the risk of displeasing you today, but with the hope of winning your approval in the future.

Certainly there was once a superstition that all that was old was true; but we are now suffering from the contrary and no less dangerous superstition that all that is old is false and all that is new is true. In fact, time has nothing to do with truth. New truth can and must replace old errors, but it cannot replace older truths. If you have a right to say that nothing is true until it has become true to you, this does not mean that it is because a truth has become your own truth that it is true; on the contrary, it had to become yours because it was, is, or will be true to every normal human mind that is able to grasp it. It was very foolish of some men of the middle ages to believe that everything Aristotle had said was true, just because he had said it. But would it not be equally and perhaps still more foolish to believe that everything Aristotle has said is false because he said it four centuries before Christ? When I read in his *Ethics* that justice is the supreme and ruling principle of social life, or that scientific knowledge is the highest form of human activity, am I bound to believe, in order to be original, that injustice is the ideal type of social life and motor driving the most perfect form of human activity? Let us, on the contrary, keep our minds open to every truth, whether it be old or new; let us joyously submit to it, whatever may be the time or the direction from which it comes. Be ready always to yield to it, resolved to stick to it, and it will spare you the burden of yielding to anybody or anything else. Truth will make you free; submission to it will make you great.

Now let us imagine a university where every student would

conduct his own studies according to the rules of the strictest moral honesty, keep his mind open to old truths, and fit himself for the discovery of new ones. One would not consider such a place as a mere nursery of future scholars, but as being already a meeting place of young scholars bound to do credit to their own university and their country.

2. The Intelligence in the Service of Christ the King

"Love not the world, nor the things which are in the world. If any man love the world, the charity of the Father is not in him. For all that is in the world is the concupiscence of the flesh, and the concupiscence of the eyes, and the pride of life; which is not of the Father, but is of the world. And the world passeth away, and the concupiscence thereof: but he that doth the will of God abideth forever." Bossuet recalls these words of the first Epistle of John[1] at the end of his *Treatise on Concupiscence,* and he adds to them this brief but pithy commentary: "the last words of this Apostle show us that the world, of which he is here speaking, is those who prefer visible and transient things to those invisible and everlasting." Allow me to add simply in my turn that, if we attain to an understanding of the meaning of this definition, the mighty problem we have to examine together will resolve itself.

We are in the world; whether we like it or not, it is a fact, and to be there or not to be there does not depend on us; but we ought not to be of the world. How is it possible to be in the world without being of it? That is the problem which has haunted the Christian conscience since the foundation of the Church, and which looms particularly large with regard to our intelligence. For it is quite true that the Christian life offers us a radical solution of this difficulty: to leave the world, to renounce it completely by taking refuge in the monastic life. But in the first place, states of perfection will always remain the portion of an elite; but more important still, the perfect themselves flee from the world in order to save it by saving themselves, and it is a remarkable fact that the world doesn't always even permit them to save it. There will always be among us souls desirous of fleeing from the world, but it is by no means certain that the world will always permit them to flee from it; for not only does the world affirm itself, it does not even want to admit that some renounce it. That is the cruelest injury that can be inflicted on it. Now, the Christian use of the intelligence is an injury of the same sort, and perhaps, among all, that which wounds it most profoundly; for the more it takes account of the fact that the intelligence is the highest thing in man, the more it longs to arrogate its homage and subject it to itself alone. To deny it this homage is the first intellectual duty of the Christian. Why and how? That is what we have to find out.

The everlasting protest of the world against Christians is that they scorn it, and that by scorning it they misunderstand what constitutes the proper value of its nature: its goodness, its beauty, and its intelligibility. That explains the ceaseless reproaches directed against us, in the name of philosophy, of history, and of science: Christianity refuses to take the whole man, and, under the pretext of making him better, it mutilates him, forcing him to close his eyes to things that constitute the excellence of nature and life, to misunderstand the progress of society throughout history, and to hold suspect science which progressively discloses the laws of nature and those of societies. These reproaches, repeatedly flung at us, are so familiar as to cease to interest us; nevertheless, it is our duty never to cease replying to them, and above all never to lose sight ourselves of what is the reply to them. Yes, Christianity is a radical condemnation of the world, but it is at the same time an unreserved approbation of nature; for the world is not nature, it is nature shaping its course without God.

What is true of nature is eminently true of the intelligence, the crown of nature. In the evening of creation, God looked at His work and He judged, says the Scripture, that all that was very good. But what was best in His work was man, created to His image and likeness; and if we seek the basis of this divine likeness, we find it, says St. Augustine, *in mente:* in thought. Let us go further, still following the same doctor: we find that this likeness is in that part of thought which is, so to speak, the summit, that by which, in contact with the divine light of which it is a sort of reflection, it conceives truth. To seize truth here below by the intelligence, be it in an obscure and partial manner, while waiting to see it in its complete splendor—such is man's destiny according to Christianity. Indeed far from scorning knowledge, it cherishes it: *intellectum valde ama.*

Unless, therefore, a person pretends to know better than St. Augustine what Christianity is, he cannot reproach us with betraying it or accommodating it to the needs of the cause by following the advice of this saint: love intelligence, and love it very much. The truth is that if we love the intelligence as much as our adversaries, and sometimes even more, we do not love it in the same way. There is a love of the intelligence which consists in turning it toward visible and transient things: that belongs to the world; but there is another which consists in turning it toward the invisible and eternal: that belongs to Christians. It is, therefore, ours; and if we prefer it to the first, it is because it does not deny us anything the first would give us, and yet it overwhelms us with everything which the other is incapable of giving us.

That there is something in Christianity which its adversaries do not succeed in grasping is clearly seen in the contradictory character of the objections that they address to it, but it is also a consolation for us to note that their objections rest on such misunderstandings. For they reproach it with putting man at the center of everything, but also with underestimating his greatness; and I am willing to admit that we may be mistaken in saying one thing or the other, but not in saying them both at the same time. And what is true of man in general is true of the intelligence in particular. I could let a person reproach St. Thomas Aquinas with having betrayed the spirit of Christianity by unduly exalting the rights of the intelligence, or reproach him for having betrayed the spirit of philosophy by unduly exalting the rights of faith, but I cannot understand how he could do both at the same time. What mystery, therefore, must be hidden in the depths of the Christian man, that his most spontaneous and unvaried steps seem so mysterious to those who observe them from without!

This mystery, for it is really a mystery, is the mystery of Jesus Christ. It is enough to be informed, no matter how vaguely, as to what Christianity is, in order to know in what this mystery consists. By the Incarnation, God became man; that is to say, the two natures, divine and human, are found united in the person of Christ. What is less well known to those who adhere to this mystery by faith is the astonishing transformation which He introduced into all nature and consequently into the manner in which we must henceforth conceive it. One ought rather to say the astonishing transformations, for this mystery includes in it so many others that one would never have done considering the consequences of it.

Let us be content here with examining one of them: that which leads us directly to the heart of our subject. From the moment human nature was assumed by the divine nature in the person of Christ, God no longer dominates and governs nature solely as God, but also as man. If among all men there is one who truly merits the title of Man-God, how could such a one not be also the chief and the sovereign of all the others, in short, their king? That is why Christ is not only the spiritual sovereign of the world, but also its temporal sovereign. But we know, on the other hand, that the Church is the mystical body of Christ: that its faithful are the members of this mystical body, that is to say, according to the doctrine of St. Paul: the members of Christ; all the faithful are, therefore, in so far as they are members of Christ, priests and kings: "*Et quod est amplius*," says St. Thomas, "*omnes Christi fideles, in quantum sunt membra ejus, reges et sacerdotes dicuntur*."[2] There is, then, henceforth, in every Christian, as an image, and even as a participation of this supreme mystery, humanity divinized by grace, reclothed, in its very misery, by a dignity at once sacerdotal and royal, which makes up the mystery of the Christian man.

Of this prodigious transformation of nature by the Incarnation we have an interpretation of incomparable profundity in Pascal, for that is what gives to his work the plenitude of its meaning. That we know God only through the person of Christ, Who was God Himself living, speaking, and acting among us, God showing Himself as man to men in order to be known by them, is too evident; but the great discovery, or rediscovery, of Pascal is to have understood that the Incarnation, by profoundly changing the nature of man, has become the only means that there is for us to understand man. Such a truth gives a new meaning to our nature, to our birth, to our end. "Not only," wrote Pascal, "do we understand God only through Jesus Christ, but we understand ourselves only through Jesus Christ. We understand life and death only through Jesus Christ. Outside Jesus Christ we do not know what life is, nor death, nor God, nor ourselves."[3]

Let us apply these principles to the exercise of our intelligence; we shall immediately see that that of the Christian, as opposed to one which knows not Jesus Christ, knows itself to be fallen and restored, incapable consequently of yielding its full return without grace, and, in this sense, just as the royalty of Christ dominates the order of nature and the order of society, so also it dominates the order of the intelligence. Perhaps we Catholics have forgotten it too much; perhaps we have never even truly understood it, and if ever there was a time that needed to understand it, it is indeed our own.

What, in fact, does this mystery teach us in regard to the ends and the nature of the intelligence?

Like the nature which it crowns, the intelligence is good; but it is only so if, by it and in it, the whole nature turns toward its end, which is to conform itself to God. But, by taking itself as its own end, the intelligence has turned away from God, turning nature with it, and grace alone can aid both of them in returning to what is really their end, since it is their origin. The "world" is just this refusal to participate in grace which separates nature from God, and the intelligence itself is of the world in so far as it joins with it in rejecting grace. The intelligence which accepts grace is that of the Christian. And it is in the abandonment of precisely this Christian state of the intelligence that the world, because of its hate for it, ever urges us to accompany it.

That is what constitutes the real danger for us. We have no doubts concerning the truth of Christianity; we are firmly resolved to think as Christians; but do we know what must be done in order to accomplish that? Do we even know exactly in what Christianity consists? The first Christians knew it, because Christianity then was very near its beginnings, and the adversary against which it fought could not be unknown or misconceived by anyone; it was paganism, that is to say, ignorance at once of sin which damns and the grace of Jesus Christ which saves. That is why the Church, not only then but throughout the ages, has especially recalled to men the corruption of nature by sin, the weakness of reason without Revelation, the impotence of the will to do good when it is not aided by grace. When St. Augustine battled against Pelagius, who called himself Christian and thought himself Christian, it was against an attempt of paganism to restore the ancient naturalism and introduce it into the very heart of Christianity, that the great doctor fought. The naturalism of the Renaissance was another attempt of the same kind and we are still, today, in a world which believes itself naturally healthy, just, and good, because, having forgotten sin and grace, it takes its corruption for the rule of nature itself.

There is nothing in all that which the Christian may not and even ought not to expect. We know that the battle of good against evil will end only with the world itself. What is more serious is that paganism may ceaselessly try to penetrate within Christianity itself, as in the time of Pelagius, and may succeed in the attempt. That is a never-ending danger for us and one which we can avoid only with great difficulty. To live as Christians, to feel as Christians, to think as Christians in a society which is not Christian, when we see, hear, and read almost nothing which does not offend or contradict Christianity; when especially life places an obligation on us, and charity often gives us the duty of not making a visible break with the ideas and customs that we reprove, all that is difficult and hardly possible. That is also the reason why we are continually tempted to diminish or adapt our truth, in order to lessen the distance which separates our ways of thinking from those of the world, or indeed, and sometimes in all sincerity, in the hope of rendering Christianity more acceptable to the world and of seconding its work of salvation.

Hence the errors, the looseness of thought, and the compromises against which, at all times, the zeal of certain reformers has rebelled. The restoration of Christianity to the purity of its essence was in fact the first intention of Luther and Calvin; such is still today that of the illustrious Calvinistic theologian, Karl Barth, who employs all his powers to purify liberal Protestantism from naturalism, and to restore the Reform itself to the unconditional respect of the word of God. We all know how energetically he pursues that aim. God speaks, says K. Barth; man listens and repeats what God has said. Unfortunately, as is inevitable from the moment that a man sets himself up as His interpreter: God speaks, the Barthian listens and repeats what Barth has said. That is why, if we believe this new gospel of his, God would be reputed as having said that, ever since the first sin, nature is so totally corrupted that nothing of it remains but its very corruption, a mass of perdition which grace can indeed still pardon, but which nothing henceforth could ever heal. Thus, then, in order the better to fight against paganism and Pelagianism, this doctrine invites us to despair of nature, to renounce all effort to save reason and rechristianize it.

It is these two perils which ceaselessly plague us, and which, lest our thought be free from all attack, sometimes reduce us to a state of uncertainty as to what is or is not Christian. We forget the golden rule which decides all issues and dissipates every confusion, and one which we ought to have ever present to thought as the light which no obscurity can resist. It is that Catholicism teaches before everything the restoration of wounded nature by the grace of Jesus Christ. The restoration of nature: so there must be a nature, and of what value, since it is the work of a God Who created it and recreated it by repurchasing it at the price of His own blood! Thus grace presupposes nature, and the excellence of nature which it comes to heal and transfigure. As opposed to Calvinism and Lutheranism, the Church refuses to despair of nature, as if sin had totally corrupted it, but she tenderly bends over it, to heal its sores and save it. The God of our Church is not only a judge Who pardons, He is a judge Who can pardon only because He is first a doctor Who heals. But if she doesn't despair of nature, neither does the Church hope that it can heal itself. Just as she opposes the despair of Calvinism, so too she opposes the foolish hope of naturalism, which seeks in the malady itself the principle of its cure. The truth of Catholicism is not a mean between two errors, which would participate in both the one and the other, but a real truth, that is to say a peak, from which it is possible to discover both what the errors are and what makes them to be so. For the Calvinist, a Catholic is so respectful of nature that he is in nothing distinguished from a pagan, save by an additional blindness which makes him degrade even Christianity itself into paganism. But the Catholic well knows that there is nothing in that, and that it is the Calvinist who, confounding nature with the world, can no longer love nature under the world which clothes it, that is to say, love the work of God while hating sin which deforms it. For the pagan, the Christian saint is an enemy of nature, who rushes furiously in a foolish rage to torture it and even to mutilate it; but the Catholic knows well that he chastises nature only out of love for it: the evil which he fights against has entered too deeply into it to be able to be plucked out of it without making it suffer. Just as Calvinism despairs of nature while believing to despair only of its corruption, so naturalism puts its hope only in corruption when it thinks it is putting it in nature. Catholicism alone knows exactly what is nature, and what is the world, and what is grace, but it knows it only because it keeps its eyes fixed on the concrete union of nature and of grace in the Redeemer of nature, the person of Jesus Christ.

To imitate the Church ought to be our rule, if we wish to put our intelligence at the service of Christ the King. For, to serve Him, is to unite our efforts to His; to make ourselves, according to the word of St. Paul, His co-operators, that is to say, work with Him, or permit Him to work in us and through us for the salvation of the intelligence blinded by sin. But to work thus, it will be necessary for us to follow the example He Himself gives us: to free the nature which the world hides from us, to make that use of the intelligence to which God destined it when creating it.

It is here, it seems to me, that we have to make a return on ourselves, to ask ourselves if we are doing our duty and especially if we are doing it well. We have all met, either in history or indeed round about us, Christians who believe they are rendering homage to God by affecting, in regard to science, philosophy, and art, an indifference which sometimes approaches contempt. But this contempt may express either supreme greatness or supreme littleness. I like to be told that all philosophy is not worth an hour of trouble, when he who tells me so is called Pascal, that is to say a man who is at once one of the greatest philosophers, one of the greatest scientists, and one of the greatest artists of all time. A person always has the right to disdain what he surpasses, especially if what he disdains is not so much the thing loved as the excessive attachment which enslaves us to it. Pascal despised neither science nor philosophy, but he never pardoned them for having once hidden from him the most profound mystery of charity. Let us be careful, therefore, we who are not Pascal, of despising what perhaps surpasses us, for science is one of the highest praises of God: the understanding of what God has made.

That is not all. No matter how high science may be, it is only too clear that Jesus Christ did not come to save men by science or philosophy; He came to save all men, *even* philosophers and scientists; and though these human activities are not indispensable to salvation, yet even they have need of being saved as does this whole order of nature which grace has come to repurchase. But it is necessary to be careful not to save them by an indiscreet zeal, which, under the pretense of purifying them more completely, would only result in corrupting their essences. There is reason to fear that this fault is committed quite often, and this with the best intentions in the world, in view of what certain defenders of the faith call the apologetical use of science. An excellent formula, no doubt, yet only when one knows not only what science is, but also what apologetics is.

To be an efficacious apologist, it is necessary first to be a theologian; I will even say, an excellent theologian. That is rarer than we might think, which will be a scandal to those who speak of theology only by hearsay, or are content with reciting its formulas without having taken time to plumb their significance. But if one wishes to make an apologetic from science, it is not even sufficient that he be an excellent theologian; he must also be an excellent savant. I say savant advisedly, and not merely an intelligent and cultivated man more or less anointed by science. If one wishes to practice science for God, the first condition is to practice science for itself, or as if one practiced it for itself, since that is the only way of acquiring it. The same holds for philosophy. It is self-delusion to think to serve God by taking a certain number of formulas which bespeak what one knows ought to be said, without understanding why what they say is true. It is not even serving Him to denounce errors, however false they may be, while showing that one does not even understand in what they are false. At least we can say that it is not serving Him as a savant or as a philosopher, which is all we are for the moment concerned in showing. And I will add that the same thing holds for art, for it is necessary to possess it before pretending to put it at the service of God. We are told that it is faith which constructed the cathedrals of the middle ages. Without doubt, but faith would have constructed nothing at all if there had not also been architects; and if it is true that the façade of Notre Dame of Paris is a yearning of the soul toward God, that does not prevent its being also a geometrical work. It is necessary to know geometry in order to construct a façade which may be an act of love.

Catholics, who confess the eminent value of nature because it is a work of God, let us therefore show our respect for it by positing as the first rule of our action, that *piety never dispenses with technique*. For technique is that without which even the most lively piety is incapable of using nature for God. No one, nor anything, obliges the Christian to busy himself with science, art, or philosophy, for other ways of serving God are not wanting; but *if that is the way of serving God that he has chosen*, the end itself, which he proposes for himself in studying them, binds him to excellence. He is bound, by the very intention which guides him, to become a good savant, a good philosopher, or a good artist. That is for him the only way of becoming a good servant.

Such is, after all, the teaching of the Church and the example she has transmitted to us. Did not St. Paul say that "the invisible perfections of God, His eternal power and dignity are, since the creation of the world, rendered visible to the intelligence by means of His works?" That is why so many doctors, who were at the same time savants, lovingly bent over the work of creation. For them, to study it is to study God in His works; never did a St. Albert the Great think to know enough about nature, because the better he knew it, the better also he knew God. But there are not two ways of knowing it: a person possesses science or he doesn't possess it, he studies things scientifically or is resigned to never knowing anything about them. St. Albert the Great became, therefore, first of all a savant, in the proper sense of the term. Of those who are astonished or scandalized, he says that, brute beasts, they blaspheme what they do not know. He knows what he is doing: he does not wait until the care of repairing an evil already committed obliges him to busy himself in his turn with science in order to remedy it. He does not believe in the policy of letting the adversaries do everything with the intention of later joining their school in order to learn laboriously the use of the weapons that will be turned against them. Albert studied the sciences against no one, but for God. When you find a man of that sort, he does not waste his time proving that the teaching of science does not contradict that of the Church: he suppresses the question by his example, showing the world that a man can be a man of science, because he is a man of God. Such is also the attitude the Church recommends to us. By making St. Albert the Great the patron of Catholic schools, she reminds us permanently that these schools ought never be afraid of placing the level of their teaching and of their scientific exigencies too high. Everything is worth the trouble of being well done that is worth the trouble of being done for God.

Still we must never forget that it is for Him that it is being done, and to forget that is the second danger which threatens us. To serve God by science or art, it is necessary to begin by practicing them *as if* these disciplines were in themselves their own ends; and it is difficult to make such an effort without being taken in. So much the more difficult is it when we are surrounded by savants and artists who treat them effectively as ends. Their attitude is a spontaneous expression of naturalism or, to give its old name, which is its name for all time, of paganism, into which society ceaselessly tends to fall back because it has never completely left it. It is important, however, to free ourselves from it. It is impossible to place the intelligence at the service of God without respecting integrally the rights of the intelligence: otherwise it would not be the intelligence that is put at His service; but still more is it impossible to do so without respecting the rights of God: otherwise it is no longer at His service that the intelligence is placed. What has to be done in order to observe this second condition?

Here, with due apology, I am going to be obliged to play the thankless role of one who denounces errors, not only among his adversaries, but among his friends. To excuse such a one, it is necessary to remember that he who accuses his friends accuses himself in the first place. The ardor of his criticisms expresses above all the consciousness of the fault which he himself has committed and into which he always feels in danger of falling again. I believe, therefore, that I ought to say, first of all, that one of the gravest evils from which Catholicism suffers today is that Catholics are no longer proud enough of their faith. This lack of pride is unfortunately not incompatible with a certain satisfaction in what Catholics do or say, nor with an optimistic air more proper in a party than in a Church. What I regret is that instead of confessing in all simplicity what we owe to our Church and to our faith, instead of showing what they bring to us and what we would not have without them, we believe it good politics or good tactics, in the interests of the Church itself, to act as if, after all, we distinguish ourselves in no way from others. What is the greatest praise that many among us may hope for? The greatest that the world can give them: he is a Catholic, but he is really very nice, you would never think he was one.

Ought not the very contrary be desired? Not indeed Catholics who would wear their faith as a feather in their hat, but Catholics who would make Catholicism so enter into their everyday lives and work that the unbelieving would come to wonder what secret force animated that work and that life, and that, having discovered it, they would say to themselves, on the contrary: he is a very good man, and now I know why: it is because he is a Catholic.

In order that we may be thus thought of, it is necessary that we ourselves believe in the efficacy of the divine work in transforming and redeeming nature. Let us believe in it, and let us say so on occasion, or at least let us not deny it when we are asked about it. That is not what we always do. If there is one principle that our doctors have transmitted to us and insistently recommended, it is that philosophy is the handmaid of theology. Not a single one of the great theologians has not said so; not one of our great popes has failed to recall it to us. And yet it is hardly the fashion to speak of it today, even among Catholics. Men endeavor rather to show that the formula does not really mean what it appears to mean. They think it clever to present the Christian who philosophizes as a good philosopher, because he philosophizes as if he were not a Christian. In short, just as he is a very good man, he is a very good philosopher: it isn't noticeable that he is a Catholic. What would be interesting, on the contrary, would be a philosopher who, like St. Thomas or Duns Scotus, would take the lead in the philosophical movement of his time, precisely because he was Catholic.

It seems to be thought sometimes that a philosophy which confessed itself Catholic would be discredited in advance, and that, in order to make truth accepted, the cleverest way is to present it as if it had nothing to do with Catholicism. I am afraid that that is even a tactical error. If our traditional philosophy doesn't find today the audience we would wish for it, it is not at all because it is suspected of being sustained by a faith, it is indeed rather because, being so, it pretends not to be so, and because no one wishes to take seriously a doctrine which begins by denying the most evident of its sources. Run through the history of French philosophy in these latter years; you will see that Catholic thinkers have been taken seriously by the unbelieving in the exact measure in which they have put in the first place what, for them, is really first: the person of Jesus Christ and His grace. Let a Pascal or a Malebranche be born to us tomorrow, I promise them that no one will reproach them for being Catholics, for everybody will know that their Catholicism itself is the source of their greatness. They will wonder: whence comes this greatness to them, and perhaps will desire the faith which has given it to them.

It doesn't depend on us that we be a Pascal, a Malebranche or a Maine de Biran, but we can prepare the ground which will favor the action of their successors when they do come. We can so act that it may become easy for their successors to surpass these great minds, by clearing the ground of difficulties which, avoidable in themselves, might otherwise retard their action. We shall do so only by restoring in their fullness the Christian values; that is to say, above all by fully reestablishing the primacy of theology.

Here, as before, and with perhaps even greater emphasis,

I will say that the great danger consists in thinking that, for the intelligence which wishes to refer itself to God, piety dispenses with technique. One might be tempted to address the contrary reproach to those who lean in that direction, and tell them that they act as if technique took the place of piety for them, but I do not think that that is what happens. Such men have not only acquired a faultless mastery of their science or art and are at times the admiration of their equals; they have also kept the most integral faith joined to the most lively piety. What they lack is that they do not know that, in order to link together the science they have acquired with the faith which they have preserved, a technique of faith is necessary along with that of science. What I see in them—rather let us say what we perceive fundamentally in ourselves—as an ever-present difficulty, is the inability of getting reason to guide itself by faith, because, for such a collaboration, faith no longer suffices; what is wanting is that sacred science which is the keystone of the edifice in which all the others ought to take their place; namely, theology. The most ardent theologian, animated by good intentions, we have said, will do as much harm as good if he pretends to "utilize" the sciences without having mastered them; but the savant, the philosopher, the artist, animated by the most ardent piety, run into the worst misfortunes if they pretend to refer their science to God without having, if not mastered, at least practiced the science of divine things. Practiced, I say, for, like the others, this science is learned only by practicing it. It alone can teach us what is the last end of nature and of intelligence, putting before our eyes these truths which God Himself has revealed to us and which enrich with such profound perspectives those truths which science teaches. As a converse, therefore, of what I said of an apologist, I will say here that it is possible to be a savant, a philosopher, and an artist without having studied theology, but it is impossible without it to become a Christian savant, philosopher, or artist. Without it, we can indeed be, on the one hand, Christians, and on the other hand savants, philosophers, or artists, but never without it will our Christianity descend into our science, into our philosophy, into our art, to reform them from within and vivify them. For that, the best will in the world would not suffice. It is necessary to know how to do it, in order to be able to do it; and, like the rest, it cannot be known without being learned.

If, therefore, we owe to our Catholicism our respect for nature, for the intelligence and the technique by which the intelligence scrutinizes nature, to it also we owe the knowledge of how to direct this science toward God, Who is its Author: *Deus scientiarum dominus.* And just as I permitted myself to recommend the practice of the scientific disciplines or artistic disciplines *to those whose vocation it is to serve God in these domains*, so also I permit myself to recommend with all my power the teaching and practicing of theology to all those who, having mastered these techniques, seriously want to refer them to God.

We must not conceal from ourselves that, in the one case as in the other, it is a question here of undertaking a long effort. Nothing less will be necessary than the collaboration of all good wills qualified to succeed therein. We are here facing a new problem, which demands a new solution. In the middle ages, the sciences were the privilege of the clerics; that is to say, of those who possessed by their very state the science of theology. The problem, therefore, did not arise for them. Today, owing to an evolution, the investigation of which is not within our present scope, those who know theology are not those who make science, and those who make science, even when they do not despise theology, do not see the least inconvenience in not knowing it. There could be nothing more natural on the part of those who are not Catholics, but nothing more abnormal on the part of those who make profession of Catholicism. For even if they experience the most sincere desire of putting their intelligence at the service of their faith, they will never succeed in doing so, because the science of faith is wanting to them. In order for them to succeed in that, it is necessary that they be taught, not how to make it (it is for them to find it), but what this sacred truth is with which their intelligence longs to be inspired.

It is important, therefore, to understand that we are living in a time when theology can no longer be the privilege of some specialists devoted to its study by the religious state which they have embraced. Doubtless the clerics ought to consider it as their proper science and retain the mastery in it, for it belongs to them in full right; and not merely retain it but exercise it in all its fullness, for it is a question of life or death for the future of the Christian life, in souls as well as in society. As soon as theology surrenders the exercise of its rights, it is the word of God which gives up making itself heard, nature which turns away from grace, and paganism which reclaims the rights that it has never surrendered. But, inversely, if it be desired that the word of God make itself heard, hearers are necessary to receive it. It is necessary that those who wish to work as Christians in the great work of science, philosophy, or art, themselves know how to hear His voice, and not only be instructed in His principles, but also and above all be imbued with them.

Here, less than anywhere else, it is neither the number nor the extent of the knowledges which is important; it will be sufficient to choose a very small number of fundamental principles, provided that the thought of those who receive them be impregnated with them, and that they inform it from within to the point of becoming one with it, of living in it and through it, as a grafted limb, which draws to itself all the sap from the tree in order to make it bear its fruit. To choose these principles, organize the teaching of them, give it to those she judges worthy of it, is the work of the teaching Church, not of the Church taught. But if the latter can in no case pretend to the mastery, it can at least present its demands and make known its needs. That is all I have wished to do, by demanding that the truth of faith be taught in its fullness and that the magisterial function of theology recover its full authority.

I would be nourishing the most naïve illusions if I thought I were now setting forth popular opinions. They are not so among the unbelieving, who are going to accuse me (some have already done so) of wishing to rekindle the funeral piles of the Inquisition and entrust the control of science to the Court of Inquisition. They are not so even among certain Catholics who, knowing that such ideas lead to such retorts, do not judge it expedient, in the interests of religion itself, to expose themselves to them. To reply to them, however, it is not necessary to reopen the discussion of what were the Inquisition and the affair of Galileo. Whatever happened in former times, the official and constant doctrine of the Church is that science is free in its own domains. No one pretends that philosophy and physics can or ought to be deduced from theology; St. Thomas even taught the exact opposite against certain of his contemporaries who were making of what we call today positive science a particular case of Revelation. To demand that science and philosophy regulate themselves under theology is first of all to ask of them to agree to recognize their limits, to be content to be a science or a philosophy, without pretending to transform themselves, as they are constantly doing, into a theology. It is also to ask of them to take into consideration certain truths taught by the Church regarding the origin and the end of nature and of man, not always with the intention of transforming them into so many scientific truths and to teach them as such (for they may be objects of pure faith) but to avoid in their researches aimless adventures, which are ultimately much more prejudicial to science itself than they can be to Revelation. The greater the authority of faith, the more those who are qualified to speak in its name ought to use prudence and wisdom before committing themselves, but the more exacting and rigorous the scientific disciplines in the matter of proofs, the more scrupulous ought they to be in putting on an equal footing all that they teach: the observed fact, the hypothesis controlled by experience, and the theory which, withdrawn from all experimental control properly so called, will be replaced tomorrow by another, although today it is imposed to all intent and purpose as a dogma. A visit to the cemetery of scientific doctrines that were irreconcilable with Revelation would take us by a great many graves. In our own lifetime, in the name of how many doctrines, abandoned since by their very authors, have we been summoned to renounce the teaching of the Church? How many false steps from which historians and savants would have been saved if they had listened to the voice of the Church when she warned them that they were exceeding the limits of their competence; that is to say, those of science itself? We ask of them nothing else: to renounce those costly and sterile experiments, and to recognize, in this sense, the primacy of theology, is precisely to renounce them.

Thus, therefore, to restore in their fullness the theological values, to do so in such a way that they descend into the thought of the savant who calculates or who experiments, into the reason of the philosopher who meditates, into the inspiration of the artist who creates, is truly to place the intelligence in the service of Christ the King, since it is to promote the coming of His reign, by aiding nature to be born again under the fruitful action of His grace and in the light of His truth. Such is the end, such also the means, and there is no other, for the only service that Christ demands from us is to aid Him in saving the world; but it is His word alone that saves. In order to co-operate with Him, let us therefore first of all listen to His word, repeat it as does the Church, and not hesitate to make it publicly when necessary. It does not depend on us that it be believed, but we can do very much toward making it respected; and if it happen that those among us who are not ashamed of the Gospel fail to get others to follow us, those who are ashamed of it can be sure not even to get others to respect them.

NOTES

1. I John 2:15–17.
2. *De Regimine Principum*, I, chap. 14.
3. *Pensées*, no. 548, ed. L. Brunschvicg (Paris: Librairie Hachette, 1920), p. 572.

3. The Distinctiveness of the Philosophic Order

Among the reasons for the discredit in which scholastic philosophy is held today there is none which goes deeper or contains more truth than the sterility of medieval thought in the scientific sphere, and the present-day difficulty of reconciling that philosophy with the conclusions of positive science. This sterility is an undoubted fact; but it was not an absolute sterility as is sometimes supposed by the ill informed. In the thirteenth century, in the universities of both Paris and Oxford, there were men who conceived the possibility of a natural science of a type either purely mathematical, comparable with that of Descartes, or empirical, like that of Aristotle; and yet they did not for a moment doubt that such a science could be reconciled with theology. For reasons doubtless complex, the attempt was a failure; and it remains true that there is not, properly speaking, one single great scientific discovery which can rightly be ascribed to the middle ages, and that even if we should succeed in ascribing several, they would prove to be due to the initiative of isolated individuals whose thinking was outside the orbit of contemporary thought.

The most important consequence of this fact is that the great uprush of science in the seventeenth century, not having received its impetus from medieval philosophy, rose in direct opposition to it. Apart from the possibly unique case of Leibniz, who had a very deep and close affinity with Aristotle, there was scarcely a thinker round about the year 1630 for whom the choice did not seem inevitably to lie between science with its proofs on the one hand, and scholasticism with its uncertainties on the other. From then onward the complaint made of the middle ages is not only that its speculations bore no practical fruit—an objection that we have already stated to be superficial[1]—but also and more particularly that it was unproductive in the sphere of thought: a very grave objection this time, especially since Peripatetic philosophy which was incapable of producing modern science, fought against it from the day of its birth, combating it in the fields of astronomy, physics, biology, and medicine, and meeting with a series of well-deserved defeats from which it has not yet recovered.

Facts such as these, of which it would be only too easy to collect historical evidence, are more than facts; they are indications of certain ideas. If scholasticism was not the mother of modern science, treated it indeed as a stepchild, it was probably not because of some kind of historical accident, but for reasons whose nature it is our task to discover. The whole question comes to this: Is its philosophic essence as such incompatible with the spirit of positive science? So the majority believe, and if it were so, we should not for a moment hesitate to abandon it; but it is our belief that scholastic philosophy has only to become more completely true to its own essence than it has ever been, in order to be reconciled with science and even to help in its development.

If we are to grasp the meaning of this problem, perhaps the simplest way will be to go back to its original data and try to find out what led to the break between the middle ages and modern thought. As we are studying it in its philosophic aspect, it is from a philosopher we must seek the explanation, and on this point no one can enlighten us better than René Descartes. The *Discours de la méthode* appeared indeed too late to kill scholastic philosophy, for the creative powers of thought had long since turned aside in other directions; but it remains true to say that it was Descartes who drew up its death certificate. He analyzed the causes; he pointed out what was obstructing its thought and so crushing out its life; he defined the rules of a method which was productive of new truths simply because it was opposed at every point to the old method: and to do all this was to do more than abandon the old philosophy—it was to suppress it by putting something else in its place. The actual way in which Descartes replaced it is sufficiently remarkable to deserve our attention.

All Cartesianism, and in a sense all modern thought, can be traced back to a winter night in 1619 when, in a living room in Germany, Descartes conceived the idea of a universal mathematics. From our present point of view the details of the method which he later evolved from it matter little. What was, and still remains, of capital importance is the spirit of that discovery, even, for the moment, one particular aspect of that spirit. A young mathematician in the ardor of his first scientific triumphs conceives the possibility, even the necessity, of applying generally to all problems indiscriminately the method which has lately brought him such dazzling success. Never in the history of human thought has there been known a shift of perspectives more tremendous or more daring than this, and on it we still live today.

It involved philosophy in a formidable adventure which, according to one's point of view, may be regarded either as the true beginning of its progress or the gravest of its crises. The first consequence of the mathematical method of Descartes, that from which all the others spring, was the obligation imposed on the philosopher to proceed always from thought to existence; even to define existence always in terms of thought. For the mathematician the problem of essence always comes before that of existence: the true circle and the true triangle are the definitions of the circle and the triangle; the figures produced in sensuous experience are only approximations to their definitions. It is not by chance that geometry is the science of sciences for Descartes as for Plato. In any case, the systematic application of the mathematical method to the real could have only one immediate result: the concrete complexity of things was replaced by a certain number of clear and distinct ideas, themselves conceived as being the true reality. To go back to the experiment of Descartes, the real from this point of view is reduced to two ideas and therefore to two substances—thought and extension. And since it is in the nature of ideas to be mutually exclusive, each containing everything that comes under its definition and nothing more, so it follows that it must be in the nature of substances to be mutually exclusive, each containing everything that comes under its definition and nothing more.

It is difficult to exaggerate the far-reaching effect upon philosophy of such a reform. Up to the time of Descartes, and particularly during the middle ages, it had always been admitted that philosophy consisted in the transposition of reality into conceptual terms. In this sense it is entirely just to describe it as an abstract conceptualism; but it is not just to accuse it of having *thingified* its concepts. On the contrary, the invariable method of the scholastic philosopher was to proceed from things to concepts: thus he required several concepts to express the essence of one single thing, according as he multiplied his points of view concerning it; and consequently no one was less liable than he to take for reality what he had extracted from the real. To convince ourselves of this we have only to consider the case of any substance. For the scholastic it consisted always of matter and form—that is to say, two concepts—although neither was matter anything apart from form, nor form anything apart from matter. It was not St. Thomas who *thingified* concepts, but Descartes: and he could not avoid it once he began to raise our concepts to the status of Ideas. He took ideas abstracted from reality and turned them into models: and it is not enough to say that reality must conform to them; they are the reality itself. The divergence between the two philosophies on this point leaps to the eye when one considers that for Descartes every substance is known because it is reduced to the content of his idea, whereas for the scholastic every substance as such is unknown because it is something other than the sum of the concepts we extract from it.

By turning the concrete into a mosaic of clear ideas, the mathematical method of Descartes raised difficulties whose solution was sought throughout the whole of the seventeenth and eighteenth centuries; in the nineteenth century it led in the end to despair—despair of philosophy itself. A universe of extension and thought can be expressed only in a deterministic philosophy to which corresponds an equally deterministic science: on the one hand, pure spiritualism; on the other, pure mechanism. From the outset nothing could be more satisfactory for science, and this is only natural; having set the method, it is bound to find itself in the results. But it is a different matter for philosophy: having given up the right to a method of its own, it must attempt to recover philosophic results with the help of a method which is not philosophic.

How can the domain of pure thought ever be in touch with the domain of pure extension when the property of substances is to be mutually exclusive? This is what Descartes does not tell us. He allows us a thought (not a soul), and extension (not a body): he is unable to account for the union of soul and body. When he offers as the solution a third idea, that of a union of soul and body whose truth may be felt but not known, he is himself contradicting his whole method of clear and distinct ideas. What Leibniz said remains true: "At that point Monsieur Descartes withdrew from the game." When others after him take up the problem of "communication of substances," they take it up on exactly those foundations laid by Descartes; consequently they involve themselves in a series of costly hypotheses, each of which, however much it differs from the rest, comes back at last to joining by a bridge fragments of the real between which the Cartesian method had dug a ditch which could not be crossed. It is, by definition, impossible to go direct from one to the other, so it is no surprise that the bridge must pass by way of God. The occasionalism of Malebranche, the pre-established harmony of Leibniz, the parallelism of Spinoza are so many metaphysical "epicycles" to solve an ill-stated problem by rescuing, with the aid of complementary devices, the very principle which makes the problem insoluble. The great metaphysical systems of the seventeenth century are pure works of art, possibly the most perfectly adjusted systems of ideas ever produced, and precisely because, like mathematics, they deal with pure ideas, they are entirely unhampered by the complexities of the real. What does hamper them is the difficulty of obtaining contact with reality. Having eliminated quality from extension, they are incapable of accounting for it when it reappears in thought. They set out in triumph from the idea, and in the end it is sensation they have failed to explain—that inferior act, suspect, even contemptible if you will, which yet reveals something which is not pure thought since it does not belong to the intelligible, and still is not extension since it already belongs to thought. The multiplicity of contradictory hypotheses required by the application of a principle may not be a proof of the falsity of that principle, but it is an indication of it. This is a case for returning to the rule of "economy of thought" dear to Ernst Mach: the increasing complications in which these theories involve inquiry call us to look for simpler theories and to give them the preference.

The problem of the communication of substances raised insurmountable difficulties when it came to passing from one order of substance to another; the difficulty of passing from one substance to another within the same order was no less, for it was exactly the same. Malebranche saw this clearly, and if he radically denies all causal efficacy—that is to say, all transitive causality—in the order of secondary causes, it is precisely because, every substance being really distinct from any other, that sort of mutual participation of substances which causality is becomes in his system an impossibility. The monad of Leibniz, a simple indivisible entelechy which can begin only by creation and end only by annihilation, has "no windows through which anything can go in or out." Nothing could be more logical, but what follows in the history of philosophy is no less so. The lesson taught by Malebranche was not lost, and it was David Hume who took it up: if we do not understand how a body can act upon a body, or a thought upon a thought, or a body upon a thought, or a thought upon a body, we shall understand no better how it is possible for a thought, even a supreme thought, to act upon bodies; for our whole idea of God is derived from our experience, and it is impossible for us to have any idea of the causality of God when we have no idea of our own.[2] The skepticism of Hume, then, is in the direct line of descent from the mathematical method of Descartes: it expresses only the impossibility of re-establishing real relations between substances once we have made a radical separation between them. After Hume, if Kant was to save a causality which could not be found in things, all that was left for him to do was to make thought impose causality upon things. In this way the Cartesian cycle was completed with the purity of a perfect curve and in accordance with the demands of its original principle: starting from mind, philosophy, after several fruitless attempts to get outside it, declared its definite intention of remaining inside. This resignation must not, however, be regarded as a triumph: it recalls that of Descartes when, having given up the attempt to prolong the life of man, he declared himself content to teach him not to fear death.

We should be strangely in error if we supposed that the effects of the mathematical method made themselves felt only in metaphysics; they spread to moral science and thence to sociology. In this the initiator was no longer Descartes but Thomas Hobbes, of whom, indeed, Descartes thought highly, though rather for his political philosophy than for his metaphysics.[3] What we are given in reality is a concrete complexity whose component parts are interdependent. Man is not only a rational animal but a political animal, because the State is the necessary condition of the perfect development of his rationality. For this reason the individual is invariably given to us in a State, outside of which he could not fully realize his essence, or even live, although the State itself has no life except in the individuals who are its very substance. It is then equally true to say that nothing is found in the individual which does not come to him from society, and that there is nothing in society which does not come to it from the individuals, since it forms them and they compose it.

Let us, on the other hand, imagine this complex reality decomposed into ideas each defining a substance: the individual would then become a thing in itself, the State would become another, and we should have a new problem of the communication of substances, as insoluble as the first. This is where Hobbes led modern thought when he defined men as isolable individuals, equal, for practical purposes, in the faculties of both body and mind.[4] As a result of this political Cartesianism, the individual found himself set up as a being by himself, and consequently an end in himself, the subordination of which to the State as a higher end became difficult, if not impossible. From that moment the political problem became what it was still for Rousseau: how to find in the individual, as such, a reason for subordinating him to something other than himself—a problem even more difficult than the squaring of the circle with ruler and compasses. It is clear that for a social atom such as Hobbes's individual the right of nature is simply freedom to make use of any means he thinks fit, in order to secure his own good:[5] every man, says the *Leviathan*, has by nature a right to every thing. How, in that case, are we to reconstruct a social body with such liberties? How can it be contrived that in the name of my own right what is mine ceases to be mine? Out of this come all the "social contract" theories which by various devices attempt to induce certain rights, laid down in the first place as absolute, to renounce themselves; which amounts to producing servitude from an aggregate of liberties.

Stated in those terms, the problem was so difficult that it could not fail to produce an abundance of attempts at its solution; but logically these were bound to lead to recognition of the contradictory nature of the problem, and to set up, one against the other, these two antinomic realities which can never be reconciled. On the one hand, we have the individual in the pure state; and as the definition of the individual as such is to exist by itself, so we arrive at the anarchic individualism of Max Stirner,[6] or the aesthetic individualism of Nietzsche. The Individual and his property. Nothing could be more logical; and Stirner proved himself a philosopher in his ability to push an idea to the purest formulation of its essence. If the individual is only an individual, then it is illogical to seek to produce the collective from the individual: the logical thing is the radical elimination of the State as a restraining force. But suppose, on the other hand, we take the collective as such; its very essence is the negation of the individual, and therefore it becomes a contradiction to construct it of individuals: and then it is Comte and Durkheim who are the true philosophers. "Man is nothing; it is Humanity which is everything." Here again nothing could be more coherent, for in a collective being as such, the individual as such can find no place; he finds himself eliminated, reduced, denied, in advance and by definition. Modern society, therefore, in so far as it attempts to reform itself on the model of its own doctrines, is condemned to oscillate perpetually between anarchism and collectivism, or to live empirically by a shameful compromise which is without justification.

The cult of antinomies in modern philosophy is not a surprising phenomenon. Kant comes up against them; Hegel lives by them and thinks that the endeavor to overcome them constitutes philosophy itself. The whole endeavor of medieval philosophy, on the other hand, was to avoid them. For St. Thomas and for Duns Scotus, the fact that they are reconciled in the real proves that they are not insurmountable, and that if we concentrate on representing the real as it is, we ought not to encounter them. So it is actually we who introduce them by our mathematical method. If there is an initial error at the origin of all these difficulties in which philosophy has become involved, then it must be the error made by Descartes when he decreed, *a priori*, that *the method of one of the sciences of the real was valid for the sum of the real.*

Such a decision was bound to entail, sooner or later, much more than philosophic difficulties: it meant the disappearance of philosophy itself. Whatever indeed be the science whose processes are set up as a universal method, we are condemned in advance to extract from that method only what it is capable of giving; and that is science, not philosophy. Few mathematicians today would concede to Descartes that his *Méditations* are, as he liked to imagine, as certain as, or even more certain than, mathematics. And yet, considered in itself and without reference to the difficulties it involves, a mathematical type of metaphysics remained a possibility, because in both cases thought proceeds by construction of ideas and belongs to the order of pure ideas. It is only with the greatest difficulty that Cartesian metaphysics can recover the conclusions of scholastic metaphysics—the spirituality of the soul, the existence of God, the existence of matter; but it does in the long run recover them, and so may keep the consciousness of its own existence. It is entirely otherwise with Kant, for whom the physics of Newton provided the standard scientific method. All physical knowledge presupposes sensuous intuition; if then it is in relation to physical knowledge that we judge of other kinds of knowledge, it is clear that where sensuous intuition is absent, knowledge also is absent. At once it stands to reason that the fate of metaphysics as a science is settled in advance. Deprived of concepts, it is left with nothing but Ideas, in whose antinomies it becomes finally imprisoned.

It was from that moment when philosophy was despaired of as a science that there began the search for its justification in an order foreign to that of rational knowledge. Kant, who would not and could not do without philosophy, attempted to find a basis for the conclusions of metaphysics as postulates of moral science. Comte, who once and for all reduced objective knowledge to the knowledge of science, but who recognized the inevitable anarchy of a purely objective thought, sought to legitimize philosophy as a subjective synthesis made from the point of view of Humanity. Finally Monsieur Bergson, realizing the necessity of getting outside the limits of the scientific order if the philosophic order was to be attained, made a gallant attempt to make his way to an intuition beyond the concept. But this very intuition—which is *experience* rather than *knowledge* of the real, and an ever fruitful method of investigation rather than a formula of discoveries—merely makes us critical of a science which considers itself a philosophy; it does not help us to construct a philosophy.[7] For although it may be necessary to achieve contact with the unexpressed, and to come back to it again and again, if we are to make any headway in philosophy, yet philosophy consists after all in what it is capable of saying about it, in spite of deficiencies of expression which have constantly to be corrected.

We cannot then be surprised to see philosophy today resigned to suicide and regarding its resignation as a triumph. From the method of one science we can extract only that science and as much of the others as can be reduced to it. From all the methods of the sciences put together we can extract nothing other than the sum of the sciences; which is all very fine, but leaves no room for an autonomous philosophy. If we take that road we come inevitably either to the absolute positivism of a Littré, which purely and simply reduces the content of philosophy to that of science, or to the idealism of Monsieur L. Brunschvicg, which reduces philosophy to a critical consideration of the stages passed through by thought in the constituting of science—the history of Mind.

Here we see philosophy arrived at a point where it seems difficult for it to go farther along the path of its own dissolution. But the last step of the outward journey is also the first step of the return, and here possibly is the point where consideration is necessary, preparatory to a new start. At first sight any idea of a return to medieval philosophy seems eminently absurd. It was that philosophy which survived with great difficulty in the dogmatic metaphysical systems of the seventeenth century; in eliminating all metaphysics, science completed the elimination of scholasticism itself. After three centuries of uninterrupted scientific progress, the same progress that relegated Aristotle's world to limbo, how could there be any question of going back to it?

And there is no slightest question of it: not only for reasons of expediency which, however compelling, would be wholly unphilosophic, but also because we are bound to condemn the scientific sterility of the middle ages for those very reasons which today make us condemn the philosophic sterility of "scientism." Aristotle also had exaggerated the scope of one science and the value of its method, to the detriment of the others; and in a sense he was less excusable than Descartes, for in this he came into open contradiction with the requirements of his own method, whereas Descartes was only carrying his through. And yet, philosophically, Aristotle's was the less dangerous error, for it was an error of fact and left the question of principle untouched: to biologize the inorganic as he and the medieval philosophers did was to condemn oneself to ignorance about those sciences of the inorganic world whose present popularity comes chiefly from the inexhaustible fertility which they display in things practical; but to mathematize knowledge entirely, and on principle, was to set strange limits to physics and chemistry, and to make impossible biology, metaphysics, and consequently moral theory. This is the point it remains for us to explain.

Since the Christian universe is a creation of God, not of man, Christian philosophy instinctively looks on these problems from the point of view of the object. Any medieval philosopher would willingly concede to Descartes that the sciences taken together are only the human mind, always one and the same, however many be the problems to which it is applied: but although the human mind in itself is always one, the things to which it is applied are not; and for this reason its methods of approaching the real must vary as much as the real itself. An Aristotelian discourse on *method* is therefore an impossibility; it is possible to speak only of a discourse on *methods*. To the order of abstract quantity corresponds the mathematical method; and even that must vary according to whether it is a question of continuous or discontinuous quantity, of geometry or arithmetic. For the order of physics its own method is appropriate, for there we have to study the movement and properties of inorganic bodies. For the order of biology yet another method is appropriate, since it deals with the study of organized beings; and so on for psychology, moral theory, and sociology. Nothing could be more incorrect than to regard these differing methods as isolated, for the method of a more abstract science dominates that of the more concrete sciences, and extends to their domain: but they are specific methods and remain distinct, inasmuch as every order of the real requires by reason of its very distinctness an appropriate mode of investigation. Thus Wisdom, or first philosophy, or metaphysics, lays down the guiding principles of all other sciences, and humanly depends on none of them: as the others study different modes of being, so it studies being itself, in its essence and its properties: it is the science of being as being; mathematics is the science of quantity; physics is the science of beings as subject to motion, biology of living beings, psychology of rational beings, and sociology of human beings living in society. Nothing could be more comprehensive or more adaptable than such an attitude, and one fails to see *a priori* why a philosophy which adopted it need have misinterpreted one of the orders of the real.

Indeed, there was nothing which compelled it to do so. Aristotle's error lay in not being true to his principle of *a science of the real for every order of the real*, and the error of medieval philosophy lay in following him in this. Committing the opposite mistake to that of Descartes, Aristotle set up the biological method as a physical method. It is generally admitted that the only positive kinds of knowledge in which Aristotelianism achieved any progress are those which treat of the morphology and the functions of living beings. The fact is that Aristotle was before everything a naturalist, just as Descartes was before everything a mathematician; so much so indeed that instead of reducing the organic to the inorganic like Descartes, Aristotle claimed to include the inorganic in the organic. Struck by the dominance of form in the living being, he made it not only a principle of the explanation of the phenomena of life, but even extended it from living beings to mobile beings in general. Hence the famous theory of substantial forms, the elimination of which was to be the first aim of Descartes. For a scholastic philosopher, as a matter of fact, physical bodies are endowed with forms from which they derive their movement and their properties; and just as the soul is a certain species of form—that of a living being—so is form a certain genus of soul—the genus which includes both the forms of inorganic beings and the forms or souls of organized beings.

This explains the relative sterility of scholastic philosophy in the order of physics and even chemistry, as well as the inadequacy of Cartesianism in the order of the natural sciences. If there is in the living being anything other than pure mechanism, Descartes is foredoomed to miss it; but if there is not in physical reality that which defines the living being as such, then the scholastic philosophy will not only fail to find it there, but will never discover even what is there. Nevertheless, it wasted its time in looking for what was not there; and as it was convinced that all the operations of inorganic bodies are explained by forms, it strove with all its might against those who claimed to see there something else, and clung to that impossible position until, in losing it, it lost itself. Three centuries spent in classing what must be measured, as today some persist in measuring what must be classed,[8] produced only a kind of pseudo-physics, as dangerous to the future of science as to that of the philosophy which imagined itself bound to it; scholasticism was unable to extract from its own principles the physics which could and should have flowed from it.

Our first duty then today is to restore to each order of the real what is due to it. In each order there is need to maintain the reality of form, without which it is impossible to account for structure. It is the principle of intelligibility in the real; positing the end for the manifestations of energy and the conditions for their fulfillment, it rules the mechanical aspect of everything, imposing on forces, even physical and chemical, certain structural laws which differentiate bodies and maintain a real distinction between the energies themselves. Still more must it play this part in botany and zoology, where the *types* are facts and laws even more manifest. But *typology* is a scientific problem which is absolutely universal, and appears in the inorganic as well as in the organic; and although the sciences today are tending in another direction, the fact is still there, and the need to reckon with it will always remain, and form is the only principle which allows us to account for it.

There is then no question of denying the hylomorphism of inorganic beings, but what does seem necessary is a radical severance of the idea of organic form from the idea of inorganic form. *Formae naturales sunt actuosae et quasi vivae*, said the Scholastics: between the Cartesian artificialism which makes animals into so many machines, and the Aristotelian vitalism which makes physical bodies into so many animals, there must be room for a mechanism in physics and a vitalism in biology. Every "nature" requires a formal principle, but not every form is living.[9] Inorganic form is a principle of structure and of arrangement of energies, but not a source of energy which is calculable, or experimentally demonstrable, nor an inner spontaneity giving rise to observable quantitative variations.

But at the same time it becomes evident that the failure of physics in the middle ages does not detract from the validity of medieval philosophy: in a sense it even confirms it, since that philosophy failed only because it was not sufficiently faithful to its own principles. There is nothing to condemn it to the astronomy of Ptolemy, to geocentrism, to motive Intelligences as the explanation of the movements of the heavenly bodies; it is not obliged to believe with St. Thomas that bodies, by reason of their substantial forms, have a fixed tendency toward a certain place; nor that the reflection and refraction of light rays are metaphors of a corporeal nature intended to express immaterial realities. There is no one so absurd as not to recognize that what is false is false. And it is not only those waste products in science that must be and have been scrapped: everything in the metaphysical and psychological order which is founded on them must be scrapped along with them. So any revaluation of the medieval tradition must start with the principles, not judging beforehand what they can or cannot give, but putting them freely to the test, in order to find how far they have value in explaining the real. The problem is not to involve them in new systems with whose unstable elements they would seem once more bound up, but to restore them in their purity and their enduring fertility, and so to prevent at least the loss of the spiritual possessions which ought to remain a permanent acquisition.

The first and most necessary of those possessions is the existence of philosophy as an autonomous discipline of thought, and of a metaphysic crowning that philosophy. The old definition holds good, as even Auguste Comte came to recognize: philosophy is the study of wisdom. It includes then within itself the sum of the sciences, each of which is trying to forge the instrument adapted to the order of the real which it undertakes to explain; but beyond the problems raised by the different modes of being, there is the problem raised by being. And it is not: How does such-and-such a thing exist? It is: What is it "to exist"? In what does existence consist? Why is there existence at all, since that given to us does not appear to contain in itself a satisfactory explanation of itself? Is it necessary or contingent? And if it is contingent, does not it postulate a necessary existence as its cause and its explanation? Such, then, is the object of the ultimate science to which the human mind rises in the order of purely natural knowledge—the science of existence beyond the sciences of the ways of existing. It is called "metaphysics"—a science which was founded by the Greeks, who clearly realized the need for it, and one which Christian philosophy will never allow to die, because it is the first and the only philosophy for which the very existence of beings seemed, and still seems, contingent—that is to say, requiring its own principle of explanation, whose nature must be studied by a science which is distinct from the other sciences, and which dominates them because its object is the problem without which there would be no other problems. As long as there is Christianity, there will be metaphysics to link the various modalities of existence with Him *qui non aliquo modo est, sed est, est*. Every science in its own place, but, above them all, the one without whose object there would be no sciences, because there would be neither any reality to be known nor any intelligence to apprehend it.

NOTES

1. See *La vie intellectuelle*, March 25, 1933, pp. 181–194.
2. D. Hume, *An Enquiry concerning Human Understanding*, VII. i, ed. L. A. Selby-Bigge (2nd ed., Oxford Press, 1902), p. 72. The whole argument of Hume in this text, which is of the first importance in the history of philosophy, is aimed directly and consciously at the occasionalism of Malebranche. Hume accepts his criticism of transitive causality, but he extends it from man to God.
3. Descartes, *Lettre de 1643*, ed. Adam-Tannery, vol. iv, p. 67, lines 10–26.
4. Hobbes, *Leviathan*, i, chap. 13, ed. W. G. Pogson Smith (Oxford Press, 1909), pp. 94 ff. The early part of this chapter is simply the application to the political man of what is said about the intellectual man in the early part of the *Discours de la Méthode*. Even certain expressions of Descartes are to be found in it. The *Leviathan* was published in 1651.
5. *Leviathan*, i, chap. 14, ed. cit., p. 99.
6. On this point see that remarkable work of V. Basch, *L'Individualisme anarchiste, Max Stirner* (2nd ed., Paris: F. Alcan, 1928).
7. The pragmatism of James, an enterprise more complicated but less philosophic, sought to submerge both science and philosophy in the common category of efficiency. In order to save philosophy, it made two victims instead of one.
8. It is clear that Aristotle's error, less serious than that of Descartes from the point of view of philosophy, was more serious from the point of view of science. To extend, like Descartes, a more general science to the less general sciences leaves it possible to reach in these last what they have in common with the first; hence a mechanization, always possible though always partial, of biology: but to turn the method of a more particular science back upon a more general science amounts to leaving the more general without an object. Now, in missing the real objects of physics and chemistry, Aristotle missed at the same time all that biochemistry teaches us concerning biological facts—which, although it is neither the whole nor the most important part, is possibly the part which is most useful. And this, as well as being a serious gap in his theory, is the thing that human utilitarianism will never forgive him.
9. It is indeed very evident that notwithstanding the error of imagination which induced certain of the Scholastics to conceive the forms of inorganic beings after the fashion of the forms of living beings, hylomorphism loses none of its value. It is sufficient to recall that every metaphysical idea arises, upon contact with the most general facts of our material universe, from a judgment made in the light of being—that is to say, the light of the principle of contradiction—and that consequently any such idea is analogical, like the idea of being itself. Such is the concept of form, realized differently in

inorganic beings and living beings. But since the human mind never thinks without appealing to the imagination and to sensuous experience, reason is naturally tempted to attach concepts which are metaphysical, and consequently analogical, to this or that image and univocal realization. It was to such an allurement that Aristotle yielded, his medical education tempting him to "biologize" form in its whole extension. But let us note in his defense that if we look up the sixth book of his *Physics* and certain passages in the second and seventh books, we can see plainly that he glimpsed the part played by quantity and measure in scientific knowledge. If he did not go farther along this path, it may be simply because of his ignorance of mathematics, of which he seems to have known only simple proportion. It is possible that this fact had a considerable influence on the general trend of his labors.

PART TWO

The Historian of Medieval Philosophy

While other choices could easily have been made, among which many would have revealed Gilson's erudition better than the present ones, I have here aimed to stress the spirit of Gilson as a historian of medieval philosophy rather than the massive apparatus of his scholarship. For example, the pages on Duns Scotus have a remarkable but deceptive lucidity; it took their author over thirty years of hard research and writing on the Subtile Doctor to achieve that equilibrium. Gilson's interpretations of St. Augustine and St. Bonaventure have earned for him a singular recognition as an objective historian—as a historian who can compare St. Augustine and St. Thomas without confusing or distorting them; or who can be faithful to the devotional character of Bonaventurean thought as contrasted with the intellectualism of the Angelic Doctor. But Gilson has been faithful not only to medieval thinkers themselves, but also to the transforming influence of Christianity on the philosophical tools that they inherited from the ancient world. The development of the idea of infinity is a case in point. A no less striking phenomenon, according to Gilson, was the liberation of metaphysics from Aristotelian science accomplished by the theology of the Schoolmen. This thirteenth-century accomplishment is for Gilson both a fact and a lesson.

4. The Idea of Philosophy in St. Augustine and in St. Thomas Aquinas

One who has some knowledge of Thomistic philosophy cannot study St. Augustine without experiencing the constant temptation to compare the two systems. The two men resemble one another as brothers but, no less like brothers, they give every impression of not being identical. Perhaps some agreement on their respective conceptions of philosophy would go a long way toward defining their resemblances and their differences. Unfortunately, such an undertaking is in its essence an endless one since it supposes a mastery of two immense systems of thought whose myriad details are for each one of them of the first importance, and of two personalities of still greater dimensions than their systems. What I have to say on this occasion consists of nothing more than a number of suggestions, open to all the corrections, additions, and deletions that they may require.

In theory, the idea that a man forms of philosophy stems only from philosophy; but, in fact, it has a great deal to do with the man himself. At least, this seems to be an evident inference in the case of St. Augustine himself. There is not a page he has written on which his powerful personality, not to say his temperament, does not reveal itself. In both the eulogistic and dyslogistic senses of the word, Augustine is a man of desires. From his infancy and throughout his whole life he sought happiness and even absolute happiness—that is to say, beatitude, the possession of a perfect good that was beyond all fear of loss. Two means were required for the acquisition of this end: *love,* which is nothing else than the very movement of a soul directed toward the good, and *knowledge,* since the supreme good, being Truth, cannot fill the soul of man with joy except by fully revealing itself to his intellect. *Gaudium de veritate:* this is the end in view, and there can be no disagreement on this point.

It is, moreover, a fact that Augustine directed himself to

this end along ways that were tortuous and painful, and that he earned his spiritual bread by the sweat of his brow. In summarizing his experience, whose history is too well known to be detailed here, one may say that it hinges entirely on his ferocious effort to give himself beatitude and on his tragic recognition that he was powerless to do so. On the other hand, since Augustine's whole work is profoundly affected by it, it is important to emphasize in his experience the dual aspect of that experience; namely, intellectual and moral.

Within the domain of the intellect, Augustine begins by striving to grasp and to possess truth by his unaided powers. Between Christianity, which is founded on an act of faith, and Manichaeanism, which holds out the promise of rationally demonstrating its way to the truth, Augustine does not hesitate: he chooses Manichaeanism. When, in his thought, the doctrine of Mani fell of itself under the weight of its own incoherence, it was in the skepticism of Cicero that he found refuge: the reason cannot do much, let us content ourselves—or let us try to content ourselves—with the little that reason can give. That this apparent state of resignation was full of internal secret suffering is sufficiently proved by the famous episode of the drunkard of Milan; and it is even more clearly proved by the later history of Augustine's own thought. In this domain the master who freed him was St. Ambrose, whose sermons in Milan revealed to Augustine the profound meaning contained in Scripture, the spirit hidden under the letter, the benefit resulting from the acceptance of the truth revealed by God and offered to man for the satisfaction of his thirst for knowledge. From the day that the young Augustine was enrolled as a catechumen, he was in possession of half of his philosophy. He knew that truth was not conquered by force, it was received. For years Augustine had vainly pretended to give himself what he did not have, instead of accepting in all simplicity what God offered him. This was the Christian revelation, interpreted by the Church, the infinite richness of whose content continued to escape him but which he henceforth knew with certainty to contain both truth and the means to beatitude.

But it is not enough to see truth. Truth must be embraced—that is, it must be loved—and one is not sure of loving truth save when he prefers it to everything else. Up to this point it was everything else that the future St. Augustine preferred. This was a more painful and disconcerting experience than the first one. Man, who cannot by himself know what he would like to know, is not even capable of loving by himself what he would like to love. The reading of Plotinus revealed to the mind of Augustine the pure spirituality of God and the soul, the unreality of evil, and the inferior nature of sensible reality. Augustine learned that the way to the truth regularly proceeds from body to mind and from mind to God. But though Augustine recognized that Plotinus was right, Plotinus yet remained for him no more than a doctor who described an illness and then health but offered no remedy. We must detach ourselves from the senses? Certainly, but how? Augustine would like to do so, he is striving to do so, but he cannot. It was then that St. Paul revealed to Augustine both the secret of his illness and the secret of the remedy. In reading the Epistles, Augustine discovered that the evil from which he was suffering was not peculiar to him; it was found in all men since the sin of Adam. The vain pride in his effort arose from the fact that, being able to fall by himself, he thought himself capable of raising himself by his own resources. Here, too, the remedy consisted in accepting what God offered and what man could not give himself. Plunged in concupiscence and the resulting disorders, Augustine looked with envy upon the serene calm of an Ambrose and the Fathers of the Desert. He then knew its source: it was grace. As faith gives to the intellect the truth that escapes it, so grace gives to the heart the purity it desires. Through grace, not only can man see from a distance the goal he is seeking, he can reach it. What Plotinus pointed out, Christ led Augustine to possess.

Such is the dual experience of Augustine and the source of all his philosophy. It would be useless to seek in Augustine anything else; for example, a metaphysical and abstract analysis of first principles, a precisely thought out demarcation of the limits and content of philosophy as such, as compared with either faith or the sciences. Of course he has touched upon all these problems, he has left us in passing important suggestions on how to resolve them, but he did not consider them directly enough to enable us to say that he resolved them. His basic point of departure was an idea that he had fully perceived, the idea of a Christian wisdom whose charter had been drawn once for all by St. Paul and which became incarnate in Jesus Christ filled with grace and truth. Hence the formula *nisi crederitis non intelligetis,* which St. Augustine never tired of repeating. This formula meant to him, first and foremost, that he who has faith has all philosophical truth in its essence, that he has this truth with an assurance that is incomparably greater than the assurance that the reason can give, and therefore that he possesses in this truth the surest possible starting point for the further work of analysis, clarification, and development on the part of his reason. Hence also the formula *da quod jubes et jube quod vis,* which completes the acceptance of faith. Just as the intellect already has within faith the whole object of knowledge, so the will already has within the act of charity the whole object of its love. In the love of God that God gives us, we have the pledge of future beatitude. This is why the entire philosophy of Augustine, including moral philosophy, is wholly developed as an untiring cultivation on the part of man of a twofold supernatural gift, a life whose profound unity is that of God Himself in us: *via, veritas et vita.*

Let us now turn in the direction of St. Thomas Aquinas. What a difference! He was born, he lived, and he died in the light. There is no trace in him of those conversions that have enriched the soul of a St. Augustine or that of a Pascal, but have also strained their thought to the point of a certain tautness, as well as removed from them the ease of a reason for which truth is its natural climate. Thomas was a man like the rest, to be sure, but a man for whom God seems to have paid a special price. The exhausting task of winning his way back from error and from evil, a task in which so many persons spend themselves, did not weigh heavily on his shoulders; he was entirely free to live for goodness and for truth. With a steady eye, and proceeding systematically across reality with that measured step that his friends came to recognize in him, Brother Thomas neglected only non-being in his journey. *Sanctificatus a veritate,* he therefore advanced guided by the truth that delivered him.

Nothing is more discouraging to the historian than such

a transparent mystery—the mystery of a Christian liberty founded on intelligence. The thought that is scrutinizing this mystery experiences no obstacle, because it is at home in mystery, and yet it is also astonished at its lack of progress. The explanation is that its depth admits neither progress nor degrees; between its center and its external limit there is no intermediate point where a lesser man might rest. Like St. Augustine, St. Thomas is master of all things in God, but the possession of the world has come to them from the same source in two different ways. Augustine paid so dearly for what he received that he clutched it to himself with a kind of fear; within the gift of faith he held onto truth as though it were at any moment on the point of escaping from him. Having at length grasped the whole that he desired for so long, he lost interest in the part. That is why, in Augustine, love regularly tends more or less to take precedence over knowledge; for this God Whom one cannot as yet comprehend as a whole one can already love as a whole. St. Thomas, no less, wishes even now to grasp the whole through love, but no fear turns him away from here and now grasping by means of his intelligence whatever part of the whole he can here and now grasp, just as he will grasp all the rest later on. He proceeds toward the beatific vision calmly by means of his thought, since to know God constitutes eternal life. To know God and, in knowing Him, in a manner to become God through the understanding, this is the method of St. Thomas. The liberty of St. Augustine is that of a freed man; the liberty of St. Thomas is that of a free man.

Such differences could not but make themselves felt in the Augustinian and Thomistic conceptions of philosophy. Both men are saints, and both are essentially theologians, which means that they are in complete agreement on the primacy of faith. St. Thomas attributes to faith the same role and dignity as does St. Augustine. Faith contains within itself the whole of the knowledge leading to salvation; so much so that he who is content with faith alone possesses in it the very substance of all the good things that he should hope for. As distinguished from philosophy, faith brings its message to all men, rich or poor, learned or ignorant, because it is to all men that salvation has been offered. But the philosopher himself finds in faith something to his benefit and he is invited to profit thereby. Whatever the power of a man's understanding may be, he is still no more than man. The task of single-handedly gathering into a system all the truths necessary to salvation that the human reason can demonstrate, without adding even the tiniest of those errors that from small beginnings become destroyers of the truth by the distant consequences to which they give rise, is a task which, though not impossible, surpasses in practice the power of any man left to his own resources. Even granting that one of us could reach such a goal, he would get there very late, after having spent all or most of his life in such an undertaking. But our need of truth is immediate, so that we might be able to begin our lives by conforming ourselves to the rules of truth.

That is why St. Thomas Aquinas is in full agreement with St. Augustine in seeking and soliciting the regulative action of faith and of revelation as the greatest boon to philosophical thought. I sometimes ask myself whether, out of an excess of zeal used somewhat rashly in his service, as well as the better to serve him, several interpreters of St. Thomas Aquinas have not made of him a sort of Christian naturalist which he never wished to be and never was. This is to be impressed too much by the criticism so often directed at medieval philosophy; namely, that it identified philosophy and theology. On the basis of the principle *philosophia ancilla theologiae*, the opponents of medieval philosophy have so often convicted it of being foreign in its very essence to all philosophy, that some of its defenders thought it a good thing to go in the opposite direction as far as such a philosophy allowed them to go. Hence arose many expositions of Thomism in which philosophy appears as a self-contained discipline, standing by itself both in its essence and in its principles, the exclusive work of the unaided reason and hence owing to faith no more than any other philosophy. If this procedure is dictated by apologetics, it is as dangerous as it is useless since, having no basis in fact, it is threatened with the constant danger of being caught in a flagrant violation of the truth. Here as elsewhere, only the truth avails. What is that truth?

It is quite true to say that there is present in St. Thomas Aquinas a properly philosophical level that it would be difficult to find in St. Augustine. The explanation of this fact would seem to lie in a much more general question, of which the problem of the relations of faith and reason is no more than a particular instance. I refer to the question of nature and grace. One would be completely mistaken in holding that St. Augustine confused the two orders, since there is no page in the writings of the Doctor of Grace that does not present grace as a gratuitous gift intended to restore, complete, and sanctify the nature from which it is consequently distinguished as by definition. Contrariwise, it seems to me that one is justified in saying that if the God of St. Augustine is no more envious of nature than is the God of St. Thomas Aquinas, since He created nature good as well as adorned it with all the gifts necessary to its perfection, it remains that St. Augustine himself is envious of nature for the sake of God. What God created was nature in its state of primeval goodness; what St. Augustine has before his eyes is nature corrupted by sin. Here is a nature that fell by its own fault and that regularly pretends to think, love, and act as though the consequences of its fall did not weigh heavily upon it. How could it have forgotten this all-important fact? His own history, ever before his eyes and recorded in his *Confessions*, was there to remind Augustine of the point. It was he, more than any other man, who wished to do without faith and without grace; it was he who on this account suffered and met defeat; it was he who in fearful self-abandonment finally threw himself into the arms of God, Who requires no more of us than He has already given us. Hence that continual defiance with which Augustine regularly looks upon nature, the suspicion with which he charges the power of reason, the constant and repeated appeal that he addresses on all occasions to the light of faith.

To this moral argument we may add a more properly philosophical one. It is quite correct that St. Augustine recognizes the existence of a nature, without which indeed grace would have nothing to save; but as distinguished from Thomistic nature, Augustinian nature does not have a defined metaphysical charter. It arises, in Augustine's eyes, much less from a right than from a fact. For example, the nature of man was in the beginning that which God had given him in creating him; but today it is different, having been corrupted by sin, so that a new nature then replaced the old one. And although it is possible to find here and there in the writings of St. Augustine traces of the beginning of reflection on at least the metaphysical possibility of a necessity internal to essences, it is not on this level that the thought of Augustine ordinarily develops. As many recognize, it is quite otherwise with St. Thomas: *formalissime semper loquitur divus Thomas.* For historical and especially philosophical reasons, which lie outside the scope of the present occasion, St. Thomas regularly supposes that any given being possesses an essence that belongs to it and consequently can exercise the activities that flow necessarily from this essence. Thus man the rational animal, from the very fact of being man, is capable of exercising activities of reason. This initial metaphysical decision has consequences not only in epistomology and in ethics but also, and perhaps principally, in the problem of the relations between faith and reason.

Everyone remembers the famous passage of the *De Libero Arbitrio* in which St. Augustine, called upon by his interlocutor to present a necessary and purely rational demonstration of the existence of God, begins by making the following surprising reply: "If it was not one thing to believe and another thing to understand, and if we did not have first to believe the great and divine things that we sought to understand, vain would have been the words of the prophet: *Unless you believe you shall not understand.* Moreover, Our Lord Himself, by word and deed, began by exhorting to belief those whom He called to salvation. But afterward, when He spoke of the gift itself that He was to give to those who believed, He did not say: This is eternal life, that they may believe; He said: *This is eternal life that they may know Thee, the one true God, and Him Whom Thou didst send, Jesus Christ.* Then, to those who already believed He said: *Seek and you shall find.* For neither can that be said to be found which is believed and remains unknown, nor does anyone become capable of finding God unless he first believe what he is afterward to know: *Neque quisquam inveniendo Deo fit idoneus, nisi antea crediderit quod est postea cogniturus.* Let us therefore, bowing to the precepts of Our Lord, seek earnestly, for what we seek under His exhortation we shall find under His direction, so far as such things can be found in this life and by persons such as we."[1]

Both the specific difference introduced by St. Augustine between reason and faith and the subordination of reason to faith even within its own domain are here fully evident. As a good Augustinian, St. Anselm gave a definitive formulation of this doctrine in his *fidens quaerens intellectum*, and he has made of it a justly celebrated application in his famous demonstration of the existence of God by means of the idea of the perfect developed in the *Proslogion*. It would be impossible to find a proof of this kind in St. Thomas Aquinas, as impossible as the attitude to which it is attached. For him the human reason, as a natural reason, is able in virtue of its essence to acquire by itself alone the whole range of knowledge belonging to the natural order. He would never say, with St. Augustine, that no one can find God by means of the reason without first believing in God's existence; for God is the cause of the natural order, and, as such, necessary for its complete metaphysical intelligibility. St. Thomas's insertion, between the act of faith and the conclusions of reason, of a reason endowed with the natural power to produce the truth, to formulate its principles, and to deduce from them their consequences, has this result, that what depends on reason within Thomism cannot at the same time and under the same relationships depend on faith. In this sense it is true to say that there exists a Thomistic philosophy which is nothing but philosophy, in that the principles on which it rests and the conclusions drawn by it from them belong to the order of reason alone, to the exclusion of revelation.

Yet even at this moment St. Thomas is nearer to St. Augustine than may at first glance seem to be the case. What Thomism adds to Augustinianism is a technical progress of great importance which saves its essence by defining it. If we refer to the text of Augustine that we have just cited, we shall there find the distinction between the act of believing and the act of knowing formulated with the greatest clarity: *sed nos id quod credimus, nosse et intelligere cupimus*. Inversely, if we refer to Augustine's doctrine of faith, we shall see quite easily that faith, essentially distinguished from the act of rational knowledge, is yet not isolated from knowledge nor condemned to remain without any influence on the activity of knowledge. For just as the divine action respects the efficacy of secondary causes, so much so that it is their foundation since God moves natures as natures, so faith respects the efficacy and the autonomy of the natural reason since, when faith moves the reason, it moves the reason as reason.

That is why we would hold to the view that the present question is a particular instance of the problem of nature and grace. For the same reason we would hold that even though Augustinian philosophy has a different ground plan and development, Thomistic philosophy is no less than it a Christian philosophy in the full meaning of the name, without thereby ceasing to be a philosophy no less fully. There is not the least doubt that Thomism is truly and unreservedly a philosophy since, on all questions that do not directly or indirectly concern the work of salvation, Thomism is the work of reason without any appeal to the light of faith. Knowledge of this sort may be comparatively without point and its pursuit idle, but the pursuit is possible and in itself legitimate. It is equally certain, moreover, that Thomistic philosophy is truly philosophical in the domain of questions that are accessible to the unaided reason but that also concern salvation; for none of the demonstrations that St. Thomas gives on any of these questions calls upon the act of faith either at the starting point of the demonstration or at any moment during the reasoning process. But the Thomistic reason is no more isolated from faith than is the Augustinian reason. However, rather than steep itself in faith in a manner that could appear to St. Thomas only as a confusion of essences, it submits to faith as to a transcendent influence that moves, directs, and fulfills it. In thus yielding with full knowledge to this influence, the reason completes itself, it does not destroy itself, since faith does not destroy the essence of the reason in order to substitute itself for it, but acts upon the reason only to confer upon it its fullness as a reason.

Let us, for example, consider any knowledge whatever, provided that it belongs among those truths that are at once philosophically demonstrable and given to man by God as articles of faith. On this subject St. Thomas teaches that it is impossible for man both to know and to believe such a truth, since if he knows it he does not believe it, and if he believes it he does not as yet know it. Hence, either he knows it or he believes it, but he could not do both at the same time. This does not remove the possible necessity of first believing that which, absolutely speaking, one is able to demonstrate. This is true both for St. Thomas as well as for St. Augustine. For such truths are demonstrable only in principle, they are not necessarily demonstrable for each one of us in the concrete. The errors and the contradictions of the philosophers prove this point only too well. Hence, he who possesses a certain truth by faith and then goes on to acquire an evident demonstration of that truth removes from his mind faith in that truth and substitutes a knowledge of it. But he does not do so except in so far as he acquires an evident demonstration of it. Moreover, if we consider together all the truths that we are able to acquire about God, then, as we know from experience, our knowledge of such truths would be seriously defective if the certitude of faith were not there to guarantee it. "For the human reason is very deficient when dealing with things divine. A sign of this is the fact that the philosophers, devoting themselves to the natural study of divine things, made many errors and disagreed with one another on many points. Therefore, so that there might be among men a firm and certain knowledge of God, it was necessary that divine things should be made known to men by way of faith, as spoken by God Himself, Who cannot deceive."[2]

Consequently, when the two doctrines are reduced to their starting points, they are found to be in complete agreement. It is necessary for man to begin with faith: "It is necessary to believe that God is one and incorporeal, which are truths that are proved by the philosophers by means of the natural reason."[3] One would be inclined to say that St. Thomas concedes a proposition of this kind if it were not for the fact that St. Thomas was the author of the proposition and had no need to concede it. Man, who sets out from faith, tends spontaneously toward knowledge: "For neither can that be said to be found which is believed and remains unknown." One could say of this proposition that St. Augustine admits it if he had not taken the trouble to be the first to affirm it.

In both systems, therefore, Christian philosophy is presented as an understanding of divine things that more and more replaces faith, at least to the extent to which it is humanly possible to do so. In both systems, whatever may have been the action of faith that precedes and prepares knowledge, it remains that knowledge as an established body of demonstrated truths owes nothing of its scientific evidence to faith. In both systems, finally, faith is always ready to take once more the place of a defective knowledge, as when an inadequate grasp of truth runs the risk of losing it.

If, then, there are disagreements between Augustinianism and Thomism, given that the principles are the same, the disagreements must be reduced either to differences in the degree of elaboration in the two doctrines or to differences of temperament between the two authors of these doctrines. For reasons that have already been indicated, it would be useless to try to find in St. Augustine a precise definition of faith, scientific knowledge, theology, and philosophy such as St. Thomas distinguishes them one from another in the *Summa*. There is no answer in St. Augustine to the question whether scientific knowledge, once established, does or does not exclude faith and whether it replaces faith or is added to it. On the other hand, the profound peculiarities of their interior lives have produced in St. Augustine and his followers a sort of pessimism with regard to the resources of the natural reason. This pessimism is not to be found to the same degree in St. Thomas Aquinas, nor is it expressed in the same tone. The Bishop of Hippo, who expected so much and received so little from the unaided reason, is especially struck by what it cannot give him. The Angelic Doctor, free as he was by walking in the light from the beginning of his life and sure of his way, could enjoy fully and fearlessly the magnificent spectacle of the wealth of truth that the natural reason, even when lacking the illumination of faith, could reveal to pagans such as Aristotle. Finally and especially, admitting with Aristotle that all human knowledge by nature begins from sensible things, St. Thomas was never tempted to condemn Aristotelian epistomology as tainted with sensualism and to attribute to a disorder of the heart—he who experienced no such disorder—

what seemed to his mind to be strictly a matter of philosophical evidence.

That is why Thomists and Augustinians are not always in agreement on the catalogue on the truths of faith that faith reserves to itself and the truths that reason can assimilate. They do not distinguish in exactly the same way the philosophical occupation of a faith that is tending toward understanding and the theological occupation of a faith that is defining and systematizing itself as faith. They do not understand in the same way the functioning of a reason which is for the Augustinians the reason of a corrupted nature, whereas in the eyes of the Thomists it has retained its essence and is for them the reason of a nature that is no more than wounded. Hence arise differences between spiritual families, to hope for whose disappearance is vain and perhaps would even be imprudent since these differences express in abstract terms the concrete and personal differences between the religious experiences that they translate into words. Hence arises as well the even more profound unity that they reveal, since this unity is based on the identity of their principles and on their irrevocable decision to root their thought in one and the same faith.

It is therefore no more than just, on this celebration of the man who was the master of the master, on this earth on which both have lived and whose language both have spoken, that we unite them in one and the same act of recognition and in one and the same love. After the passage of so many centuries, the Christian philosopher who thinks or prays, whether he wishes it or not, thinks with the understanding and prays with the heart of St. Augustine and of St. Thomas. He owes to them this even more priceless gift, that henceforth his thought can be completely at one with his prayer. Hence it is not necessarily in the silence of a cell nor in the turmoil of a university chair, it is not even necessarily under the vault of a church, it can also be on the shore of Ostia or on the road to Naples that the fraternal presence of these great souls can be felt. For myself, I never rediscover them anywhere so well as on the extreme point of one of those Italian promontories, those sun-beaten rocks whose every crack sustains fresh and green vegetation and which St. Thomas Aquinas more than once beheld from the shore of the Tyrrhenian Sea. The time is noon. The brilliant sun of a May day sets everything in clear and sharp relief, like the definition of an exacting intellect. Near at hand everything lies revealed in the clear evidence of its essence and enjoys the peace of its order. Farther off, the glance of the eye moves toward distances so brilliant that they are lost in their own expanse and disappear in the very excess of the light that covers them. What is more beautiful than this earth, this earth on which the source of distinctions is the very same as that of unity? Suspended between the heavens and the sea, some birds look down upon it from on high and glide like angels, until one of them, moving off with a great sweep of wings, answers the call of the sun, mounts, and, cutting the blue with his flight and his cry, rises to meet the light.

NOTES

1. *De Libero Arbitrio*, II, chap. 2, no. 6; *Patrologia Latina*, vol. 32, col. 1243.
2. *Summa Theologiae*, II–II, q. 2, a. 4. Cf. *Summa Contra Gentiles*, I, chap. 4.
3. *Sum. Theol., ibid., Sed Contra.*

5. The Future of Augustinian Metaphysics

The fifteenth centenary of the death of St. Augustine will not fail to concentrate once again the attention of historians and philosophers upon his work. Many books have already appeared in honor of the occasion, and the present year* will see many more. There will never, it is true, be too many; in the first place because the immensity of the task exceeds the efforts of any single individual writer; secondly and especially, because the very character of his work is such that it cannot live without the collaboration of interpreters who study it, assimilate it, and transmit the results of their labors to others. But this work of interpretation, a work of fundamental importance, would avail nothing without the complementary work of appreciation and assessment. Will this fifteenth centenary, we wonder, rest content with the historical statement of the existence, once upon a time, of a doctrine belonging to the past, classified and superseded, or will it mark a fresh outburst of vitality of Augustinian thought, a third or fourth renascence, heralding a new period of life? This is the question that we propose to consider, by asking ourselves whether the thought to St. Augustine retains still today something of its original fertility, or whether it is now nothing but an object of curiosity for the diversion of the historian.

I. THE OBSTACLES

We may well ask ourselves whether Augustinianism has any future before it. In the first place, it is a Christian philosophy: this expression does not simply mean that his was the philosophy of a Christian, for a man may be a Christian and a philosopher without holding a Christian philosophy; such a thing has happened–René Descartes would be a quite good instance. What, on the contrary, is characteristic of the

* That is, 1930, when the fifteenth centenary of the death of St. Augustine was celebrated all over the world.

thought of St. Augustine is that, in his case, revelation is the source, rule, and even the very food of his rational thought; he holds faith to engender reason, and dogma, taken as such, to engender philosophy. Not by any means that he confuses belief and knowledge, or even philosophy and theology, for to believe in the dogma, and to deduce from it the consequences it implies, is, for him, no more philosophizing than it would be for any of our contemporary positivists. But to let reason go out to meet faith, to account rationally for his faith to himself, to construct, under the influence of a supernatural and transcendent light, a system of ideas which, though purely rational in themselves, would yet be impossible without this light, is what he had always meant to do, and what he did with wonderful success.

At the same time we cannot but recognize that his very success is one of the most serious obstacles standing in the way of Augustinianism today. *Nisi credideritis, non intelligetis* is and will always remain the charter of every Christian philosophy. It is what distinguishes a Christian system not only from anti-Christian systems, but even from systems merely compatible with Christianity. Now, in proclaiming this principle and repeatedly asserting it with his well-known emphasis, St. Augustine appears to cut himself off from the communion of philosophers whose fundamental principle is that every philosophy, properly so called, is amenable to reason only. When we ask St. Augustine to prove to us the existence of God, he asks us in his turn first to believe in it; can we make the same request to our contemporaries without losing our qualification to be philosophers? And if Augustinianism presupposes Christian faith as a necessary condition, are we not driven to the conclusion that, at best, it is but a philosophy good enough for Christians?

But there is an even more serious question: we may well ask whether even for Christians, and more especially for Catholics, such a philosophy is still good enough. There has been a good deal of talk about "St. Augustine's exile"—wrongly, we hold, for there have always been, and there will always be, Augustinians among us; but we should fail of the most elementary intellectual honesty if we hid from ourselves the suspicions and the sort of disfavor of which St. Augustine, *qua* philosopher, has been the butt in the minds of many Catholic thinkers. The causes of this situation, which, unless we are much mistaken, is a patent fact, are complex and numerous. A complete history of Augustinianism—an ocean added to the ocean of Augustinian study itself—would be needed to disentangle these causes; but we may at least try to define the main causes, or at least those most directly accessible to observation.

Taking the question as a whole, it would seem that the principal difficulties confronting the progress of Augustinianism spring from one of its essential characteristics: its fundamental condition of incompleteness. Considered under this aspect, it appears, compared with Thomism for instance, as structurally quite different. All those who have had to teach the philosophy of St. Thomas know how little margin he leaves to the imagination of his interpreter. In expounding him, almost everything we may add of our own invention is false; interpreting him means essentially to get to know him, to understand him; it means never, or hardly ever, to complete him. If we venture to do so, we learn sooner or later to our cost that whatever we attribute to a master like him rarely amounts to more than an average intelligent misunderstanding. Hence the remarkable stability of Thomism in the course of history: its teaching has developed but little, fixed as it is by its very perfection, resting upon the evidence of its principles, and rounded off by the rigorous completeness of its deductions. The history of Thomism up to the present is indeed the history of the thought of St. Thomas Aquinas, whereas the history of Augustinianism is by no means the history of the thought of St. Augustine.

However great St. Augustine is—and St. Thomas himself would have been scandalized at being placed above his master—he is far from having left us a complete system of philosophy. Neither he nor his time felt the need of it, and the character of his teaching can be understood only if we put ourselves back into the conditions under which it was conceived. It is difficult for us nowadays to realize St. Augustine's starting point and what a prodigious effort he had to put forth to set himself free from difficulties which, thanks to him, had ceased to exist for a man of the thirteenth century: the refutation of radical skepticism; the discovery of spiritualism in opposition to the

Manichæan materialism; the solution of the problem of the existence of evil. We must never forget that St. Augustine took years before he came to conceive the bare possibility of a non-material reality and the compatibility of an imperfect universe with a perfect God. Little wonder that the painful conquest of these fundamental principles should have appeared to him, for the very reason that it allowed his reason henceforth to move freely within his Christian faith, as the equivalent of a complete philosophy. Once in possession of these key positions, he clung to them with the full conviction that reason under proper guidance would have no difficulty in finding its way, provided it followed the light of faith.

In fact, as St. Thomas has justly observed, St. Augustine had but re-thought and deepened, from the point of view of a Christian, the essential elements of Platonism. He had done so with genius, but with an intuitive rather than systematic genius. By putting into circulation principles without the series of consequences which explain but at the same time limit them, he left behind him a philosophy rich in undefined possibilities, but incomplete, poorly protected, and for that reason exposed to all sorts of deviations. It is a fact of experience that Augustinians are rarely disciples of St. Augustine, and yet if it is made a matter of reproach against them they do not protest without reason: for they indeed begin with him, but are compelled to leave him, since he himself so often is content to make no more than a beginning. Augustinians are always conscious of having set out along the master curve, but they sometimes forget at what moment they went off at a tangent. Jansenius, Malebranche, Gerdil are so many tangents of Augustinianism; they are not St. Augustine.

To limit ourselves here to the sphere of pure metaphysics, we should say that the two most dangerous temptations imperiling the integrity of its essence to which Augustinianism has yielded are Cartesian idealism and modern ontologism.

Whether Descartes did or did not come, directly or indirectly, under the influence of St. Augustine, is a purely historical question, which in the present state of the texts cannot perhaps be wholly solved. Personally, we believe in the existence of a direct influence, but it matters little as far as the question we have raised is concerned. Whether Descartes did or did not study St. Augustine, the fact remains that his method condemned him to follow in metaphysics the road of St. Augustine. We hope to show that the converse is not true, and that the metaphysic of St. Augustine does not condemn the Augustinian to follow the Cartesian method. Herein lies, if we may say so in passing, the justification of Cartesian Christian thinkers, at whom it is fashionable to be scandalized, although they flourished not so very long ago. If we take the trouble to examine their manuals used for instruction in seminaries without any scandal, and, as far as we know, without any harm being done, it will be seen that not one of them followed the method of Descartes; but what they all find behind Descartes and cling to is St. Augustine. St. Augustine is Descartes *minus* the "Method" and the impossibilities which it entails; Descartes is the attempt to invest the "Method" with the very substance of St. Augustine. Hence strange deformations inflicted upon Augustinianism, which are all the more dangerous as their principles are rarely apprehended.

It is a remarkable fact that scholastic philosophers today are constantly mistaken concerning the meaning of the Cartesian method. They usually do not penetrate beyond the appearances, and when a right feeling for what is foreign to them in Descartes's system leads them to attack it, they aim, by preference, in the first place at his methodical doubt. Kleutgen and Zigliara, so acute when they are dealing with St. Thomas, are guilty of surprisingly naïve mistakes in this matter. They insist upon proving that the first principles of knowledge, such as the principles of causality or of identity, are inaccessible to methodical doubt, as if Descartes had not proclaimed this fact before them. Mistaking entirely the Cartesian meaning of the term *principle*, they fight with shadows and win but the shadow of a victory. Perhaps this explains why, convinced as they are, they have been so little convincing. In reality, it is necessary to go farther back and to deal, behind the *cogito*, first principle of the Cartesian metaphysics, behind even the doubt which prepares it, with the mathematical method that demands both and justifies them to Descartes' satisfaction.

Descartes is essentially a man who attempted and carried through an experiment on the following notion: What happens to metaphysics, if we apply to it the mathematical method? In our opinion, what happens to it is that you destroy it. Descartes did not hold that view; on the contrary, he believed himself to be the first to save it; but his very illusion was possible only because, under certain aspects, Augustinianism lent itself to the experiment.

If there is an incontestably Thomistic and, generally speaking, medieval, principle, it is the principle *a posse ad esse non valet consequentia.* But the mathematician, as such, is convinced that *a posse ad esse valet consequentia.* Not only does the consequence hold for him, but it is the only consequence that holds; nor can anything be more natural, since he works only upon ideas. There is no difficulty about it, as long as he confines himself to the strictly mathematical order. Applied to that aspect of the real for which it is designed, his method yields full results; but as soon as he universalizes his method and decides to apply it to the totality of reality, Descartes entangles himself in singular difficulties. To start with, he wagers, without a shadow of possible justification, that there is nothing in things that escapes the mathematical method; then, bound to model reality on his ideas, instead of modeling his ideas on reality, he is driven to recover things only through concepts and to have no other starting point but thought. There precisely Augustinianism presented itself for the Cartesian mathematical method as the only road opening out upon metaphysics.

St. Augustine too had a method, quite different, we believe, from that of Descartes, but it had led him to results which could be utilized by the new philosophy. Like Descartes, he had at first relied on pure reason; again like Descartes, he had doubted, not only as a matter of method and exercise, but really and painfully; again like Descartes, he had issued from his doubt, thanks to the triumphant evidence of his *si fallor, sum;* like Descartes, finally, he had from the evidence of thought, held by direct grasp, drawn the certitude of the spirituality and immortality of the soul, as well as the proof of the existence of God. Why should not Descartes, when by his method he had closed for himself the Thomistic road, have taken that of Augustinianism, which asked for nothing better? By setting out upon it, he, who had no right to start from anything but thought, recovered, without leaving for a moment the sphere of thought, all the conclusions of the traditional metaphysics, even, as he believed, the existence of the external world. That is the reason why the philosophy of St. Augustine, passing over into the system of Descartes and profiting by the new glory shed upon it by this genius, came to make common cause with a method which was not its own, joined forces, willy-nilly, with idealism, and, by losing its essence in such an apparent triumph, lost at the same time its fertility.

The second metaphysical tangent of Augustinianism is ontologism. Zigliara, who has done more than anyone to discriminate between these two doctrines, has nevertheless not hesitated to write with his customary loyalty: "That St. Augustine has very often used expressions which at first sight seem to favour and even openly to affirm ontologism, I would certainly not deny, for it would mean denying a very obvious fact." Perhaps something that goes deeper than mere expressions may be here in question, and without believing, any more than Zigliara does, in an even moderate ontologism of St. Augustine, we believe that we must go back to the very structure of his teaching in order to explain this fresh contamination and to purge his doctrine of it.

Once St. Augustine, for reasons which we shall have to state more in detail, had chosen as his starting point the evident fact of the existence of the soul, he was bound to pass through the soul in order to reach all other spiritual substances, and more particularly God. His position is, therefore, from the very start very different from that which was later to produce the metaphysics of St. Thomas. It is true that, in both doctrines, it is by the analogy with the soul that God is best known; but the point of bifurcation between Thomism and Augustinianism lies farther back, at the point where the knowledge which the soul has of itself is defined. According to St. Thomas, the soul is, for man as he is in this life, less known than the body; for St. Augustine, even in this life, the soul is better known than the body. When, therefore, his thought attempts to rise to God, it will quite naturally find its starting point or its footing in the soul, for the consideration of the body only serves to lead the soul to itself, whence it can then attain to God.

One consequence of this initial position, which in its turn rests upon the Augustinian conception of the union of soul and body, is that on such a theory every proof of the existence of God must rest in the last resort on a certain content of thought. St. Augustine has no other way open to him, but he sees in this direction a short and effective means of reaching his object. One of the possible contents of thought, capable of supporting a proof of the existence of God, might have been the very idea of God, considered as an effect, the cause of which required to be discovered. St. Anselm, Descartes, and even Hegel were later to take that road; St. Augustine had the presentiment of it, even prepared it, but did not himself tread that path, for a reason perhaps deep enough to warrant our attempt later to determine it. The fact on which he fastened as the witness in ourselves of the existence of God was the true judgment. His analysis, often repeated, of the characteristics of necessity, immutability, and eternity, which formally define truth as such, is well known; the antinomy between the contingency of the subject as the vehicle of truth on the one side, and the necessity of truth itself, whatever its object, on the other, can only be solved by the admission of a subsistent truth, the cause of all truth, which is God.

Nothing could be more impressive than such a metaphysical analysis, especially if followed through the meanders of his closely packed argument in the actual text of St. Augustine; yet it is burdened with a heavy load of epistemological difficulties. Those who endeavor in all conscience to reconcile the Thomistic with the Augustinian theory of knowledge fail to observe that at the end of their efforts they have either eliminated the Augustinian proof of the existence of God or have introduced into Thomism a proof which cannot find room there without changing the whole structure of the system: the proof by the truth, not in things (which St. Thomas admits) but in thought (which Albert the Great still admits, but St. Thomas admits no longer). And the reason for this is clear. For the Augustinian proof to have its full effect, it is necessary that, somehow or other, the human intellect, which conceives the truth, should not be the immediate sufficient cause of its truth; if it is, there is no necessity for it to affirm the existence of God as cause, and then the way opening through thought is blocked at the very entrance. Doubtless there would remain the search for God in the order of causality, as cause of the intellect itself (which Albert the Great was to attempt), but St. Augustine does not even try this, because the only operation of the intellect which requires the affirmation of God as its sufficient reason is the conception of truth. He has, therefore, always to come back to the true judgment, or, what comes to the same thing, the intellect, so far as it is capable of conceiving truth. Unless, therefore, the immediate presence of God is imprinted as, so to say, a negative impress on our judgments, there is no proof of His existence. In writing these lines, we are trying to keep as close as possible to the thought of St. Augustine, and we certainly use terms very much less forcible than the expressions he uses himself.

The essential feature of such a position, whatever its ultimate interpretation, is a definition of the human intellect which leaves us nothing wherewith to account for the existence of truth. If St. Augustine had simply held that man cannot know truth without an intellectual light given him by God, his analysis of the contingency and insufficiency of human thought would be lacking in a precise object; but if, as the consensus of the most important texts shows, this is the point on which his proof rests, it must necessarily follow that divine illumination (to give it its traditional name) must reach thought directly. For either it reaches it directly, and in that case we grasp at the same time the sufficient reason of truth and God, Who is its foundation, or it reaches it indirectly, and in that case we are equally incapable of attaining to the existence of God and of accounting for truth.

This is both the central and the vulnerable point of the Augustinian metaphysics. Precisely because St. Augustine was at the very antipodes of ontologism, he is poorly protected against it. He never dreamed of restraining those who might attempt to go off at the tangent followed later by Gerdil and Gioberti. It occurred to him so little that, as Zigliara himself admits, he calmly supplied them with the weapons, or at least with the pretexts. To say that we "know in God," or that we see His hidden light, is this not tantamount to inviting the metaphysician in search of a mystical intuitionism to treat God as the very light of our thought, as the natural and first object of this thought, so that, instead of knowing Him through things, we know things through Him? This deviation begins from the end of the twelfth century onward, under the influence of Arabic neo-Platonism, and especially of Avicenna; dammed in by the efforts of St. Bonaventure and of St. Thomas Aquinas, it spreads in the seventeenth century with Malebranche, thanks to the influence of Cartesian idealism, and reaches its height in the nineteenth century under the impulse of German idealism.

In these circumstances, it is not a matter of surprise to observe the unexpected and yet undoubted phenomenon described as "St. Augustine's exile." It is certainly an unexpected phenomenon to find St. Augustine an object of suspicion within Catholicism itself, where everyone respects and loves him to an extent that makes him almost indistinguishable from it. It is no less a painful fact because it gives the impression of an inner disruption of that Christian thought whose indivisible unity is a matter of daily experience for all those who live it. To remedy the situation, the Thomists try with as much persistence as ingenuity to bring St. Augustine over to them. Nothing can be more legitimate as long as it is a matter of showing that Thomism accounts equally well, or better, for all that is true in Augustinianism. But it is an operation not without danger for Thomism itself, if carried out by hands other than the infallible hands of St. Thomas himself, for Thomistic thought is sometimes contaminated in its essence by contact with a thought other than its own; and it is always fatal to Augustinianism, which, if the operation is successful, disappears by assimilation in an essence different from its own.

Augustinians have another remedy. They protest; they attack; they denounce the situation. Yet it is they who are responsible for it. The true Thomist has at his disposal a complete, coherent Christian philosophy; he lives in an atmosphere where his metaphysical thought and his religious life can expand and grow in perfect freedom. It is his duty to join the Augustinian in conclusions common to both, but it is also his right to do so by ways which are peculiar to him. As to the legitimacy of the ways preferred by the Augustinian, it is for the Augustinian, not the Thomist, to prove it. All that he needs do to succeed, it seems to us, would be to be not less, but a little more, Augustinian. In face of this negligence of the philosophers to take in hand the task which is theirs, the historian, whose proper function is merely to preserve intact the deposit of tradition, has the impression of a dangerous abstention; he hopes, therefore, to be forgiven for doing what he can to palliate it.

II. THE MEANING OF AUGUSTINIANISM

The difficulties which at the present time beset Augustinianism are not an ill for which we need to find remedies, for St. Augustine himself is not affected by any ill; all that is needed is to return from the Augustinianism of the Augustinians to that of St. Augustine. This task is not easy. There is room for asceticism even in the most abstract metaphysical thought, for a change in point of view means a change in habits. We have, therefore, by no means the pretension of convincing the reader of the true meaning of Augustinianism by simply setting before him what we believe it to be, not only because with the best will in the world we may be mistaken, but also because, even if we were right, we should have to let time do its work and allow ideas to come to maturity of themselves. The real question is whether at this time of the day we can reverse the engine and find St. Augustine as he was, before three centuries of idealism had passed over his teaching. If it is possible at all, the essential operation, in order to do so, consists in eliminating the method of Descartes from the system of St. Augustine.

The important point before all else is to understand that the two philosophies have no essential relation, and altogether, if there is any relation between them, that it is, so to say, unilateral, not between St. Augustine and Descartes, but between Descartes and St. Augustine. While admitting that the first principle of Cartesianism is the universal application of the mathematical method, with the resulting idealistic method, we can admit as equally evident that nothing of the sort is to be found in St. Augustine. Now, it follows therefrom, on further reflection, that even when the two philosophies employ the same concepts and arrange them in the same order, they do not mean the same things. Whether the *si fallor sum* of St. Augustine has or has not led up to the *cogito ergo sum* of Descartes, it cannot be charged with the same implications. Pascal congratulates Descartes on this fact. One might feel disposed, perhaps, to congratulate St. Augustine.

By placing the *cogito* at the beginning of his metaphysics as the fundamental basis of the entire edifice, Descartes is committed beforehand, in the name of his mathematical method, to attributing to thought whatever is contained in his clear and distinct idea, and, correlatively, to attribute to it only what is thus contained in it. In this sense, the *cogito* is as rich in exclusions as in affirmations; it is but the first of that series of conceptual snippets which substitutes progressively a mosaic of abstractions for the continuity of reality, digs impassable trenches between the aspects of the concrete, and requires the invention of illusory bridges for the attempt to cross them again. This is not the place to set out the numberless difficulties in which the *cogito* entangles metaphysics; what matters is to observe that the very *cogito* of Descartes —that is, the one of all Descartes's steps which we would most certainly expect to furnish a concrete reality in all its proper substantiality—furnishes actually only that part of the reality which can be retained in idea, for whatever part of the *ego* the idea does not contain it denies: *a non nosse ad non esse valet consequentia.*

When, on the contrary, we consider the attitude of St. Augustine, it appears as very different from that of Descartes, and each of his theses displays a fruitfulness which Cartesianism destroyed by its very rigidity. To begin with, instead of being a method practiced upon ideas, Augustinianism is an inquiry concerning the concrete content of thought. It is true that, for St. Augustine as much as for Descartes, man apprehends himself only through his ideas, but St. Augustine does not hold in anticipation that his inner experience will divide itself into a certain number of simple natures and defined essences; taking man altogether, he observes him, and while he formulates him in ideas, he models his ideas on the empirical content that he has observed. Hence the fundamental character of his work, which, it must be said, Cartesianism has not only not safeguarded, but systematically destroyed. In proportion as the teaching of St. Augustine aimed at being a metaphysic, it is a metaphysic based upon a psychological empiricism, or, if preferred, a metaphysic of inner experience. Hence its extreme suppleness, its power of rebirth, and the very incompleteness which left a permanent possibility of progress open before it.

This essential characteristic is displayed in the thought of St. Augustine from its very beginnings. It too opens with doubt; but this doubt is not methodical or intentional, still less a pretense, like that of Descartes; St. Augustine is the prey of doubt, uncertain and almost despairing of finding truth. What is, for the French philosopher, but the initial step in a regulated order of thoughts is for St. Augustine a concrete and painful experience, an illness from which he has suffered and of which he has cured himself. Hence the remedy he has discovered and now offers us is no more necessary than the illness itself: his *si fallor sum* appears in its place whenever skeptical uncertainty threatens him as a possible danger, but its place is not at the beginning of a general exposition of his teaching, because the radical preventive of doubt is much less the *cogito* than the act of faith. Whoever believes in God and His word holds a truth infinitely richer and more fruitful than the *cogito*: "I believe, therefore I know" is better as a first principle than "I think, therefore I am."

For the same reason, the Augustinian empiricism discovers in the *cogito* something very different from what the mathematical method of Descartes discovers in it, for Descartes is committed once and for all to find in it nothing immediately but the essence of thought to be defined, whereas St. Augustine finds in it the whole of man to explore: man, that is, the body, the soul, and grace. The point is of such importance as to warrant special emphasis.

Three centuries of idealism have produced in us so intimate an adaptation to the Cartesian method that, wherever we observe its absence, we seem to observe an empty gap. Here, however, we encounter a solid. What St. Augustine discovers is, in the first place, his thought; but instead of denying—

even provisionally—what it is *not*, in order to define it better, he takes together with it all that it is not, and wherein he finds it, to compare it with and locate it in. Thus, his thought is that of a man who thinks, and a man is a body among other bodies, just as much as a spirit among other spirits. Analyzing his thought means for him analyzing the beings which are presented in it quite as much as analyzing it itself. He finds there all the degrees of reality taken in its complexity and its hierarchic order: inorganic being which only is; the plant which is and lives; the animal which lives and feels; finally man, who lives and feels and thinks. Thought as it apprehends itself directly is, therefore, in this case a life of a higher order than the others, and it apprehends consequently the others in itself, not in the manner of Descartes as something foreign to its essence, but as inferior virtualities which it cannot but have realized, since it apprehends itself as occupying the highest degree. The *sum* of St. Augustine affirms at one stroke the existence of man—not only of one half of him, destined to struggle desperately to rejoin the other half.

It is at this point, it seems to us, that the original deviation inflicted by modern Augustinianism on the authentic Augustinianism must be sought. There is a great temptation to see in it nothing more than an inconsistent idealism. Yet, if we may be allowed to use an expression unknown to St. Augustine, his philosophy is fundamentally just as realist as that of St. Thomas Aquinas. It is possible to read St. Thomas through the spectacles of Hume; the thing has actually been done. It is also possible to read St. Augustine through the spectacles of Descartes, and the St. Augustine obtained in the second case is about as good as the St. Thomas obtained in the first. We confess to disliking the word *realism*, though it is often difficult to avoid using it; perhaps someday, when it has been purged of certain meanings, it may be used without fear. What cannot in any case admit of the slightest doubt is that every substitution of abstract concepts for reality, and of a geometrical analysis for the investigation of concrete experience, is repugnant to the very essence of authentic Augustinianism. Another method may be preferred, but in that case we ought to realize that we are no longer Augustinians.

If this matter had been fully appreciated, the illusion of

an ontological St. Augustine, or a St. Augustine tending to ontologism without fully committing himself to it, would never have arisen. Malebranche (whom we do not, by the way, consider as an ontologist), Gerdil, Gioberti, and many others believe they can justify their point of view by a skillful exegesis of Augustinian texts on divine illumination. The Thomistic interpreters, like the eminent Zigliara, attempt the opposite operation by the same method. This method may have to have its day, but in the last resort it is worth only as much as the whole ideology on which it rests. All that such analyses establish is that at times the letter of St. Augustine invites ontologism and at others rejects it. But what is the significance of the letter? To discover it, we have to deal with his ideas. And here again it seems to us that every ontologism presupposes an idealist interpretation of Augustinianism and falls to the ground together with that interpretation.

Assuming it be admitted that St. Augustine's method is as we have described it, what do we find as the necessary starting point of our search? Facts, and nothing but facts. These facts may be, and often are, facts of inner experience, they may be ideas—but ideas taken not as principles of deduction, but as the basis of induction. The problem of the existence of God enjoys no privileged position in his teaching. It is, indeed, a unique case in respect of the reality at stake and consequently also in respect of the nature of the datum which allows us to attain to it, but this datum differs from other data only in content, not in nature. Like being, like life, like sensation, like thought, truth is a fact; like other facts, it is presented to our empirical observation; like other empirical observations, it demands of metaphysics the discovery of its sufficient reason; and if God alone can furnish its sufficient reason, we shall have proved the existence of God. Nothing here ever leaves the strictly philosophical order to pass over into mystical intuition and to substitute it for philosophical thought. The mystical order is certainly anticipated, hoped for, prepared for, but we have not got there yet; we are even still so far from it that it is never by pure philosophy that we can reach it: the order of knowledge has first to be superseded by the order of charity.

Every ontological interpretation of St. Augustine presupposes, then, a more or less complete misunderstanding of his radical empiricism. This explains also why such an interpretation believes itself able to introduce idealism into it. The *primum cognitum* of St. Augustine is not God; it is man within the universe, and, within this universe and this man, the experience of a true judgment. But it must be added that this *primum cognitum* is not even the *primum reale;* on the contrary, it becomes intelligible only on condition of finding its sufficient reason in a transcendent fact which provides its explanation. It is of the very essence of Augustinianism to affirm that this transcendent fact has left on man its mark and impress, that this impress is decisively legible for us only in true thought; but an impress is not the seal, and to forget that is the sure way of destroying Augustinianism. Far from taking his starting point, like Gioberti, from a *primum cognitum,* which is, *pro tanto,* the First Being, St. Augustine starts from a complex *cognitum,* in which he distinguishes by analysis an order of reality which postulates in its turn that of the First Being. Once this Being is apprehended and posited, it becomes possible to set off into an order which is not that of deduction, but rather of production; and even then it must be remembered that the start is taken not from a principle, but from the consequence, since we ourselves are only a consequence. Whatever, then, the letter of St. Augustine may be—and we have tried elsewhere to explain what it signifies—it cannot signify ontologism, unless it implies the negation of the entire thought of St. Augustine: the doctrine of divine illumination is not the vision of the First Cause, but the induction of the First Cause, starting from an effect; namely, truth.

But we have to proceed, we think, even farther on that road in order to give back to the Augustinian empiricism its proper character. Among the losses it has suffered in the course of history, perhaps the most surprising loss is that of its religious inspiration. An Augustinianism without grace is surely a strange metaphysical monster. Yet it has seen the light of day, and again we owe it to Descartes. Not by any means that Descartes ever dreamed of denying grace, but since it eluded the grasp of the mathematical method he had to relegate it to an extra-philosophical order and had to isolate it as another piece of that conceptual mosaic which for him was reality. For St. Augustine, on the contrary, the initial *sum* contains the supernatural order given in his experience and his being, as well as the natural order into which the supernatural is inserted. He cannot forget in his philosophizing that his first attempt to attain to truth and beatitude ended with an appeal of the reason to faith and of the will to grace. The congenital impotence of our intellectual light to apprehend truth, a correlative impotence of our will to compass the good until truth and goodness are accepted as the gifts of God, instead of being conquered like the spoils of the victor, had been St. Augustine's experience, undergone with an inner clarity of evidence unparalleled by anything else. Why, then, should a consistent psychological empiricism refuse, how could it avoid, to take this fact into account as much as the others?

St. Augustine never dreamed of avoiding it, any more than Maine de Biran, one of the most authentic of his race, while under the threat of his approaching death he felt the sting of his conscience and found in it an unimpugnable sign of the presence of grace. He felt it as soon as it was there and immediately surrendered to it. More fortunate, St. Augustine surrendered earlier; that is why the supernatural order by which he had access to truth was for him always an integral part of his philosophical inquiry. It is grace which turns knowledge into wisdom and moral effort into a virtue, with the result that instead of regarding Christianity as a belated crowning of philosophy, he sees in philosophy an aspect of Christianity itself, since it is the Way, the Truth, and the Life. Considered under this aspect, Augustinianism is something else and something more than a Christian philosophy; it is its very charter and enduring model. Beside it there are anti-Christian philosophies to be found, or philosophies compatible with Christianity; but to be Christian *qua* philosophy, a philosophy must be Augustinian or nothing. His metaphysic of nature completes a metaphysic of grace, because nature is given to the Christian in grace, which, working in him inwardly, manifests itself there in the manner of a cause revealed by its effects.

Thus restored in the purity of its essence, the philosophy of St. Augustine seems to us capable of setting out upon a new and fruitful course, but only on condition that those who undertake to promote it exercise care not to betray it. To put a stop to the painful sense of St. Augustine's exile, all that is needed is that those who have exiled themselves from him should return to him; they will find him where he has never ceased to be—at the very heart of Christian thought, side by side with St. Thomas Aquinas, who may have differed from him, but has never left him.

The fact is that both are indispensable. Those who judge of the history of Catholic thought from the outside may see in the present-day triumph of Thomistic philosophy nothing more than an accident of history or an incident in the ideological game. But, if we admit that a sole religion is bound to find expression in a sole *magisterium*, and ask which metaphysician can be regarded as the model and norm of a Catholic philosophy, whom could we choose but St. Thomas? Him and no other; not even St. Augustine. The perfection and completeness of his work protect it against the ceaseless deviations to which Augustinianism remains exposed. Considered in its living workings, Thomism is completed; the framework within which its future progress can be realized is set up. Augustinianism has yet to be completed, and by reason of its very nature will always remain in that condition. Nothing could be more logical and even necessary than that the Catholic Church should have chosen St. Thomas as her official Doctor, but we should fly in the face of facts and of her spirit in thinking that the choice of St. Thomas meant the exclusion of St. Augustine. Far from contradicting each other, the two doctrines complete each other, and their complementary nature does but indicate the infinite wealth of the religious reality whose rational exploration they attempt. God alone is necessary, and numerical diversity emerges simultaneously with the emergence of the contingent. All that matters is simply to know whether Augustinianism is something contingent that Christian thought can easily do without. We do not think so; it remains to give shortly our reasons for thinking so.

Like the work of St. Augustine, the work of St. Thomas is that of a saint. For a variety of reasons, some of which are co-essential with his work, it takes longer to become aware of this in his case than in the case of St. Augustine. Still, of all the discoveries we enjoy by living for a long time in close contact with him, one of the most certain is that of him, as of his master St. Dominic, it is true to say, "*Aut de Deo, aut cum Deo.*" What is apt to disguise in part this obvious truth is partly St. Thomas's intellectualism and partly what might be called his "physicism." The famous utterance of St. Paul about the *invisibilia Dei* has become for him, as it were, the program which philosophy has to accomplish. Watching him in his exploration of the nature of *ea quæ facta sunt*, we are apt to forget what he is searching for. Yet it is equally true to say that it is nothing but God that he searches for and that it is there that he is searching for Him. Taking man as he conceives him within nature as he finds it, St. Thomas asks himself the question, before all else, whether a universe like ours carries with it its own sufficient reason, and, if not, where it is to be found. Hence his entire theodicy is essentially cosmological. Search is sometimes made for a key to the system of St. Thomas, and after having conscientiously explored the *Summa Theologica* its supposed discoverer generally offers us a concept. But the object of Thomistic philosophy is not ideas; its object is things, for a real philosopher always speaks of things; it is the professors of philosophy who talk of ideas. The fundamental object, the primary experience on which St. Thomas continually bends his exploring gaze, is the fact of physical change. He wants to know its nature, its conditions, its causes. Convinced as he is that here is, not the only reality, but the most obvious reality for man as he is, the philosopher selects this as the best starting point because it is the most evident and accessible. Not that St. Thomas has any illusions as regards the knowledge of God that such a metaphysic can give us. If we start from the most crudely sensible fact in order to attain to the purest intelligible, no wonder that in such circumstances we end in a *quia est* whose *quid est* escapes us. But at least this *quia est*, and the little we induce concerning the *quid est*, cannot elude our grasp; they participate in the evidential and solid nature of the initial fact on which the entire structure rests. It would be rather naïve to ask on what grounds St. Thomas selects this philosophy; for a philosopher does not select his philosophy, he accepts the only philosophy he holds to be true. At best we might perhaps take into consideration the circumstances in which he found himself, the contamination which Augustinianism had undergone, and the state of confusion that its teaching presented, but these would be in the last resort merely accidental reasons which would make no difference to the essential question. If St. Thomas had thought that the philosophy of St. Augustine were the best, it would have been easy for him to restore its essence; if he preferred to do something else, the reason was that he visualized the possibility of a truer system.

Having said that much, the fact remains that by the very act of choosing the way he considered best he precluded himself from at the same time following another. St. Thomas was not an eclectic, ready to stitch together pieces borrowed from different philosophies to give them the external appearance of a system. He was a true philosopher, and though agreeing with St. Augustine on the meaning of the problems as well as on the formula of their solution, he yet did not consider himself justified in adopting it for the technical proof of these solutions when this seemed to him unsatisfactory. Every choice implies a limitation. Basing his efforts strictly upon the cosmological foundation of his theodicy St. Thomas was precluded from basing it upon its psychological foundations. It is a question not merely of the practical difficulty of exploring two such different fields of research, or the difference of aptitude required for the task, but of the divergence of the roads followed by St. Augustine and St. Thomas. They can meet again in the same conclusions, but the roads leading to them, though constantly crossing, never follow at any point the same direction. All that immense field of inner observation, wherein St. Augustine has no rival, would remain fallow if he were to be abandoned; none of the tracks he has started would be pursued; those ascensions that God has prepared for the heart of man would cease to be an object of meditation by the philosopher as such; all sorts of possible ways to God would be definitely closed which it is perhaps better to keep open for the greater good of Christian thought.

What it is consequently important to grasp is that the program of Christian philosophy is the same for both St. Thomas and St. Augustine: *invisibilia Dei per ea quæ facta sunt*. It is in no case possible for man to start from God to deduce from Him the creature; on the contrary, he must mount from the creature to God. The course recommended by St. Augustine—and herein lies his personal contribution to the treasure of tradition—is the path to God, leading through this particular creature which is man, and in man, thought, and in thought, truth. But this means, quite beyond speculations about the nature of truth and its metaphysical conditions, a sort of moral dialectic that, taking as object of its search the search itself by man of God, endeavors to show the presence in the heart of man of a contingency much more tragic and disturbing than that of the universe, because it is the contingency of our own beatitude. Even when we know how and why we are capable of truths, we still need to know why we are capable of the desire of truth; we need to understand the presence in us of an appeal by God who, working in our soul, creates in us a fruitful restlessness, moves, stirs our soul, and leaves it no rest until it has finally put itself into His hands. That this opens a field of inexhaustible fertility to analysis and metaphysical reflection is sufficiently proved by the recent controversies about the possibility of a natural desire of God in man. St. Augustine opened the way, but the Augustinians mistook it when, setting out on it themselves, they mistook his description for a demonstration and their emotions for proofs. It is for them to create an entire technique, to set up a metaphysic of charity able to meet the strict demands of Thomism; to give to nature what belongs to nature, and to grace what belongs to grace; able to discriminate between moral asceticism and the knowledge which it conditions; and, while observing better than hitherto the distinction of plans and orders, to *verify* Augustinian teaching, in the full sense of that word: adding to its truth in the future the truth which it contained in the past, instead of merely confirming, and sometimes of diminishing, that truth. One of the great features of superiority in Thomism is that it possesses enough creative power to assimilate the results of Augustinianism; the only question of the moment is whether Augustinianism has retained enough creative power to assimilate, without destroying itself, the decisive advances made by St. Thomas Aquinas.

We venture to hope so. We are personally convinced that

other ways may be possible, and even that they may have advantages over that followed by St. Augustine; but we are not prepared to assert that that of St. Augustine is impossible, or that it offers nothing but disadvantages. It is impossible not to be struck at once by his extraordinary philosophical vitality. St. Anselm left, in our opinion, the right road, when, abandoning the fundamental problem of the origin and of the ontological foundation of the idea of God, he shifted the burden of proof to the inner necessity of the concept itself. His mechanism for deducing God carries no conviction and gives the impression that what is of value in it lies rather in what it hides and neglects than what it places in the forefront and shows. It is not in the *Proslogion* but in the *De Veritate* that he lays his hand upon that secret door behind which God stands. Yet St. Anselm is an outstanding witness to that tenacious conviction in the heart of man that there is a divine sign by which the creature can recognize his Maker: *signatum est super nos*. By following on the footsteps of St. Anselm in their turn, Descartes, Malebranche, Leibniz, Hegel bear each one witness in his own manner to the persistence of this sentiment. Pascal and Maine de Biran, on the other hand, attest the vitality of the moral and religious dialectic. Philosophical thought does not usually pursue with such pertinacity roads leading nowhere. It may grope, it may err and lose its way, but, if need be, it is capable of turning back, to make a fresh start and recover itself.

This is, we think, what Augustinianism can and ought to do, and the progress of Thomistic thought is vitally interested in the doing of it. It would be easy to show how much Augustinianism could gain in precision, in discipline, and enrichment of every kind by contact with Thomism, but St. Thomas himself is there to prove that a St. Thomas is impossible without a St. Augustine. All that the Master has gathered from his illustrious predecessor, not by way of an external eclecticism, but by a real absorption and assimilation, disciples could gather in their turn, if a renewed Augustinianism offered them something to assimilate. But to do that, Augustinianism itself would have to become assimilative and creative, as it was in St. Augustine. It is capable of so becoming; it will so become, once it realizes that its function is to do well what has been badly done by modern idealism, to re-establish it on the foundations of a psychological realism which is its natural basis, alone capable of bearing its erection. If it is thus assimilative and creative, an immense future opens out before it. It can secure to contemporary thought the legitimate possession of truths whose presence this thought feels confusedly without being able to grasp them, because it grasps them together with errors; by means of Augustinianism, Christianity can once more accomplish its purifying, liberating, creative task. Everything invites it to this task; everything is waiting for it. Let Augustinianism embark upon this task, and in proportion as it will be true, it need fear nothing from anyone, from the Church less than from all the rest. The unity of Catholicism is not at stake; it is not waiting to be brought about; it exists. For the last six centuries Thomism and Augustinianism have gone side by side; six centuries—fifteen centuries: it counts for little in the life of the Church. They may still go for long together in exile; what they cannot prevent is that every one of their successful efforts to be more completely themselves will bring them more closely together, for their source is at the same spot, on Calvary; and their goal is at the same spot, on Thabor.

6. The Spirit of St. Bonaventure

We have followed to its goal the way on which St. Bonaventure set philosophic thought; and as we arrive at the promised end it looks as though we have not so much traveled in a straight line as circled round a mysterious center; our essential task has been to determine exactly the point where that center is, and there take our stand. This is the reason why we so often had to take a step backward whenever St. Bonaventure's thought took a step forward, and so often had to cast forward into the future to establish the significance of some point his thought had just attained. Because of a deep-lying analogy—above all, because of the Augustinian element so strongly active in both of them—St. Bonaventure's method is closely related to Pascal's. Often it may happen that they explain the same thing following a different order, and each of these orders is legitimate because in each the mind is moving about a center whose position grows ever more precise as the movements of thought that bear upon it are more numerous and more diverse in their starting points.

"Order," as Pascal was to say, "consists principally in digressions upon each point to relate it to the end and keep the end always in sight."[1]

This "order of the heart," with all the totally unforeseeable conclusions it involves, is St. Bonaventure's as well as Pascal's. It is possible, by abstraction and to meet the exigencies of doctrinal exposition, to draw out a regular line of questions; but to consider any point in this line as separable *de facto* or *de jure* from all or any of the others would be to conceive an utterly false idea of his thought. *Each* of the ideas which we have set out with a prior idea before it and a subsequent idea following did in reality contain *within its own compass* all that went before it and all that was to come after it, and could not rightly be considered save in strictest connection with its past and its future. This is true of all his ideas save one—the idea of the center by relation to which all the others find their place and their definition.

To express the spirit of St. Bonaventure in isolation from the doctrine in which it finds expression cannot, therefore, consist in summarizing that spirit in a formula, or in fixing a definite road for the march of his ideas: for his thought traverses innumerable roads, and consequently cannot be bound within a formula. We can express the spirit of St. Bonaventure only by showing the end toward which all digressions tended and in view of which alone they come to unity.

But even to show this end is still not enough. It would be a betrayal of St. Bonaventure if we left in any mind the impression that the abstract and so to speak geometrical determination of that central point enables us to know it as it requires to be known. Philosophy has not for its end to teach us to determine the center of things, as we determine the center of a circle by showing the lines which must pass through it; its end is rather to assure us the possession of this center by conferring upon us the habit of mind whereby we turn toward it inevitably no matter what the point at which we find ourselves, and the aptitude to relate any other point to the center once we have established our mind in it.

Wisdom, in its highest acceptation, is the inexpugnable occupation of the center of things by the purified soul; but philosophy, in its legitimate acceptation, is the science of the roads which lead to Wisdom, and the formation which enables the soul to traverse those roads. It is more true of this philosophy than of any other that its spirit needs not only to be described but still more to be accepted, willed, and obeyed before it can be truly known. To know how the summit of Alvernia is reached, it is not enough to be able to rattle off a description of all the roads that lead to the summit; rather we must choose one of these roads and set our foot upon it with the firm resolution to travel it to the end. The closer we approach the interior dispositions that St. Bonaventure demands of his reader, the better we shall understand the sense of the formulas he employs and the root reason of the ways he chooses.

It may be added that, for the man who is able to bring these dispositions to life in himself in their perfect form, the universe and the soul are immediately ordered into a totally unified system.

Let us begin with the center, which is Christ;[2] we shall immediately find that we can enter into the right relation with everything, starting from Him; and, likewise, if we start from any other thing we shall be brought back to Him. Being can be conceived only as either absolute or contingent; contingent being implies the existence of absolute being; and absolute being—since it contains by definition all the conditions required in order to be—must necessarily be of itself, conformed to itself and for itself; in other words, absolute being cannot be sufficient unto itself without at the same time being its own original cause, its own exemplar cause, and its own final cause.

Now, it is clear that within such a substance the origin holds the place of principle; the exemplar, of means; the final cause, as its name indicates, of end; and as it likewise appears that the Father is the Principle and the Holy Spirit the End, it follows of necessity that the Son is the Means. Thus the Father is the original foundation, the Holy Spirit the completion, and the Son the mental word; and it is because He is the eternal truth, at once principle of being and of knowing, that we, in our turn, find ourselves faced with an intelligible to be known and an immutable rule whereby to judge it. The measure of God Himself, the measure of things, the measure of knowledge, the Word is the central point at which the metaphysician must take his stand, and if we have placed exemplarism at the center of metaphysics, the reason is that the Exemplar Himself is, as it were, at the center of God.[3]

Let us now put ourselves in the position of the physicist who defines the principles of nature rather than the rules in virtue of which we judge it. As the heart is the center of the microcosm, the source from which the vital spirits spread outward into the body through the arteries, and the animal spirits through the veins; as the sun is the center of the macrocosm, the source of heat and of all the kinds of generation that take place in the world, so the Word became the center of the universe by being made flesh and dwelling among us. We know that He is also the means whereby the soul is united with God in ecstasy during this life, and the theologian can very readily show that He is also the means of eternal beatification: *Agnus in medio aquarum est Filius Dei, Filius dico, qui est media persona a qua omnis beatitudo.*[4] To have chosen, once for all, such a center of reference, and never to admit any other center—this cannot fail to have a profound influence not only upon the general economy of such a doctrine, but also upon its smallest details; to forget this central fact is to lose comprehension of the whole system.

In relation to such a center man can see both his origin and his goal, and so arrives at the recognition that he has a history. He sees his life as a passage between a beginning and a conclusion; and this certitude is capital—its effect upon his other certitudes is such that it completely transforms them. Not only has the life of man a history; the universe as a whole has a history; and in this case, too, the man who grasps the truth realizes that he can never again think as if he knew it not. You cannot reason about a universe whose astral revolutions are counted, are each one of them events willed by God and chosen by Providence, as you would about a universe whose essential facts would be exactly what they are even if it had existed from all eternity. And to make it more impossible still to forget this truth, the history of the universe is seen by us as a drama in which we have a part, a drama whose conclusion, after all digressions and divagations, must be our beatitude or misery for all eternity.

Once the soul has come to awareness of this terrifying truth, it can never again forget it; nor can the soul ever again think of anything at all save as this truth bears upon it. All that it knows, all that it feels, all that it wills, lies under the illumination of this tragic certitude. Where the Aristotelian merely saw the satisfying of curiosity, the Christian sees the deciding of a destiny. St. Bonaventure is profoundly penetrated with this sense of high tragedy: it is this that confers upon his doctrine its character of tension, and upon the expressions he uses the poignancy we feel in them. He thinks, precisely because it is for him a problem of eternal life or death to know what one *must* think; he trembles at the mere imagined possibility that he might, in a moment of distraction, lose sight of it. It is his agony to see that practically no one is thinking about it, and that man made by someone who is God, remade by the blood of the same God, is ever busy at his own unmaking—as if all that can choose between nothingness and being did, in blind folly, choose nothingness. The intellect must be an instrument of salvation and nothing besides. In so far as it puts Christ at the center of our history, as He is at the center of universal history, it must ever remember that on nothing whatsoever can a Christian think as he would if he were not a Christian.[5]

Let us consider the very idea of philosophy. It cannot begin without Christ, for He is its object, and it cannot attain completion without Christ, for He is its end. Thus, it has a choice between systematically condemning itself to error or taking count of facts which henceforth totally inform it. The Christian philosopher knows, to begin with, that his faculties of knowing have not a coefficient of value of their own; as a consequence he knows that the evidences of things will be more or less easily accessible to him according to the point of perfection at which he himself is. The intellect, in short, thinks more or less well according as the soul is more or less completely purified of its stains; and one could not treat an argument, such as St. Anselm's proof of the existence of God from the idea of the perfect, as if its acceptance depended solely upon the definition of the terms which compose it, or upon their comprehension by any intelligence at all. Man understands only what he deserves to understand, and the same argument which seems a sophism to a materialist intellect may seem evident to that same intellect once it has been stripped clean, purified, and turned toward God.

For a reason of the same sort the Christian philosopher will realize that the expression of natural phenomena—and particularly of their metaphysical conditions—cannot be the same in his eyes as they would be if he left God out. Of two possible conclusions, of which one attributes more to nature or free will and less to God, while the other attributes more to God at the expense of nature or free will, he will always choose the second, provided only that it does not contradict either free will or nature.[6] He would rather find himself in error through humility than risk a sin of pride; for there is no great harm in underrating oneself, whereas it is a crime to underrate God.

The repercussions of such a principle in such a system as St. Bonaventure's are of necessity multiplied so that no part of his system is unaffected by them. *Attribuere quod est Dei creaturae periculosum est.* If one reflects upon it, that is why the world could not be eternal, why the angelic substances could not be devoid of matter, why form could not be drawn from matter without pre-existent seminal reasons, why human knowledge could not find any absolute foundation without that illumination which is the source of necessity and certitude, why philosophy could not succeed without the light of faith, why virtue could not be attained without the help of grace, why nature must remain incomplete without the immediate and special concurrence of God. The doctrinal conservatism of St. Bonaventure and his anxiety in face of the danger to faith from innovators in philosophy or religion are but the most general manifestation of this fundamental tendency: one cannot place God in the center of thought without taking account of His presence every time one thinks, and the Christian soul judges of things only in relation to God.

Let us now see what is the condition of such a soul when it has achieved completely what is thus proper to it. Filled with a sense of the intellectual and moral wretchedness in which it is, it comes to understand the true cause of its state when it finds in Scripture the story of man's fall. From that moment it knows that there is nothing healthy in itself, that the task of its whole life must necessarily be to find healing from its sickness and cleansing from the stain which infects it, and by infecting it contaminates the whole universe.

From this comes that atoning discipline of the Christian life in its most perfect form—Franciscan poverty giving life to the intellect, with the eradication of the passions, interior unification, and ecstasy for its crown.

The flaw is not annulled, but a watchful discipline, progressively stabilizing the human soul in its regained perfection, maintains in it and in things the divine order which has now been restored by the concurrence of grace and freedom.

The wayfaring man thus finds himself separated from God Who is to be his reward; his intellect, even made perfect, cannot attain the face-to-face vision which would fix it once for all upon its object. This is the secret of that incessant movement which draws the mind from one object to another without any object ever being able, or even seriously looking as though it would be able, to hold the mind finally. But an intellect, even condemned to move, can at least regulate its movement and settle, once for all, the objects upon which it may rightly look. This, in one word, is the Christian soul in its state of perfection.

Hierarchically arranged, reaching out to God and rightly ordered to Him, it moves back and forth according to its own individual, personal rhythm, between the ecstatic contact with God by love and the intellectual contemplation of God in the exterior or interior mirrors which reflect Him. Too rarely for its liking, and for a few too short moments, it is in immediate contact with its God; but even when that direct contact is broken the soul is charged with new desires and new energies driving it to seek, again and again, the contact it has lost.

St. Bonaventure sees the soul illumined by grace turning majestically, like a sun which can never fix its light in one single point nor cease its revolving, but which yet follows an ordered course as if the twelve houses of the heaven it traverses were the only places worthy of its passage.

An intellect ill-disciplined lets itself be drawn in unrelated directions by a movement leading it nowhere; the hierarchized intellect, on the other hand, turns about God; it has fixed forever the spiritual constellations which make its zodiac and, having fixed them, it passes ceaselessly from one of its houses to another without ever leaving the luminous orbit which they constitute. What are these signs? We know them already, for they are necessarily the same objects upon which along with St. Bonaventure we have concentrated the effort of our philosophic reflection, plus certain others upon which rational reflection can take no hold, but which the soul illumined by grace can contemplate to its own advantage: the consideration of corporeal beings, then of spiritual substances; the consideration of the ways of knowledge conceived by the mind; of the moral virtues, then of the laws instituted by God; of the divine graces which give the soul its hierarchy; of the unsearchable judgments of God; of His mercies, likewise, which are as incomprehensible; of the merits which will be rewarded, and of their rewards; of the sequence of times revealed by Scripture and the order that the soul finds in them; of the eternal reasons, finally, which bring this contemplation to its term in God and unite it with the first sign of the mental zodiac—the beings of which these exemplars are the models.[7] Thus, ever moving on the orbit proper to it, the contemplative soul ever finds itself in one or other of these signs, yet never stays in any.

Now, it follows of necessity that such a transformation of the intellect involves a correlative transformation of the universe. Natural science claims to give the universe its true meaning by multiplying to infinity individual phenomena and the theories which account for them; Christian philosophy, on the other hand, gives the universe its true meaning by subordinating it to its true end, which is to show forth God to man, and to lead man to God. For one who never loses sight of the goal of beatitude, this world can have no other *raison d'être* than to give us a foretaste of what is to come. Ceaselessly St. Bonaventure expressed this thought in every possible form; but the expression which is most striking in its Franciscan homeliness, he found when he defined man's task as the organization of our earthly exile into a sort of suburb of the heavenly kingdom, in such wise that every day we might savor in advance something of the eternal beatitude: *Si haec caelestia gaudia jugiter in mente teneres, de hoc exilio quoddam suburbium caelestis regni construeres, in quo illam aeternam dulcedinem quotidie spiritualiter praelibando degustares.*[8]

If we give this formula its fullest meaning, and if further we suppose an intellect infinitely subtle and flexible given wholly to its realization, we shall see how naturally it implies the analogical universe of St. Bonaventure with its correspondences and its proportions founded in the very essence of things, penetrated through and through, and strengthened by the influx of light—that noblest analogy of the spirit in the world of bodies. Whether they concern the soul or things, all the doctrines that we have in turn examined are seen to issue from one sole and single fundamental preoccupation; creatures are what they ought to be in themselves in the exact measure in which they are what they ought to be for God.

Perhaps this is the deepest-lying reason why St. Bonaventure's doctrine has often remained ungrasped by even the best-informed historians. A misunderstanding so frequent cannot be purely accidental; and its cause may be worth a closer search. All the great philosophical doctrines are strongly systematized, but for all that they are usually made up of a series of fragments linked together, each of which retains something of its true meaning when considered separately. We may think we understand Comte if we know only the *Positive Philosophy*, or Kant if we know only the *Critique of Pure Reason*, or Descartes if we have read his *Metaphysical Meditations*, or St. Thomas if we have studied his philosophy and not his theology. And while undoubtedly each of these supposed understandings is at some point incomplete, the mere fact that self-deception of this sort is possible, or even that a historian can think he is free to choose what seems to him most interesting in the system he is studying, proves that the fragments of the system thus mutilated retain an interest and a meaning.

It is quite otherwise in such a doctrine as that of St. Bonaventure. In it, the totality of the system means so much that the mere notion of fragments has no meaning at all. You can either see the general economy of his doctrine in its totality, or see none of it; nor would a historian be led by the understanding of one of the fragments to desire to understand the whole, for the fragments are quite literally meaningless by themselves, since each part reaches out into all the rest of the system and is affected by the ramifications leading to it from the system as a whole. That is why incomprehension waits inevitably upon those historians who set out, for example, to discover the mind of St. Bonaventure upon the proofs for the existence of God, or upon the relation of reason and faith; for the true sense of St. Anselm's argument is only to be seen in such a doctrine at the very threshold of ecstasy, and the critique of Averroist Aristotelianism finds its true basis only in our realization that avarice and curiosity (which is intellectual avarice) have a common root in the concupiscence and will to self of original sin.

Paradoxical as the assertion may seem, I hold that it is the extreme unification of Bonaventure's doctrine which has made it look incomplete and unsystematized; it is easier to deny that the details form part of a system than to grasp the system in its entirety and think out each detail in function of the whole.

What is true of the doctrine considered in itself is equally true of the position it occupies in the history of philosophic thought in the thirteenth century. If we do not see the interior logic of the doctrine, it could scarcely occur to us that it has played a really active part, and in consequence occupies a place which history is bound to take into consideration. This is the perfectly simple and natural explanation of an extraordinary defect in even first-rate historians—describing the movement of ideas in the thirteenth century, they pass over St. Bonaventure in silence, or else see nothing save passivity, lack of constructive power, or of power to unify by its own principles, in the medieval Augustinianism of which he gives the most complete expression.[9] Impotence and anarchy; this is the surprising summarization of the intellectual effort to which we owe the *Breviloquium*, the *Itinerarium*, and the *Hexaëmeron*—three works whose closeness of thought and solidity of structure grip the intellect ever more powerfully as it enters more deeply into them. A misunderstanding of this nature is too grave to be left without some effort to clear it up.

It might, of course, be that a certain conception of philosophy in general and of scholastic philosophy in particular is at the base of these judgments upon medieval Augustinianism. Looked at from the rationalist point of view of modern philosophy, St. Bonaventure's doctrine does undoubtedly appear as the most medieval of medieval philosophies; and so, in certain aspects, it is. No thirteenth-century thinker set himself more systematically to reduce the sciences to theology and put them entirely at its service; and no one took more literally than he the mission entrusted by the popes to the University of Paris: *theologia imperat aliis ut domina et illae sibi ut famulae obsequuntur*.[10]

Looked at from the point of view of Thomist philosophy, St. Bonaventure's doctrine would seem to be disqualified for an analogous reason. Assuredly Thomism was modern from the moment of its birth—in this sense, that, established of set purpose on the common ground of the human reason, it professed to resolve philosophical problems by methods common to all. By accepting the *Organon* of Aristotle as the criterion of true and false in philosophy, Albertus Magnus and St. Thomas made it possible for Christian theologians to communicate *as* philosophers with those who were philosophers only. Discussion was now possible between a Thomist of the University of Paris, or Naples, or Cologne, and an Arab, a Jew, or an Averroist: a proof for one of them was a proof for all of them, and, in fact, many doctrines were held by them in common as truths rationally demonstrated.[11]

On the other hand, if you set St. Bonaventure's doctrine against these philosophies, it is for them quite literally not a philosophy at all. Refusing to accept unaided reason as a common ground, it cut itself off from the communion of unaided human minds. Into Bonaventure's system one can enter only by an act of faith.[12] Therefore, it necessarily met the opposition both of those who would not make an act of faith at all and of those who would do so but only for the salvation of their souls and not for the development of their philosophy. If by philosophy we mean pure reason, there is no Bonaventurean philosophy, and from that point of view it is but just to treat it exactly as if it did not exist.

But at least we must realize that this is a dogmatic point of view which we are free to choose for our own, but not free to regard as history; the judgment of value must follow the establishment of the facts and not condition it. First we must observe that the historian cannot accept the purely negative interpretation of the facts proposed by the philosopher. To show that St. Bonaventure confused philosophy with theology might mean two very different things. First, it might have the bad sense, that he was incapable of distinguishing the two disciplines: in this event we should regard him as having failed to realize the fundamental distinction between them, and as thereby of necessity condemned not to know where he stood in the matter. But in fact we know exactly what his attitude on this point was: either you can establish the formal distinction between philosophy and theology, and so make of philosophy simply a collection of truths mingled with errors invented by the human mind; or else you can preserve a positive meaning for the word "philosophy," and in this case you must in practice abandon the distinction between it and theology in order to make a study of nature according to the principles suggested to reason by revelation. But recognizing the fact, the very formula we use invites us to reflect upon the primary interpretation that history offered us. If confusion reigns in St. Bonaventure's thought it is a confusion of a very special kind. For in a certain sense, as we have shown, it is true to say that there exists a formal distinction between philosophy and theology in his doctrine, but when he has established this distinction as real, he puts it aside as illegitimate. There is thus not a negative confusion, nor a simple absence of distinction, but a positive condemnation of the distinction. St. Bonaventure was not unaware of it; he knew it, and would have none of it; so that we must modify the terms in which the question is usually expressed.

If we adopt the first of the two hypotheses which we have just said to be possible, the historian has no difficult choice to make: he writes off Bonaventure and his followers as theologians who do not even know what philosophy may be, and all the philosophers he consults are at one in neglecting the system. The rationalists do not agree with the Thomists in so far as they would reduce the whole content of human knowledge to that of the reason, but rationalists and Thomists are agreed in reducing the whole content of *philosophy* to that of the reason. Thus, St. Bonaventure's doctrine, not being a philosophy, need have no place in the history of philosophy.

But if we adopt the second interpretation, the problem becomes more complex, because two different conceptions of philosophy are offered to us, and two quite different kinds of doctrines claim their place. St. Bonaventure can no longer be considered as unaware of the existence of philosophy. He knows it exists. But he holds that precisely *as* philosophy it is vitiated by its claim to exist apart. He denies it as an autonomous discipline; he affirms it as a subordinated discipline, gathers it up and integrates it in an organism of supernatural ideas and influences which transfigure it and thereby bring it to its right completion. Thus there is no question of a suppression, but only of a transmutation of philosophical values; and the only reason which could justify a historian in considering St. Bonaventure's attempt as a mere nullity would be the conviction that he had failed. If, in fact, the denial of a separate philosophy (in St. Albert's sense) had sterilized philosophic thought, history would have no more to do than note the fact; it would observe that the conscious and explicit integration of philosophy in theology had led to an impotence for the construction of one of those coherent systems wherein the multiplicity of the facts of experience is reduced to unity. Whether this is true of St. Bonaventure's system is the question we must now ask.

To answer this question by a strictly historical method we must judge it not by a conception of philosophy different from its own, but in relation to the ideological development of which it is the perfect flowering. In order to make clearer the line of our argument, we may contrast two different interpretations of the evolution of philosophy in the thirteenth century. One, which we may consider as classic, sees all that took place in the perspective of Thomism: the thirteenth century began with the Augustinian tradition, but, threatened by the invasion of Averroism and reacting with Albertus Magnus against this invasion, absorbed from it all that was true in the system of Aristotle. The thesis of the anarchy of Augustinianism is necessarily involved in this, since obviously, if Augustinianism had been adequate, Thomism would have had no reason to exist.

The second interpretation sees the scholasticism of the thirteenth century as reaching its height in two summits: the powerful movement at work within Christian thought threw up two high peaks, to say nothing of the secondary heights which formed a double chain about them: of these two peaks, one is the doctrine of St. Bonaventure; the other, that of St. Thomas Aquinas. We have said elsewhere what the signification of the second has appeared to us to be; here we should like, in the light of the examination made in this book, to insist upon the historic significance of the first.

The argument usually used to thrust St. Bonaventure outside the frontiers of the history of philosophy consists simply in dubbing him a mystic; and it is precisely to this argument that we appeal to bring him once more within that history. St. Bonaventure is essentially a mystic; but he is at the same time a philosopher, because he conceived the project of systematizing knowledge and being in terms of mysticism; indeed he is a great philosopher because, like all great philosophers, he followed out his idea to its conclusion in a real synthesis. If the mystical feeling is to be considered as an integral part of human nature, the content of the philosophy of mysticism may very well evolve because our representation of the universe evolves; but never will any doctrine do more complete justice to the experiences which are the eternal source of mysticism, nor be more comprehensive or more systematically organized than St. Bonaventure's; and if, as is still more evident, mysticism forms an integral part of the Christian life, no doctrinal synthesis will ever be found in which the aspirations of Christian mysticism receive a more abundant satisfaction. You might complain that there is too much mysticism in Bonaventure's doctrine; you can never say that there is not enough, for mysticism permeates the whole. But in permeating the whole it systematizes the whole, and it is this which confers upon this doctrine such richness in such unity.

Compare the doctrine of St. Bonaventure with that of the greatest medieval mystic before him—St. Bernard. Dante, who had an almost infallible instinct in his choice of the personages required by his argument at every point, chose St. Bernard as the incarnation of the highest form of Christian life that it was possible for him to conceive. In fact, no choice could be better justified than that of St. Bernard as guide to the summits of the spiritual life, for he is not only a mystic, he is the mystic pure and simple, without a trace of philosophy. His will to ecstasy involved the denial of everything beside and the successive suppression of all aspects of nature and all manifestations of life. Hence his prodigious asceticism leading him to these two principles: in the matter of sleep, he would not spend the *whole* night without it; in the matter of food, he would force himself to eat in spite of the disgust he felt for food. Hence, also, an asceticism of the mind parallel with that of the body. For him to restrain curiosity implied the deadening of the senses in such wise that exterior stimuli no longer gave rise to sensations; or, if by chance sensations were produced, they left no trace in the memory, and in the end were not perceived. We learn as a fact that he did not even know the structure of the chapel to which he went every day. Curiosity of the mind was disciplined as rigidly as that of the senses, and by this we must not understand simply that the study of the sciences for their own sake seemed to him useless, but that even the use of *fides quaerens intellectum* was a source of anxiety.

The fixity of his hostility to Abelard had no other reason than Abelard's efforts to interpret dogma. He accused Abelard of wanting to destroy faith because Abelard wanted to understand it in the measure in which it is understandable. It is he who stigmatized Abelard as a rationalist in the modern sense of the word, and he was believed. That is why St. Bernard's mysticism developed in its totality along one single line. Stripped bare, purely interior and psychological, it had something classic, in the French sense, about it. The psychological analyses of our interior wretchedness, the knowledge of ourselves, the moral ascesis whereby we climb the steps of humility and descend the corresponding steps of pride, the way of the meditations which lead us from the love of ourselves to the love of God for us, then to the love of God for Himself and for us, and finally to the love of God for Himself; the ascent of desire to ecstasy by the consideration of Providence, the terror of the judgment and the certainty of God's mercy; some gripping pages on the joys of that indescribable experience which alone gives our life its true sense: this, for all practical purposes, is the essence of his mysticism, which is all depth and intensity.

St. Bernard goes straight to his goal and wastes no time on any secondary consideration. He does not call Nature to his aid, but, on the contrary, excludes it from the field he chooses to explore, and systematically closes his eyes to the beauty of the world of sense; the walls of his mysticism are as bare as the walls of a Cistercian chapel; he is not curious to know whether human knowledge comes by way of abstraction, as Abelard and Aristotle taught, or by way of illumination, as St. Augustine had it. What St. Bernard taught was not a system, not an elaborated doctrinal scheme, but simply an interior life and its formula; and because mysticism is much more a matter of doing than of speaking, it was natural that Dante should have chosen him as guide to the topmost heights.

Between St. Bernard and St. Bonaventure, medieval thought was transformed by an immense labor of development. Not only did St. Bernard's disciples—like William of Saint-Thierry or Isaac Stella—carry on the discussion and develop the analysis of the mystical life, but the work of thinkers like Hugh and Richard of St. Victor exceeds in breadth and solidity anything previously produced by the medieval West: their writings were veritable summas of mystical inspiration, and the *De Sacramentis* and the *De Trinitate* were the immediate sources of Bonaventure's synthesis.

Between them and St. Bonaventure lay also the *Summa* and the teaching of Alexander of Hales; now that his text has been restored, the student can study in detail the influence upon the disciple of the master's thought. Such works bear ample witness—a witness that grows ever more irrefutable as they are more deeply studied—to the intense vitality of Christian thought toward the end of the twelfth and the beginning of the thirteenth century. We can no longer view that age as an age of chaos with scattered groups of thinkers busying themselves without order or direction and so leading nowhere and constructing nothing. It is clear that, as early as the great age of St. Victor, Christian thought was definitely set upon the way that leads to St. Bonaventure. While its inspiration is essentially theological, it makes no bones about using the terminology or even the doctrine of Aristotle; but always with the express condition that none of his constitutive principles should take the place of the traditional principles of Augustinianism. The better Aristotle's teaching comes to be known, the more numerous will these borrowings be seen to be; those of St. Bonaventure are continual: the distinction of act and potency, and the theory of the four kinds of causes—to take only two examples in a hundred—were suggestions which he was to develop fruitfully in all sorts of ways. He was even to utilize them in the interpretation of the words of St. Francis. But for all this use of Aristotle, it remains true that until the Thomist reform one regular and continuous movement of Christian thought was giving birth to works of increasing amplitude, animated by the spirit of St. Augustine, but in their systematic structure of a remarkable novelty when compared to the profound but fragmentary efforts of St. Augustine himself. Not to see how continuous is this progress through the years preceding the triumph of the Thomist synthesis is as if one were to see nothing between the *Theologia Christiana* of Abelard and the work of Albertus Magnus.

It is surely right to hold that St. Bonaventure's synthesis marks a capital stage in this progress. The Thomist synthesis resolved the Aristotelian crisis by a sudden about-face; and its victory gives us at this distance the impression that it overwhelmed medieval Augustinianism. But as the publication of texts continues we can see, following St. Bonaventure, a whole series of thinkers whose work was to maintain, to deepen, or to develop the metaphysical principles which were the basis of his teaching. Mathieu d'Acquasparta, John Peckham, Eustache d'Arras, Guillaume de la Mare, Gauthier of Bruges, Pierre-Jean Olivi were, in varying degrees, under his influence and paved the way for the new doctrinal synthesis of the fourteenth century—that of Scotus especially, of which the interpretation still remains lamentably uncertain. The whole work of Raymond Lulle is completely unintelligible apart from the symbolism of St. Bonaventure and his doctrine of intellectual and moral illuminations. With Jean Gerson this doctrinal influence extends to the domain of spirituality and piety; it was to spread still further and occupy the Christian conscience for centuries; and it would not be absurd to ask whether what is today known as the French school of spirituality does not derive in part from the Franciscan school whose spirit is Bonaventurean. It is not yet possible to write the history of the influence of his doctrine, but what little we know makes it certain that it was remarkably fecund.

The illusion of perspective, which today makes it so difficult to discern his influence, masks equally what was truly definitive in his doctrine. In certain points the principles upon which it was founded might develop in the course of time a whole series of new consequences; but if we consider even the edifice raised by St. Bonaventure, we see it as something unique and completed—the ultimate issue of a tendency which had no further goal to reach. And in this sense it may be said that if the success of Thomism seems at a distance to have brought the development of medieval Augustinianism to an end, it may be simply because with St. Bonaventure the mystical synthesis of medieval Augustinianism was fully formed, just as that of Christian Aristotelianism was fully formed with

St. Thomas. Like all the great systems, each impresses us as something complete and final in itself, yet as capable of endless development by reason of its power of assimilating new elements of reality. The philosophy of St. Bonaventure is in this sense final: the profound and characteristic tendency of medieval Augustinianism was to place the mystical element of the doctrine in the foreground, subordinating all the rest; and with St. Bonaventure this tendency for the first time achieved full expression. The desire for ecstasy and the knowledge of things were two elements sustaining and enriching each other: and in Bonaventure they are finally developed in a vast structure into which is built the totality of human experience as it had been inherited by philosophy—a doctrine of knowledge, a theory of the metaphysical principles of nature, above all, a rule of action, and all this penetrated, sustained, held in unity by an inspiration so perfectly one that the mind rises from the humblest operations upon material objects to the highest inpourings of grace without the faintest breach in the continuity of its movement.

This undoubtedly is its gravest fault in the eyes of many of our contemporaries. Philosophy must treat of nature; mysticism can treat only of grace, and is, therefore, the business of none but the theologian. But we should be clear, to begin with, as to the meaning of the word "nature." We can, of course, use this word to mean the collection of facts given to us through the senses, with an *a priori* supposition that they contain within themselves the sufficient reason of their being and their own interpretation. In this sense the notion of the transcendent or the supernatural is evidently meaningless: but we may well ask whether the notion of philosophy itself is not equally meaningless. All that is, is in nature, and is therefore natural—but only if the idea of the supernatural, the desire and the need for the supernatural are not an integral part of nature: only if the exigency of the thing excluded is not engraved in the very substance of that from which it is excluded; only if we ignore, and indeed specially train ourselves to ignore, those questions which are ever springing up in the depths of the human heart, questions which we repress in the name of that very nature which asks them so insistently. All is as if man and things contained virtually in themselves the sufficient reason of what they are; a being can always be explained by another being, and the totality of being would be self-explanatory if only the totality were given to us. The eternal silence of the infinite spaces no longer terrifies us; we are grown deaf to the appeals which still spring up when we least expect them from the depths of the human soul. Nothing remains but physics and in consequence all that is belongs to science alone; the radical elimination of the transcendent is the elimination of all metaphysics and hence of all knowledge that philosophy can call its own.

But there is another point of view. According to it, Nature is to be defined as the totality of what is given to the mind, without any *a priori* exclusion of the conditions it requires in order to be understood. This is the true beginning of metaphysics and thus the only order of speculation in which it is possible to assign a specific content to philosophy; it is the science of the conditions required by, but not contained within, the totality of that which is given. But this inevitably implies the transcendent, and this as inevitably the supernatural. This transcendent—which the formula of pure naturalism excludes by definition—is no longer held to be a thing whose whole essence consists in its inability to form part of any experience: and its opposition to nature is no longer that of a term to its contradictory; the supernatural thus becomes an experience that we have not yet had, temporarily in eclipse, because nature itself is in darkness. It is not yet a datum but it will be one. It may even be said in a certain sense that if it is not yet a datum, at any rate its place is marked by signs so clear that an integral empiricism has no right to ignore it.

But from this point also the supernatural may be presented to philosophic reflection in a twofold aspect. Either it may be supposed that its latent presence acts only to conserve and move beings in their proper nature in such a way that it remains possible to make a separate description of their nature as science knows it, omitting the economy of the divine influences sustaining it and making its existence possible; this is St. Thomas's method. Or, on the other hand, it may be supposed that the supernatural perfects beings in their own nature so that it perpetually completes them and reveals them to themselves, and that it is impossible to describe them in themselves without recourse to it; and this is the method of St. Bonaventure. This is why for all that his doctrine remains a philosophy, it yet has the special quality we feel in it and differs from other metaphysical systems by what is deepest in it.

If, in fact, it is the transcendent and the supernatural which constitute the very heart of the real, and if the real cries out this truth to us unceasingly by its manifold insufficiencies, the highest task of metaphysics must be the reintegration in the economy of nature of all the supernatural that it requires to become intelligible to us. Like all true philosophies, St. Bonaventure's starts from experience; it thrusts its roots down to the furthest depths of our insufficiency and the insufficiency of things; but it sees this insufficiency only to see beyond it: for the evil presupposes that there is a remedy unless we are to grant that the universe is meaningless and evil incurable. Thus philosophy may either despair of things and of itself, or seek the explanation of the universe where it is to be found; but it cannot choose this latter part unless it sees, as the essential object of its effort, the discovery and the elaboration of that element of the divine implied by nature. This is precisely the work St. Bonaventure set himself to accomplish. With a delicate logic which in the extent of its exigencies will never be surpassed, he develops the complete philosophy of that supernatural apart from which nature and man would remain insoluble enigmas. This is the glory that shall not be taken from him. In his powerful, complex philosophy, knowledge enlightens charity and is fed by it. Paris does not destroy Assisi, and Assisi does not reject Paris. But if the somber plaint of Jacopone de Todi here loses its point, it is because the doctor comes down from his professorial chair and goes to meditate upon Alvernia. Upon the summit of Alvernia and not on the slopes of the hill of St. Geneviève, he sought to fly in the track of the seraph with the six wings; and if he owed his knowledge to the University of Paris, it was in the soul of St. Francis that he found his inspiration.

Hence St. Bonaventure's doctrine marks for us the culminating point of Christian mysticism and constitutes the completest synthesis it has ever achieved. Thus it must be clear that it can never be properly comparable in any point with the doctrine of St. Thomas Aquinas. Obviously it would be absurd to deny their fundamental agreement. They are both Christian philosophies and every threat to the faith finds them united against it. As against pantheism, both of them teach creation from nothing and maintain that the gulf is infinite between absolute Being and contingent. As against ontologism, both deny explicitly that God can be seen at all by the human mind in this life, and *a fortiori* they deny that habitual knowledge of God which ontologism attributes to us. As against fideism, they both set the most thorough effort of the intellect to prove the existence of God and interpret the data of faith. As against rationalism, both co-ordinate the effort of the intellect with the act of faith and maintain the beneficent influence of the habit of faith upon the operations of the intellect.

The agreement between them is deep-lying, indestructibly proclaimed by tradition, which has submitted it to the test of the centuries: an agreement such that no one even in the time of the worst doctrinal conflicts has called it in question. But if these two philosophies are equally Christian, in that they equally satisfy the requirements of revealed doctrine, they remain none the less two philosophies. That is why, in 1588 Sixtus V proclaimed, and in 1879 Leo XIII repeated, that both men were involved in the construction of the scholastic synthesis of the middle ages and that today both men must be seen as representing it: *duae olivae et duo candelabra in domo Dei lucentia.*

The attempts sometimes made by their interpreters to transform their fundamental agreement into an identity of content are, from the start, futile and doomed to fail. For it is clear that since the two doctrines are ordered from different starting points, they will never envisage the same problems in the same aspect, and therefore one will never answer the precise question that the other asks. The philosophy of St. Thomas and the philosophy of St. Bonaventure are complementary, as the two most comprehensive interpretations of the universe as seen by Christians, and it is because they are complementary that they never either conflict or coincide.

NOTES

1. *Pensees*, no. 283; ed. L. Brunschvicg, p. 461.
2. St. Bonaventure, *In Hexaemeron*, I, 1 and 10 (*Opera Omnia*, ed. Quaracchi, vol. V, 1891, pp. 329, 330).
3. *Op. cit.*, I, 12–14; ed. cit., vol. V, pp. 331–332.
4. *Op. cit.*, I, 38; ed. cit., p. 335.
5. Because, even when a Christian agrees with an unbeliever on the material content of some truth, he sees in that truth the transcendent foundation that remains unknown to the unbeliever and he attaches more importance to the knowledge of that foundation than to the knowledge of that truth in itself.
6. *In II Sententiarum*, d. 26, a. unicus, q. 2 Respondeo (ed. minor, Quaracchi, 1937, pp. 655, 656). Same remark on the hyleomorphic composition of the angels: *In Hexaem.*, IV, 2; ed. cit., vol. V, p. 351.
7. *In Hexaem.*, XXII, 40; ed. cit., vol. V, p. 443; also VI, 19, p. 363.
8. *Soliloquium*, IV, 1.4 (in *Decem Opuscula*, ed. minor, 4th ed., Quaracchi, 1949, p. 128).
9. For an expression of this view, see P. Mandonnet in *Revue des Jeunes*, X, 1 and 2, 1920, pp. 159–160, 524–525, 526.
10. See E. Gilson, *Etudes de philosopie médiévale* (Strasbourg: Université de Strasbourg, 1921), pp. 44–49.
11. See below, pp. 181–183, 271–274.
12. Is it necessary to add that the doctrine of St. Bonaventure is nevertheless *not* a fideism? Fideism substitutes faith for reason, whose efficacity it denies; whereas Augustinianism demands the aid of faith for the good use of reason as reason.

7. John Duns Scotus[1]

John Duns, called Scotus from his country's name, was born in 1266 at Maxton, in the county of Roxborough (Scotland). Sent to the convent of Dumfries in 1277, he joined the Franciscan Order in 1281. John studied at Oxford shortly before 1290, was ordained a priest at Northampton March 17, 1291, and studied at Paris (1293–1296). After his return to Oxford he began to teach theology (1297–1301). His first teaching at Oxford is represented by the *Lectura Oxoniensis*, still unpublished, but whose final redaction by the master is known under the title of *Opus Oxoniense*. In 1302 the young master returned to Paris and, in order to pass his Parisian doctorate, he publicly "read" for the second time the same text. As a result of this teaching we have a second redaction of his Commentary, known by the title of *Reportata Parisiensa*. Banished from France in 1303, with many others who, like himself, had taken the part of the Holy See against Philip the Fair, Duns Scotus returned to Paris in 1304, there became doctor in theology in 1305, and was sent to Cologne in 1307, where he died November 8, 1308. In addition to his two Commentaries on Peter Lombard, we have from his pen a series of writings on logic, important *Questions on the Metaphysics*, *Quaestiones quodlibetales*, and a treatise *De primo principio*. Even if the less important works were not taken into consideration, the immensity of the effort accomplished by a master dead at the age of forty-two would still be overwhelming.

A. METAPHYSICS AND ITS OBJECT

His premature end certainly deprived us of writings where we would find the complete expression of his thought, and whose absence is cruelly felt. On some important points we are sometimes reduced to knowing only his conclusions, without being able to say how he justified them. On the other hand, the general inspiration of his philosophy is clear, and we can assign to it, without risk of any very grave error, a definite place in the history of medieval philosophies. With Avicenna, and against Averroes, Duns Scotus considers that the object of theology is God, whereas the proper object of philosophy, or rather of the metaphysics crowning it, is being as being. Even our theology does not bear upon God as God, but upon God as knowable by the most perfect of the concepts we can form of his nature; namely, that of "infinite being." The metaphysician deals only with being *qua* being. Moreover, even being *qua* being partly escapes the intellect of the metaphysician. Strictly speaking, being as such is an absolute, without any determination which restrains it to a certain mode of determined being. Now it happens that man has to draw his knowledge from the sensible. The human intellect, therefore, knows about being only what it can abstract from sense data. We have no direct intuition of being, both material and immaterial, in its entire indetermination and generality. All our metaphysics is therefore an abstract science of being as being, constructed by an intellect attaining only one of its aspects, which is not even the highest.

Such being the situation, the only way to find for metaphysics an object endowed with a sufficient unity is to posit a notion of being so abstract and indeterminate that it may apply indifferently, always in the same sense, to everything that is. That is why metaphysics cannot intend to attain that act of existing (*ipsum esse*) which, according to St. Thomas, is the core of every being. Existents are, in the last analysis, irreducibly distinct from one another; they cannot provide metaphysics with an object truly one. In order to save the unity of its object, and consequently its own possibility, metaphysics must consider the notion of being at its ultimate degree of abstraction, where it becomes applicable in one and the same sense to all that is. This is what we mean when we say that being is "univocal" for the metaphysician.

The univocity of being imposes a certain method in the demonstration of the existence of God. Some deem it necessary to start from the existence of sensible things to infer from it the existence of their cause. Assuredly, if we start from physical bodies, we will finally succeed in proving the existence of their primary cause, but whether it be that of their movement or even of their existence, it will remain a physical cause. This is what happens in the philosophy of Aristotle, where the Prime Mover, primary cause of the universe, is itself included in it. In other words, if it is the function of physics to prove the existence of God, the God whose existence physics can demonstrate does not transcend the physical order; as a keystone is gripped in the arch, this God is gripped in nature, even if it holds together only through him. To attain a primary principle which causes the world in its very being, one cannot build upon *sensible being*, but on *being*.

The univocal notion of being as being is therefore the condition of the very possibility of a science transcendent to physics and the indispensable point of departure for metaphysics. It is an abstract notion, and the first one of all, since, as Avicenna says, being is what falls first in the intellect. It is therefore a universal notion, but the metaphysician does not envisage it from the point of view of its universal predicability. The nature and conditions of the predicability of our concepts are logical properties; their study does not concern metaphysics, but logic. On the other hand, since the metaphysician disregards the individuating conditions of sensible beings, he does not consider them as a physicist either. The kind of being considered by the metaphysician is neither a particular physical reality nor a universal taken in its logical generality; it is the intelligible reality which the very *nature* of being as being is. Avicenna had clearly established that, of themselves, "natures" are neither universal nor singular. If the nature of a horse was singular in itself, there could only be one horse; if it were universal in itself, no individual horses could exist; consequently, as Duns Scotus likes to repeat with Avicenna, natures are just what they are. The same is true with regard to the nature of being: it is everything that being is, and nothing but that.

Taken in its logical predicability with respect to all that is, being is the emptiest of forms; no matter how it is considered, no *real* knowledge can come from it. On the contrary, the being of the metaphysician is a reality; it is rich in possibilities, and being wrapped up in it is not to get into a deadlock. Being as being has properties, the first of which are its modes. The modes of a nature, or essence, are its possible intrinsic determinations. Let us take an example. Here is a luminous ray;

it can be varied in color; the colors which diversify it add to its nature of luminous ray, which is only that of light itself; they are therefore extrinsic determinations for it, they are not modes of light as light. On the contrary, if we increase or diminish its intensity, a certain light will become more or less luminous without anything being added to its nature or subtracted from it: intensity is therefore a mode of light. There are likewise modes of being—that is, as the very name indicates, "manners of being"—which are only being itself, diversely modified, but modified as being. The two primary modes of being are the finite and the infinite. This first division of being includes all the others. It is, in fact, anterior to the Aristotelian distinction of being into the ten categories, for every category is a determination, therefore a limitation, so that the being to which the categories apply enters by full right into the finite modality of being. For the metaphysician, to demonstrate the existence of God is to prove that the "infinite being" is, or exists. Limited by the very nature of its object, which is being, metaphysics could not claim to go any further, but it can go that far.

B. THE EXISTENCE OF GOD

To achieve this the metaphysician will proceed in two phases: he will prove first that a Primary exists in the order of being, then that this Primary is infinite. Note in passing that this way of defining the problem is sufficient evidence of Avicenna's influence, whose customary manner of designating God is to call him *Primus*. This doctrinal affinity will last as long as the problem will be to prove that there is a First in the order of being. Among the many modalities of being considered as being is the couple possible-necessary. Proving the existence of a primary being will therefore be done also in two stages: proving the necessity there is for thought to posit a first necessary being, then proving that this first necessary being is an existent.

Such demonstrations cannot be made *a priori*, that is to say, starting solely from the definition of God, as St. Anselm wished. It might even be said that it is more impossible in Duns Scotus's doctrine than in any other, since the Scotist argumentation must bear solely upon the notion of being, not on the notion of God. These demonstrations will therefore be *a posteriori*, that is to say, going up from effects to their cause; but the effects from which they start will not be the contingent beings given in sensible experience. Not only would the proofs based on them not permit us to get out of physics; they would not even allow us to get out of the contingent. The necessity of the prime cause of contingent effects is but a hypothetical necessity, because it rests upon the actual existence of beings which might not exist. The solid base on which the proof will be built up must therefore be some modality of being considered as being, not the contingent existence of some existent.

The first proof is based on these complementary properties of being, "causality" and "producibility," or aptitudes for producing and being produced. Let us start from the fact that some being is producible: how will it be produced? It can only be produced by nothing, by itself, or by another. It cannot be by nothing, for what is nothing causes nothing. It cannot be by itself, for nothing is cause of itself. It must therefore be by another. Suppose that it be by A; if A is absolutely first, we have our conclusion. If A is not first, it is a secondary cause, therefore it is caused by another. Let us suppose that this other cause is B; the reasoning will be the same for it as for A. Either, therefore, the reasoning will continue thus *ad infinitum*, which is absurd, since then nothing would be producible for lack of a primary cause, or it will stop at an absolutely primary cause, which is what had to be demonstrated.

The same argumentation makes it possible to prove that it is necessary to posit an ultimate final cause, which itself has no final cause, but is the final cause of all the rest. Thirdly, it can be proved by the same method that being itself requires a supreme degree of perfection and eminence. The next step consists in proving that what is First in one of these three orders coincides with what is First in the two others. The Prime Cause, the Ultimate End, and the Prime Being must be posited as one and the same First. This is a necessary metaphysical conclusion. There still remains for us, however, to prove the actual existence of this Prime Being. A truly metaphysical demonstration must rest upon the very nature of the being at stake. In the present case, our intellect is grasping the nature of a primary cause; it is therefore positing a prime uncausable cause as being at least possible. Two hypotheses remain open to us concerning it: it exists or it does not exist. These two hypotheses are contradictory, and of two contradictory propositions one must be false. Let us suppose, then, that this uncausable cause does not exist. Why should it not exist? Would it be in virtue of a cause of its nonexistence? But the primary cause has no cause. Would it be that, possible in itself, it would be incompossible with another? But then neither this other nor itself would be possible: now it is possible by definition. In reality, if an uncaused primary cause is possible, it is possible by itself. In other words, such a being is the only conceivable cause of its very possibility. Hence the conclusion of Duns Scotus: if a Prime Being is possible, it exists.

This is not a "physical" argument, but it is no "logical" argument either. It deals with intrinsic properties of the very nature of being *qua* being as conceived by the metaphysician. The possibility of that whose being is causable does not necessarily bring with it its actual existence, but that which excludes all cause, either extrinsic or intrinsic, with regard to its own being, cannot not exist: *excludendo omnem causam aliam a se, intrinsecam et extrinsecam, respectu sui esse, ex se est impossibile non esse*. As has been said, if primary being is possible, it exists. The conceptual character of these arguments should not hoodwink us concerning their nature. Duns Scotus knows that one can start from the empirical fact that there is movement produced and effects caused; he also knows that one can validly conclude from these factual data in favor of the existence of a prime cause; but that, to him, is not metaphysics. Starting from existences is starting from the real, certainly, but from what there is contingent in the real. As for me, says Duns Scotus, I prefer to propose premises and conclusions drawn from the possible; for, if one concedes those taken from act, one does not thereby concede those taken from the possible, while, if one grants those taken from the possible, those taken from act are granted at the same stroke. And the reason for this is simple; one can conclude from the necessary to the contingent, but not inversely; now, the proofs drawn from actual existence are conclusive enough, but they remain contingent, whereas the proofs drawn from possible beings give necessary demonstrations.

The infinity of this Primary, which exists, is still to be established. The same roads lead to this new conclusion. A primary and consequently uncaused cause is not limited by anything in its causality; it is therefore infinite. More, first in the order of perfection, this necessary being is intelligent; it is even the Primary Intelligent, therefore the supreme Intelligent, that knows all that can be known; there is therefore an infinity of intelligibles in the primary intelligence and consequently the intellect which embraces them all simultaneously is actually infinite. Finally the infinity of the First is proved to us by the natural inclination of our will toward a supreme good and of our intelligence toward a supreme truth. Our will would not incline toward an infinite good as toward its real object if the nature of this infinite good were contradictory and could not exist; the possibility of such an attraction in the will implies that its center of attraction is at least possible. It is the same with regard to intelligence. Not only, as a matter of fact, does the idea of an infinite being not seem to us contradictory, but it seems to be the very type of the intelligible. Now it would be extraordinary if no one were to perceive the least contradiction in this primary object of thought even though our ear immediately discovers the slightest dissonance in sounds. It is even because the idea of infinite being seems to us so perfectly intelligible that St. Anselm's argument preserves some value; it would not be perfectly intelligible were it not first a really infinite being answering our intellection. It is therefore certain that the Prime Being whose existence we have affirmed in the conclusion is an infinite being.

C. INFINITY AND CONTINGENCY

After proving its existence, metaphysics has said most of what it can say about the Infinite Being. To study its nature belongs to the theologian. Like St. Thomas, Duns Scotus considers our philosophical knowledge of the divine attributes relative and frail, but he considers it to be better founded on reality than is generally supposed. This is a point to be kept in mind by those who compare Duns Scotus' thought with Descartes's. These two philosophers have in common an acute feeling for the importance of the infinity of God; but while Descartes concludes from it the negation of all distinction, even of reason between the divine attributes, Duns Scotus considers the distinction generally admitted between these attributes insufficient. The fact is, the tendency to bring out the transcendence of the creator with regard to the creature is balanced in the mind of Duns Scotus by another tendency to stress the entity of forms. All the divine attributes are one because, each of them sharing in the infinity of the divine being, they all are infinite. This is the pre-Cartesian aspect of the Scotist God, but there is in him another aspect which is as anti-Cartesian as possible. Duns Scotus maintains that there is in God at least a virtual foundation for the distinction that we posit between his different attributes; namely, the "formal" perfection corresponding to the names by which we designate them. Since "natures" have an intelligible entity of their own, there is a formal distinction between the natures answering the various attributes of God, and this plurality of formal entities does not break up the absolute unity of Infinite Being.

Having thus posited a necessary being as the first cause of all that is, Duns Scotus finds himself at the same starting point as Avicenna, but when it comes to explaining the relation of finite beings to the infinite being, he separates from the Arabian philosopher. For Avicenna, the possible emanated from the necessary by way of necessity; for Duns Scotus, whose doctrine in this case becomes a radical anti-Avicennism, the possible comes from the necessary by way of liberty. The God of Duns Scotus is a necessary being because he is infinite being. Now, between infinite being and finite beings, all ontological relations are radically contingent. In a doctrine which is based on univocal being and not upon analogical acts of being, a dividing line other than the act of being must be drawn between God and creatures. The role played in Thomism by the existential purity of the divine act-of-being is played in Scotism by the divine will. The infinite essence of God is the necessary object of God's will. There is, in the God of Duns Scotus, no voluntarism with respect to God. There is no trace of voluntarism in him even with respect to the essences of creatable beings. Even in the moral domain God is in some way bound by the first two commandments of the Decalogue, which are the expression of the natural law and correspond to an absolute necessity. In Scotism, divine liberty is emphatically not the enlightened despotism of the Cartesian Lawgiver whose will freely promulgates even necessary and eternal truth. In Scotism, the will of God intervenes to bridge the ontological gap there is between the necessary existence of Infinite Being and the possible existence of finite beings. In the universe of Avicenna, because the First was necessary, all the rest enjoyed a conditional necessity; in the universe of Duns Scotus, because the First is infinite, all the rest is contingent. Between the necessary and the contingent the only conceivable link is a Will.

In a curious text wherein Duns Scotus describes a hypothetical generating of essences in God, we see that, at the first moment, God knows his own essence in itself and absolutely; in the second moment the divine intellect produces the stone, conferring upon it an intelligible being, and God knows the stone (*in secundo instanti producit lapidem in esse intelligibili, et intelligit lapidem*); in the third instant, God is compared to this intelligible and a relation is thus established between them; in the fourth moment, God in some way reflects on that relation and knows it. It is therefore clearly a posteriority of finite essences in relation to the infinite essence of God which is here at stake. Since God's essence is the only necessary object of God's will, there is not one of these finite essences whose existence should be necessarily willed by God. God creates if he wills to do so, and only because he so wills. To ask the reason why God willed or did not will such-and-such a thing is to ask the reason for something for which there is no reason. The sole cause for which the necessary being willed contingent things is his will, and the sole cause for the choice he made is that his will is his will; there is no getting beyond that. The only conditions this liberty observes are to will essences such as they are, to choose only compossible essences among those that are to be produced, and to preserve unchangingly the laws which have once been decreed. With the exception of the principle of contradiction and of the intrinsic necessity of the intelligible forms taken in themselves, the will of God is therefore absolute master of the decision to create or not to create, as well as of the choice and combination of essences to be created. With respect to what is not God, the divine will is not necessarily ruled by the good; it is on the contrary the choice of the good that is subject to the will of God. If God wills a thing, that thing will be good; and if he had willed other moral laws than the ones he established, these other laws would have been just, because righteousness is within his very will, and no law is upright except in so far as it is accepted by the will of God. One could not go any further without ending in Cartesianism; but in order to go further, one should first reject the very essence of Scotism, which lies here in the formal distinction there is between the intellect of God and his will.

D. SPECIES AND INDIVIDUALS

The duality of tendencies which leads Duns Scotus strictly to subordinate existences to God while accentuating the distinction he maintains between formal entities affects his conception of essences themselves. We have seen that, while maintaining the divine Ideas, Scotus stresses their ideal posteriority with regard to the thought of God. In this sense Duns Scotus was less of a Platonist than St. Thomas had been. But once the essences are posited in the divine intellect, Duns Scotus attributes more proper and distinct entity to forms than St. Thomas had done. His realism of forms is first expressed in his famous theory of "formal distinction," which had always been present in the doctrine of the plurality of forms. Duns Scotus conceives this distinction as intermediary between a mere distinction of reason and a real distinction. It must not, however, be confused with the Thomist distinction of reason *cum fundamento in re*. The basis for the formal distinction of Scotus is the actual presence, in reality, of formally distinct entities. Since Scotus does not accept the real composition of essence and existence, he can attribute several formal entities to any being without disrupting its actual unity. The "formalities" thus conceived are therefore both really distinct formal entities in the thing and really one as sharing in the actual being of the whole subject whose parts they are. This, moreover, is in agreement with the way in which, in Scotism, the formation of concepts is explained. Scotist concepts answer this distinction between forms in the unity of concrete subjects. The universal, as we conceive it, clearly results from the abstraction our intellect works on things; but, Duns Scotus observes, if the universal were a pure product of the intellect without any foundation in things themselves, there would be no difference between metaphysics, which bears upon being, and logic, which deals with beings of reason. Better still, to the extent that it deals with concepts, all science would be simply logic: *omnis scientia esset logica.* It is to avoid this consequence that Duns Scotus considers essence as equally indifferent to the universal and to the individual, but as containing virtually both of them. The distinction introduced by Scotus between formal entities has therefore its foundation in things; the intrinsic indetermination of essence provides us with the very material out of which the agent intellect draws its universal concepts, but which the metaphysician rediscovers intact in the very structure of reality.

It must therefore be admitted that the real is in itself neither pure universality nor pure individuality. The very fact that we can abstract general ideas from it shows that it is not pure individuality. If species had not already a certain unity, although inferior to the numerical unity of the individual, our concepts would not correspond to anything. Inversely, the same common nature of the species is still found in individuals, but, this time, determined by their principle of individuation. In accounting for the possibility of individuals, Duns Scotus still had to start from the "nature" or "common essence," neither universal nor particular, which the metaphysician considers. Solving this problem, therefore, inevitably consisted for him in adding an individuating determination to the essence. That determination could not be a form, for all form is common to the individuals of one species; it must therefore be added to form from within. In fact, says Duns Scotus, it is its ultimate actuality. The famous "hecceity" of the Scotists is the ultimate act which restricts the form of a species to the singularity of its individuals.

E. INTELLECT AND WILL

Duns Scotus's desire to guarantee as completely as possible the originality of the individual is closely related to his conception of the pre-eminence of will and to his doctrine of liberty in man. For him as for St. Thomas, it is certainly the will that wills and the intelligence that knows, but the fact that the will can command acts of understanding seems to him to decide in favor of the primacy of the will. No doubt we only will what we know, and in that sense the intellect is the cause of the will; but it is only its occasional cause. On the contrary, when the will commands the intellect, it is clearly the will that causes intellection, even though that act taken in itself is an act of the intellect. And if we consider an act of will taken in itself, it is certainly true that the knowledge of the object willed is anterior to the volition in time, but it is nevertheless the will which is the primary cause of the act. The cognition of the object by the intellect is but the accidental cause of our volition.

This affirmation of the primacy of nobility of the will over the intellect in man announces a more voluntarist than intellectualist conception of liberty, and that is precisely what we find in Duns Scotus's doctrine. Just as he had insisted upon the radical indifference of the divine will with respect to the existence of created finite beings, so he endeavors to attribute solely to the human will the total causality of the voluntary. It is the will alone, Scotus says in a striking formula, which is the total cause of volition in the will: *nihil aliud a voluntate est causa totalis volitionis in voluntate*. It is true that we have to know an object to will it and that it is the good that we know to be in that object that makes us will it; but it is equally true that if we know that object rather than another, it is because we will to know it. Our cognitions determine us, but we first determine the choice of our cognitions. Even when the decision of the act seems irresistibly drawn by the knowledge we have of an object, it is first of all the will which has desired that knowledge, and, in the end, it is the will alone that bears the total responsibility for the decision.

Thus Duns Scotus's thought, which at first glance may seem closely related to St. Thomas', is on the contrary distinguished from it in more than one respect, and it is not empty subtleties or simple pettifogging words that separate the two doctors. Both theologies make use of the same stock of concepts borrowed from Aristotle's philosophy, but the edifices constructed with those common materials are very different in style.

They differ first, if not by the idea their authors have of philosophical demonstration, at least by the value they attribute to it. It is not in this case a question simply of sorting out what is accessible to reason and what must be reserved for revelation, but of what one has the right to call demonstration within the very domain reserved for reason. It is understood that the Trinity or other dogmas of this kind cannot be rationally demonstrated. But in what is ordinarily considered as demonstrable there must also be a distinction between the demonstration taken as it is possible in itself and the demonstration taken as it is possible for us in the present state of our human condition. For some reason or other, our intellect, which, by its very nature, should be capable of intellectual intuition, finds itself restricted to abstractive cognition. Even the whole range of being *qua* being is no longer accessible to it. Since the sole kind of being which it directly grasps is sensible being, the philosophers naturally mistook sensible being for being itself, with the consequence that they attributed to being itself characters which are proper to sensible being only. Hence, we find in the mind of Duns Scotus a general appreciation of the work of the "philosophers" which affects his own doctrinal positions. The science of sensible being naturally leads to a metaphysical doctrine of universal necessity, whereas the consideration of being *qua* pure being leads to a metaphysics of the radical contingency of finite being. Theologians have, for the same reason, been liberated by theology from the limited outlook which was naturally that of the philosophers. The liberation of metaphysics is achieved in Scotism by the new task imparted to it by the theologian: to demonstrate by philosophical reasons the existence of the Infinite Being.

The philosophical consequences of this new situation were manifold. After Scotus, a new importance is attributed to the notion of infinite. In theology, there appears a marked tendency to withdraw from the competency of the metaphysician all the problems whose ultimate answer hangs on the infinity of the divine being. Philosophers can know that there is an infinite being, but concerning the essence of God precisely *qua* infinite, only the theologians have something to say, and this only to the extent that revelation provides a starting point for their speculation. Because he considers finite beings in the light of Infinite Being, the theologian knows that God is absolutely omnipotent; that He is free to create or not, and to act through secondary causes or not; that He is omnipresent to all creatures and free to set up any moral code He pleases so long as it deals with rules of human conduct whose relations to His own essence are not necessary ones. Nothing of what depends on the free decisions of this absolutely free God is philosophically deducible. The very condition of some natural beings falls under this rule. What does not belong to them strictly in virtue of their essences cannot be deduced from their nature; consequently, it is no object of philosophical demonstration. The immortality of the human soul is a point in case. Philosophical reasons may show it to be probable, and even more probable than its contrary, but they cannot demonstrate it as a necessary conclusion.

NOTES

1. The student who wishes to thread his way through the texts of Duns Scotus will need to make use of the detailed references that are here omitted: see E. Gilson, *A History of Christian Philosophy in the Middle Ages* (New York: Random House, 1955), pp. 454–464, 763–767.

8. Theology and the Unity of Knowledge

The problem of the unity of knowledge will be considered in the essays which follow* from the point of view of science, then from that of philosophy. We will approach it from the point of view of theology. Now since natural theology is included in metaphysics, it should be included in the philosophical approach to the problem. Let us, therefore, take it for granted that we are supposed to deal with the kind of theology that is part and parcel of religion. It is sometimes called revealed theology because it rests upon the assumption that a supernatural being—that is, God Himself or some divine messenger—has revealed to men truths naturally inaccessible to human understanding. Several religions rest upon their belief in such a revelation which they consider contained in one of several sacred books. Their theology is the discourse about God born of the effort of believers to achieve some understanding of revealed truth.

If there is any man capable of mastering the knowledge of all the theologies developed by the theologians of all religions, he is better qualified than we are to handle this vast problem. We shall therefore content ourselves with discussing it, in a very summary way, from the point of view of the theologies which we happen to know, or rather, with which we happen to be acquainted. These are the Christian theologies of the West, especially the doctrines developed by Christian theologians from the second century after Christ up to the time of the Reformation. It is our sincere hope that we shall not be charged with mistaking the limits of our own information for the limits of the subject.

Supposing, therefore, that there are such theologies, and that they may have exercised a perceptible influence on the history of the problem under discussion, we shall ask ourselves

* The reference is to the papers of Niels Bohr and John H. Randall, Jr., in the Columbia University bicentennial volume edited by Lewis Leary.

the following question, whose terms we are accepting as we received them: "Is the world of knowledge a chaos, or a cosmos, or something in between, and does theology particularly favor one of these answers to the question?"

I

Christian theologies arose at the confluence of two distinct doctrinal traditions: the biblical account of the creation of the world by God as described in the book of Genesis and the philosophical answers given by Greek philosophers to the problem of the origin of the cosmos.

Among these answers, two happened to be of exceptional importance. From the second century up to the first half of the thirteenth century, the only philosophical cosmogony known to Christian theologians was the myth developed by Plato in the first part of his *Timaeus*. It was, in fact, a sort of philosophical "genesis" of the universe well made to attract the attention of theologians. Reduced to its essentials, it consisted in describing the world as a cosmos molded out of matter by a divine artist, the Demiurge, after the pattern of intelligible Ideas. Countless theologians have repeated the two lines written by an unknown Platonist and known to Christians ever since the third century: there are three principles, matter, Ideas, and the Demiurge. Since it was the mark of an artist, the world of *Timaeus* was bound to be a cosmos.

The second philosophical universe known to Christians was that of Aristotle. Unlike the myth of the *Timaeus*, the doctrine of Aristotle was not a cosmogony; it was a cosmology describing the world such as it is now, always was, and always will be. A finite cosmos, made up of concentric spheres, the universe of Aristotle is eternally kept in motion by its desire for the perfection of a Prime Immovable Mover, whose nature it is to be a Self-Thinking Thought. Since, in Aristotle's own terms, the thinking of this divine mind "is one with the object of its thought," the self-cognition of the Prime Mover should probably be conceived as a perfectly unified world of knowledge. As to the universe of things, although the presence of matter introduces into it an element of chance and of unintelligibility, it makes up a completely self-contained whole. Everything in it, as Dante puts it, is being eternally rolled—

even as a wheel that moves equally—"by the love that moves the sun and the other stars."

II

These two philosophical worlds, inherited by Christian theologians, are usually considered the universes of Christian theology in the middle ages, and, most certainly, they were integrated to it by theological speculation. Yet a simple remark makes it evident that the Greek cosmos could not enter the Christian world of knowledge without undergoing deep transformations. The God of the Bible was very different from either the Prime Mover or the Demiurge. In order to simplify a very complex picture, let us consider only two individuating differences of the Christian God: first, He was an unknown God; secondly, He was a Creator.

Concerning the first point, let it be recalled that the God of the Scriptures was an essentially nameless God. According to the Jewish tradition, the tetragrammaton, which consists of the four consonants included in the "incommunicable name" of God, represented a name known to the high priest only, transmitted by him to his successor but whose pronunciation had somehow become lost during the course of centuries. In the twelfth century, the Jewish theologian Moses Maimonides admitted the fact that no one then knew how to pronounce it. Accordingly, they would designate the Lord as Adonai, as a substitute for the forgotten name of God.

More boldly, the Christians used a variety of names considered by them as so many renderings of the tetragrammaton: Jehovah, Yehowah, Yahweh. Yet even the Christians never pretended to retain the secret which the Jews themselves considered as lost; moreover, whatever the pronunciation of the name, countless difficulties arose from its interpretation. All these difficulties revolved around the famous text of Exodus 3:13–14, in which, being asked by Moses for His name, the Lord cryptically answers in words the received translation of which usually runs as follows: I AM WHO AM, and HE WHO IS. One of the oldest interpretations is also the simplest one: I am who I am and you have no business to know more about me. Most Christian theologians, however, interpreted the same words in a more metaphysical way;

namely: I am He whose very nature it is to be. In conceiving HE IS as being itself, a Christian theologian conversant with the Greek philosophical tradition found himself again on familiar ground. For indeed the notion of being was far from unknown to philosophers. Unfortunately, as early as the fourth century before Christ, Aristotle was already describing it as "the question which was raised of old and is raised now and always, and is always the subject of doubt; viz., what being is." To say that God is unknown, or to say that God is being which, in turn, is something practically unknown to us, was to say very much the same thing.

It is perhaps significant that the unknowability of God became one of the favorite themes of the Greek Fathers of the Church. Since we cannot possibly follow the details of this history, let us observe its outcome at the moment when, in the ninth century, the Latins came into contact with the writings of the mysterious author whom we call Denys the Aeropagite. In a famous passage of his *Divine Names*, VIII, 4, Denys had asked himself this puzzling question: How do we know God since He cannot be perceived by sense, nor be grasped by understanding, nor be considered one of those objects which we universally call beings? Incidentally, let us note that the question goes much farther than the usual one: can *we* know God? What Denys is asking, in the truest Plotinian tradition, is if God is knowable *in Himself*. Still more precisely, he is asking how we can know an object which, in itself, is raised above both being and intelligibility.

To this question the only possible answer is: no, we cannot know such a being because no one of the terms which we can use correctly applies to an object which is, in fact, above definition. Negative theology thus became one of the features common to all Christian theologies. After affirming that God is this and that, one must presently add that He is neither this nor that, and finally conclude that He is no one of the things that are because He is beyond them all. Even in the theology of Thomas Aquinas, wherein God is identified with the pure act of being, it is specified that, although it be certainly true to say of God that He is, we do not know the meaning of the verb *is* when applied to God. In another passage, as if afraid to let men imagine themselves endowed with a positive knowledge of God, Thomas bluntly states that "neither the Catholic nor the Pagan knows the very nature of God as it is in itself." How could a unified world of knowledge be possible if the very cause of the world escapes cognoscibility?

III

Almost all Christian theologians agree that God is unknowable in Himself, and that our knowledge of Him is negative. We do not know that which God is. On the other hand, since theologians do speak about God, a positive moment must inevitably enter the structure of any theology. As has already been suggested, the most positive of all the concepts which Christians have considered as more or less applicable to God is the concept of being. Hoping that our desire to be brief will excuse what would otherwise be an absurdly ambitious question, we now ask: What is the most striking difference between the Greek notion of the deity and the notion of God common to practically all the seventeenth-century philosophers? The best answer we can imagine is that, apart from Anaximander, who in a rather cryptic statement said that "the first principle of all things is infinite," no known Greek philosopher ever posited an infinite being as the cause of all that which is, whereas Descartes, Leibniz, Malebranche, and practically all the other metaphysicians of the seventeenth century conceived of God as the primary cause of all that which is, and they did so on the strength of the principle that, if there is a God, He must needs be an infinite being. The remark applies even to the only one among these philosophers who was not a Christian, namely Spinoza. God, Spinoza says, "is a being absolutely indefinite, that is a substance consisting of infinite attributes, each of which expresses eternal and infinite essence." What can be the cause for this radical change in perspective? The only answer we can imagine is that this cause is to be found in the theological speculation which, starting from the biblical notion of a Creator of all beings, led the men of the middle ages to conceive infinity as a *positive* perfection of being.

This notion could hardly have been included in the Greek philosophical heritage. To a Greek mind, an infinite being was a boundless one and, consequently, an unfinished and an imperfect one. Because it was finite, the cosmos was perfect in its own way; and because the Prime Mover was able to cause motion during an infinite time, by allowing itself to be eternally desired, its power could be called a limitless energy, but Aristotle would have been very much surprised to hear his own Prime Mover called an infinite being.

More remarkably still, this notion was not included in the biblical heritage common to both Jewish and Christian theologians. Even today it comes as something of a shock to a theologian to hear it said that this simple formula, God is infinite, is nowhere to be found in Holy Writ. The experiment is a simple one to try, and the result is always the same. After a moment of incredulity, the Christian theologian painfully digs out of his memory, or more probably from some biblical concordance, a few texts to the effect that, wherever you may happen to go, God is there, or that His wisdom is without limits and that His days are without number, but that God is infinite, this simple proposition has never been quoted as extracted from the Bible by any Christian theologian whom we can remember.

What, then, is its origin? We must modestly confess that, personally, we do not know. And this might well be the strangest point in this curious story: the history of the notion of infinity has not yet been written. Let us hail from afar this promised land which only a younger generation of historians can hope to enter, but foolish as it always is to imagine what an unexplored country will look like to its first explorers, we can hardly refrain from risking one or two guesses concerning what our successors will know.

In the first place, they will probably attribute some importance to the fact that, as early as the second century after Christ, the creation of the world by the Christian God was unanimously interpreted as a production *ex nihilo*. The import of this notion becomes obvious when one considers the new relationship between the world and its cause which necessarily followed from it. There is such a thing as the notion of a "great chain of being" running throughout the whole of the Western tradition, but its meaning is not in Christian theologies what it had been in Greek philosophies. To a Christian, the continuity of the great chain of being is one of order, not of being. No ontological link can possibly insure any kind of continuity between the being of a Creator and that of the creatures which His power has made to be from no antecedent matter, element, or entity of any kind. Something had to be done to the notion of being in order to adapt it to a God so utterly different from the Prime Mover of Aristotle and from the Demiurge of Plato.

A second possible incentive to conceive infinity as a perfection might well be found in the speculations of Plotinus and of Proclus which eventuate in the curious chapter of the *Divine Names*, IX, 1, where Denys shows that if greatness, selfhood, similarity, and immobility are rightly attributed to the Christian God, then smallness, dissimilarity, and motion should also be attributed to Him. We shall presently see the reason for this remark.

A third and last approach to the problem, and perhaps the most promising of all, could be found in the reflection of the theologians on the peculiar consequences that follow from the notion of perfection when it is applied to being. For indeed, to be perfectly something is to be determined and limited by the essence and quiddity of that thing, but to be perfectly being taken precisely *qua* being is to overcome all conceivable determinations and limitations. Here again the speculation of Denys in the *Divine Names*, XIII, 1, assumes a paramount importance. God, says Denys, is posited by theology as being both one and perfect, but His perfection is in fact a superperfection, different in kind from the perfection of any creature. Whereupon, in his commentary on the text Thomas Aquinas observes that, while the Greeks were right in opposing perfection to infinity in creatures, we are no less right in affirming, with Denys, that God is perfect as "extending beyond all limits and neither included nor comprised within any one." This conjunction of the two seemingly contradictory notions of perfection and infinity is typical of the world of Christian theology, but it was not achieved in a day, nor even in a century. From what little we know about its history, we would incline to place the term of this evolution in the second half of the thirteenth century, probably toward its end.

In his *Summa Theologiae*, Thomas Aquinas asks himself

the question: Is God infinite? His answer is that God *is* infinite because "He is His own subsisting act of being." Yet, even Thomas Aquinas seems to have conceived of the notion of infinity as essentially negative. It simply points out the nonexistence of limits in the divine being. In other words, after saying that God is the pure act of being, we are not adding anything positive to His notion by saying that He also is infinite. The act of being is something positive; the pure act of being is the most positive of all conceivable notions; to say that it is boundless or illimitable adds nothing positive to its notion.[1]

IV

It is in the Questions on the *Sentences* left us by the now half-forgotten Henry of Ghent that we meet for the first time the long-expected question: Does infinity point out something negative or something positive when it is predicated of God? And Henry's answer was: something positive. What was new in this answer was not the notion that the divine being is infinite; nor was it that infinity is an exclusive property of the divine being; the novelty consisted in this, that for the first time, instead of being conceived as the negative counterpart of a positive perfection, infinity was understood as being, itself and in itself, a positive perfection. We use a negative name to designate infinity because finite beings are the only ones of which we have direct experience, but this is not the only meaning of the word infinite. God is infinite in the sense of this term in which it points out something whose progress never ceases to proceed farther without ever reaching an end where it stops. Thus understood, infinite is something truly positive in real being. Henry was so fully conscious of the import of his own words on this point that he boldly challenged the traditional argument of Aristotle that the cosmos in which we live is finite *because* it is perfect. Henry does not deny the finiteness of the world, but he does deny that it owes its finiteness to its perfection. The cosmos is finite simply because it lacks this power of true infinity to extend farther and farther indefinitely. In affirming the finiteness of the world, we deny its infinity: in denying that God has limits, we affirm His infinity.[2]

After Henry of Ghent this new notion of a positive infinity of the divine being becomes part and parcel of the theology of Duns Scotus and, straightway, it yields consequences directly relevant to our own problem. According to Scotus, the notion of infinite being is precisely the object of our human theology, since the most perfect of human concepts applicable to God is that of being qualified by infinity. In other words, infinity is the very thing that makes God the unique divine being which He is. Nothing can be more simple than such a general division of being: on the one side, the infinite being, God; on the other side, all the finite beings, that is, all that which, since it is finite, is not God.

It is one of the principles always present in the mind of Duns Scotus that there is no proportion between the finite and the infinite, nor vice versa. The immediate consequence of this principle is that, although the essences of created things do not depend on the divine will, the choice which God makes of finite essences and His decision to create them by His infinite power are absolutely free. In other words, we are introduced by Duns Scotus into the radically contingent universe familiar to the students of modern philosophy. At the same time, all hope to achieve a wholly unified interpretation of the world of knowledge has to be given up. Assuredly, taken in itself and such as it is, this world is intelligible, but if God had decided to create another world, it would be both different from, and just as intelligible as, the world which God has in fact decided to create. Because there is no proportion from the finite to the infinite, any attempt to assign to the universe the ultimate reason for its intelligibility is bound to find itself confronted with an absolutely free decision of the divine will.

V

We all know the modern version of this Scotist theology; it is what we call the metaphysics of Descartes. The same notion of an infinite God is this time applied, beyond the existences, to the essences themselves. True enough, nothing could have been more contrary to the authentic intentions of Duns Scotus, who never admitted that the eternal essences of possible beings could be submitted to the divine will; but Descartes simply carried the fundamental intuition of Duns Scotus to its ultimate implications. There is no more completely unified world of knowledge than that of Descartes. Everything in it finds its natural place and receives its perfectly intelligible explanation. The evidence of the mathematical method leaves nothing unexplained and the result is a unified system of the world. What more could one possibly ask for? Nothing, were it not for the fact that the perfect unity of this world of knowledge owes its intelligibility to a free decision of the divine will. God is infinite and all-powerful; since we understand them, the principles of mathematics are finite; since they are finite, they are creatures; since they are creatures, they ultimately depend upon a free decree of God, Who established them in the world as a king establishes laws in his kingdom. Everything is intelligible in the world of Descartes, except its very intelligibility.[3]

The new notion of infinity seems to have brought about similar results in an entirely different way through the speculation of Nicholas of Cues. The ultimate conclusion of Nicholas appears clearly from the very title of the best known of his works, *On Learned Unknowing*. And why should this learned ignorance be the last result of theological reflection if not because human knowledge is all a question of relations and proportions? Now the world which we strive to understand is both the work and the image of an infinite God, Who Himself, precisely *qua* infinite, is out of proportion with anything. The infinite is a maximum, but since it has no contrary, it must also be the minimum. In short, the infinite is the coincidence of the opposites.

Now what is true of God must also be true of His works. With deep insight, Nicholas realized that the logic of Aristotle, dominated as it was by the principle of contradiction, had been a fitting instrument to explore the finite universe of the Greeks, but that the new Christian universe required interpreters of a different type, fully trained in a new logic of the coincidence of the opposites. For the first time since the beginning of philosophical speculation, Nicholas thinks, the old saying of Anaxagoras is finding its complete justification: *quodlibet est in quolibet;* everything is in everything. Literally understood, this means that the infinite greatness of the whole is totally present in the infinite smallness of any one of its parts. But then how could we achieve the exhaustive cognition of anything? As we have said, there is simply no proportion between the finite act of a human intellect and the infinite object which it ambitions to grasp. Every one of our intellections being a finite approximation of an infinite reality, the exhaustive cognition of any single object, let alone of the whole world, is an absolute impossibility. Hence the last word of Nicholas of Cues on this problem: "The quiddity of the things, which is the truth of beings, is inaccessible in its purity; all philosophers have investigated it, but nobody has discovered it such as it is; and the deeper we shall steep ourselves in this ignorance, the nearer we will find ourselves to truth." In the doctrines of Nicholas the negative theology becomes a negative philosophy and a negative science because the notion of infinity is beginning to invade the created universe after having so long been considered as an exclusive attribute of God.

Just as we found Descartes in the wake of Duns Scotus, we can now find Pascal in the wake of Nicholas of Cues. This time at least both the texts and the doctrine are so well known that it should suffice to recall one of them in order to make clear that there is a doctrinal continuity between them or, at the very least, a continuity of inspiration: "For in fine, what is man in nature? A nothing compared to the infinite, an all compared to nothing, a mean between nothing and everything. Infinitely removed from understanding the extremes, as far as man is concerned the end of things and their beginning are invincibly hidden in an impenetrable secret, identically incapable as he is of seeing the nothingness from which he is drawn and the infinite wherein he is engulfed." Just as Nicholas of Cues had introduced the infinite into the radically contingent world of Duns Scotus, so also Pascal is now introducing the infinite into the very texture of the radically contingent universe of Descartes. In both cases the result is the same. Man loses himself in the smallest thing as in a maze and he becomes to himself the most inextricable of all mazes.

VI

Let us now return to our initial question—whether the world of knowledge is a cosmos, a chaos, or something in between. Since it was incumbent upon us to discuss the problem from the point of view of theology, we suggest that the answer should run about as follows: The world of knowledge is neither a chaos, nor a cosmos, nor anything in between. The notion of cosmos, conceived as a finite whole achieved by some admirable artist similar to the Demiurge, or eternally moved by a Self-Thinking Thought similar to the Prime Mover of Aristotle, has ceased to be applicable to the world of experience ever since the universe in which we exist became the free creation of an infinite being.

To ask the question in terms of whole and parts is by no means an unreasonable attitude. We all imagine the world of knowledge as such a finite cosmos. There is not a single man who, engaged in the pursuit of any branch of knowledge, does not somewhat resemble those pioneers who, fully resigned never to achieve the complete exploration of a country, cannot help feeling that it is all a matter of time. But when it is a question of learning, is not this an illusion? At the end of a long life of study, do we know really *more*, or would not it be more true to say that we know *otherwise?* The same objects are still there, or more of the same, but the landscape has become different and we feel that, were we to enjoy a much longer life than man normally is allowed, the world of knowledge would go on changing indefinitely, never more complete, never more perfectly well-rounded than it is now, but always and always different.

This feeling for a universe of adventure and of creation rather than of totality, for a world of history and of change, rather than for any cosmos conceived, according to our dictionaries, either as the "sum total of experience" or else as a "self-inclusive system characterized by order and harmony"; in short, this growing indifference toward the Greek love for finite totality—cannot we consider these as typical of our own times? As Paul Valéry so aptly remarked, "If we had *the whole,* what could we do with it? *Absolutely nothing.* Our mind would be out of a job." Valéry was no Christian; he heartily detested Pascal, and yet his remark was that of a man living in a Christian universe. It even was the remark of a heart full of the Christian longing for that which men feel to be beyond all conceivable beyonds.[4]

In the light of such notions, the problem at stake has simply ceased to exist. Assuredly we still believe that there is order in reality and that, without order, no world of knowledge is in any sense possible, but we have ceased to think that the relation of countable parts to a whole is the highest type of intelligible order. We have even ceased to imagine that what is deepest and best in any finite part can be expressed in terms of quiddities and exhaustively expressed by means of abstract definitions.[5] The world in which Christians have learned to live is no less perfect than the Greek cosmos ever was in the minds of the Greeks, but its perfection comes to it from the infinity of its cause which, being beyond all, perfects all.[6] No conceivable image could picture to us such a world, yet we do need images, and since our preferred image of the world is a perfect sphere, let us also remember that it is a sphere whose center is in infinity.

NOTES

1. This was enough to render God completely unknowable to any creature, at least to the extent that knowledge is comprehension. Thomas Aquinas maintains that, even in the beatific vision, which is the sight of God face to face, His essence cannot be comprehended. Assuredly, this sight of God fully appeases all the desires of man; hence its beatifying nature; but since no finite cognitive power is adequate to an infinite object, God seen face to face cannot be comprehended: "*Virtus finita non potest adaequare in sua operatione objectum infinitum*" (*Summa Contra Gentiles*, III, chap. 55).
2. Henry of Ghent, *Summae Quaestionum Ordinariarum* P. II (Jodocus Badius Ascensius, Paris, 1520, vol. II, fol. xiii, ro–vo). The only scriptural text which Henry finds to quote in favor of the divine infinity is Wisdom 7:14: "For she [Wisdom] is an *infinite* treasure to men." In the same passage (fol. xv, ro Z) Henry quotes another text borrowed from Exodus 33:19: "I [the Lord] will shew you all good," to which Henry adds this commentary: "*Ostendam tibi omne bonum. Infinitum vero significat ipsam con-*

summationen omnino perfectionem omnem continentem." Infinity is thus identified with the aptitude indefinitely to add more perfection to any amount of given perfection without any conceivable limit.

3. The typically Greek attitude of Gassendi is interesting to compare with that of Descartes. In the "Fifth Set of Objections" to the *Meditations* of Descartes, Pierre Gassendi had observed that "he who says that anything is infinite attributes to a thing which he does not comprehend a name which he does not understand." On the contrary, Descartes maintained that all that which is finite is subjected to the free will of God. In his answers to the "Sixth Set of Objections," after reaffirming that it is because God willed "the three angles of a triangle to be necessarily equal to two right angles that this is true and cannot be otherwise," Descartes justified this extraordinary statement by the general principle that, "on account of God's immensity, it is clear that nothing at all can exist which does not depend on Him." As can be seen, Descartes has carried much farther than Duns Scotus the subordination of the finite to the divine will. Intelligibility stands on the side of the finite; to transcend it is, by the same token, to transcend intelligibility.
4. See the penetrating remarks made by Lionel Trilling on Henry James' definition of "the romantic" in *The Liberal Imagination* (New York: The Viking Press, 1950), pp. 267–268. His reference to Dante is perfectly relevant, and others could naturally be added, for instance the medieval theme of the "quest," for the Holy Grail or for the faraway princess of Triboli. All this is of a piece with what Henry James described as "the things that, with all the facilities in the world, all the wealth and all the courage and all the wit and all the adventure, we never *can* directly know."
5. A general interpretation of contemporary existentialism would be relevant to the present problem. We must content ourselves with recalling that the work of Kierkegaard was an essentially Christian reaction to a theological problem. Following a classical pattern, what was at first theology has become philosophy; yet, even apart from the Christian existentialism of Gabriel Marcel, the apparently philosophical doctrines of Karl Jaspers and of Martin Heidegger could be understood as so many attempts to provide a non-Christian answer for the questions raised by a Christian universe and, more precisely still, by the Christian condition of man in such a a universe.
6. Thomas Aquinas maintains that "God comprehends himself perfectly." (*Summa Theologiae*, I, q. 14, a. 3.) This means that God knows Himself as perfectly as He is perfectly knowable; but since "the strict meaning of *comprehension* signifies that one thing possesses and includes another," it can be said that, in this sense, "everything comprehended is finite"; consequently, God cannot be said to comprehend Himself in this sense. He is not

"finite to Himself," that is, at least, not in the sense that "He understands Himself to be something finite." The only acceptable meaning of the formula is that God "knows Himself as much as He is knowable," or, in other words, that His knowledge is infinite and adequate to the infinity of His being.

9. Historical Research and the Future of Scholasticism

What changes in our conception of scholasticism have been brought about by fifty years or so of historical and critical research? What do these changes suggest about the future of scholasticism? These are assuredly large questions; and my only excuse for attempting to answer them is that I accepted them exactly as they were put to me. There may have been temerity in my acceptance, but at least I hope you will not believe me rash enough to have assigned myself such a task.

It was in 1850—that is, a century ago—that Hauréau published his *De la Philosophie scolastique,* to be followed by his *Histoire de la philosophie scolastique* in 1872 and 1880. Since then studies on the medieval philosophies are without number. In 1900 there appeared De Wulf's *Histoire de la philosophie médiévale;* in 1905, Picavet's *Esquisse d'une histoire générale et comparée des philosophies médiévales;* in 1921, Grabmann's *Die Philosophie des Mittelalters;* in 1929, Geyer's *Die patristische und scholastische Philosophie.* Other titles easily come to mind, and this without including the many books devoted to the philosophies of St. Thomas Aquinas, St. Bonaventure, John Duns Scotus, and William of Ockham. But in the midst of such an abundance of histories of medieval philosophy, how many histories of medieval theology are to be found? As against twenty volumes on the philosophy of St. Thomas Aquinas, how many historical expositions of his theology are there? During the past hundred years the general tendency among historians of medieval thought seems to have been to imagine the middle ages as peopled by philosophers rather than theologians.

There are many reasons for this fact. And first, dogmatic reasons. In a sense, it can be said that the separation of philosophy and theology goes back to the middle ages: St. Albertus Magnus and St. Thomas Aquinas have clearly established the distinction of their respective objects. Both have written philosophical treatises and commentaries on Aristotle, in which natural reason alone was at work. Moreover, when their disciples later on had to write such commentaries or questions on Aristotle, they naturally made use of the philosophical views which they could find scattered through the theological works of the masters. Thus, for instance, the *Quaestiones super Duodecim Libros Metaphysicae* of Antonius Andreas, an immediate disciple of Duns Scotus, constitutes in fact a sort of exposition of the metaphysics of Duns Scotus. To a lesser degree, even the questions of Duns Scotus on Aristotle's *Metaphysics* had already been something of that kind. Yet, apart from the curious group of the so-called Averroists, who do not seem to have invented much, scholastic philosophy was always conceived, in the middle ages, as a preparation for theology. As a rule, a philosopher then was a future theologian; and because he was fully aware of the fact, the philosophy which he was teaching was that of his future theology. The great change took place in the seventeenth century, when Descartes decided, not at all to oppose theology—on the contrary, he felt sure his own conclusions would help Christian faith better than the scholastic philosophers had ever done—but to philosophize as though there were no such thing as theological wisdom. In other words, Descartes felt convinced that a new metaphysics, better adapted to the new mathematical physics, should be substituted for the antiquated philosophy of the scholastics, which rested on the antiquated physics of Aristotle. Henceforward philosophers would only know, while theologians would only believe. Philosophy would be an exclusively scientific knowledge of the world in the light of natural reason alone; theology would simply teach men how to achieve salvation through grace and in the light of revelation.

Naturally, since it was being attacked as a philosophy, scholasticism had to counterattack as a philosophy. This movement had already begun in the sixteenth century, and it was accelerated toward the end of the seventeenth. The great theologians of the middle ages were then progressively turned into so many metaphysicians.

In 1667, writing under the pseudonym of *Ambrosius Victor*, André Martin, a priest of the Oratory, devoted the five volumes of his *Philosophia Christiana* to the purpose of making St. Augustine a philosopher. In 1679 there appeared the *Philosophia juxta Thomae Dogmata* of Antoine Goudin, a work which has been followed by innumerable *Cursus Philosophiae Thomisticae* down to our own day. In 1746 J. A. Ferrari defended the philosophy of Aristotle *rationibus Joannis Duns Scoti subtilium principis*. What a long road had been covered since the middle ages! Duns Scotus had devoted himself to using Aristotle in order to interpret faith; in the eighteenth century his disciples were using him in order to defend Aristotle. In 1782 Carolus Josephus a Sancto Floriano published his *Joannis Duns Scoti Philosophia*, which was by no means the last of its kind. Then, as today, the aim was to oppose a philosophy to a philosophy; and that is why the theologians of the middle ages, who never wrote a philosophy while they were alive, have composed so many after their death.

To these dogmatic reasons may be added historical ones. The more scholasticism became a distinct philosophical discipline, the more it became difficult for the history of philosophy to neglect the middle ages. If there had been philosophies of St. Augustine, of St. Albert the Great, and of St. Thomas Aquinas, no general history of philosophy could afford to ignore their existence. Furthermore, it was scarcely possible to overlook the great and evident difference that distinguishes modern philosophy in its very beginnings from Greek philosophy at its termination. Metaphysics, as it came out of the middle ages, was different from metaphysics as it had entered the middle ages. Something, historians would think, must have taken place in philosophy, and this even in the faculties of theology. That is why historians have been prompted to write so many studies which oscillate between theology and philosophy, and to treat medieval theologians as if they had been philosophers. In point of fact, these historians were doing the best they could, without being too much concerned over speculative distinctions; their job was to find medieval philosophy where it existed, and they did it.

But, understandable as all this may have been, the question may be asked whether this attitude of the historians can be considered a medieval view of the middle ages. Clearly, it could not. The general attitude of the great doctors of the thirteenth century appears to be faithfully defined by St. Bonaventure when he distinguishes (*In Hexaemeron*, XI, 7) four types of writings, each with its own rank and value. There is, first, Sacred Scripture, which contains that which it is necessary for man to know in order to save himself. There are, secondly, the writings of the fathers, aiding in the interpretation of the Scripture. There are, thirdly, the commentaries on the *Sentences*, aiding in the interpretation of the fathers. There are, fourthly, the books of the philosophers, aiding in the interpretations of the commentaries on the *Sentences* or of the *summas* of theology. Now there is no doubt that the testimony of St. Bonaventure must be taken with some reservation; for, particularly after 1273, he expressed his antipathy toward philosophy and the philosophers with considerable sharpness. Yet his testimony remains valid. For indeed it is a fact, as some have noted, that philosophy does not occupy the prime level of importance in the thought of St. Bonaventure; but in the thought of what theologian worthy of the name has philosophy ever occupied such a prime level? Certainly not in that of St. Thomas Aquinas. After we have introduced all the corrections that history may require, the fact remains that the hierarchical order described by St. Bonaventure does not appear to have been contested by a single medieval master of theology. There is first Scripture; there are then the fathers, as interpreters of Scripture; there are the theologians as interpreters of the fathers; there are finally the philosophers, to understand the theologians.

It was therefore natural that, for the last forty years, historians with a theological education should recall this fact for those historians whose education was primarily philosophical. Their reaction can be summarized in the criticism directed by one of them against a book on the "philosophy" of St. Bonaventure. What you call philosophy, this critic said, is nothing but a mutilated theology. He was right, and the criticism applies equally to every book dealing with the "philosophy" of St. Thomas Aquinas, Duns Scotus, or Ockham. Let us therefore state our first conclusion. The research in medieval thought, which began by being concerned with the philosophies of the middle ages, is tending more and more to restore these philosophies within the theologies which contain them.

There is a second development in historical research, which is all the more remarkable since it seems to contradict our first conclusion. Some hundred years ago, historians had no difficulty in speaking of *a* scholastic philosophy. Hauréau even tended to reduce this scholastic philosophy to a single problem, as though everything within it were a variation on the common theme of the nature of universals. Nearer our own day, there are those who have gone so far as to hold that the doctrine of St. Thomas Aquinas was to such an extent the common doctrine of his age that one could expound it by using only the texts of his contemporaries. But in fact the progress of historical studies has led us to differentiate medieval doctrinal positions. Without denying that which is common in the Aristotelian technique of the medieval theologians, we are beginning to realize the distinctive and individual way in which each of them made use of this common technique. Every great medieval doctrinal synthesis appears to us more and more in the light of its own originality; and there is no doubt that we see these doctrines as more distinct from one another than they appeared to our predecessors.

Even the unity of the schools now appears as less rigid than we once thought. We would no longer think of St. Albert the Great as of a man who tried to be a Thomist by anticipation, and failed; and we should experience some hesitation today in saying what our predecessors saw no reason to doubt —namely, that Giles of Rome belongs to the school of St. Thomas Aquinas. Now, in the eyes of the historian, this progressive differentiation among scholastic theologies seems to be related to the fact that these various theologies have used various philosophical instruments. This is the point of the old scholastic maxim: *Qualis in philosophia talis in theologia.* Hence, our very effort to return to theology has placed us in the presence of as many distinct philosophies as there are distinct theologies. This fact is so important that it deserves to be examined attentively.

In a sense it accounts for the stress put by so many historians on the philosophical aspect of medieval theologies. The very nature of scholastic theology calls for it. Since theology is an *intellectus fidei,* it is quite natural that diverse ways of achieving this understanding, within the unity of faith, should produce diverse theologies. The "philosophies" of the theologians, therefore, even after being restored within their theologies, will continue to occupy in the future an important place in the history of medieval thought. But it will not be the same place as that occupied in the past. For history has taken a decisive step. The lesson of experience is that the more the historian separates philosophy from theology in medieval doctrines, the more scholastic philosophy tends to shrivel into a general technique that becomes increasingly poorer in originality and, in the end, identifies itself with the philosophy of Aristotle as seen by Avicenna or Averroes. It is no wonder that the historians who are the most anxious to extract from medieval texts a philosophy that is entirely free of theology are usually the same historians who insist upon the oneness of scholastic philosophy, or at least upon the existence of a scholastic "synthesis," of which it is possible to say that it was the common philosophy of the thirteenth century in its entirety. And, from their own point of view, these historians are correct. Act and potency, form and matter, the fourfold division of causes, metaphysics as the science of being, truth as the grasp of being such as it is—here are so many master theses, to which others might easily be added, which define a philosophical interpretation of the world common to all our theologians. The position of the above-mentioned historians, therefore, is true. But if this were the whole truth, we should have to conclude from it that the Christian middle ages remained philosophically sterile and that, as some indeed still imagine, they did no more than repeat *ad nauseam* a more or less deformed Aristotle.

It is at this point that the second conclusion to be drawn from the lessons of historical research requires our attention. Experience teaches us that the more we reintegrate the philosophies of the middle ages within their theological context, the more their originality becomes apparent. This same fact can be expressed in many ways. For example, one may say that it is while serving theology that philosophical thought became creative; or one may say that, in the golden age of scholasticism, the more a master was a great theologian the more he was a great philosopher. The fact itself is what is important, and the fact is this: All the decisive steps of progress made by Western philosophy in the middle ages were made in relation to points of doctrine, in which the *intellectus fidei* in some way evoked philosophical originality. At the same time, therefore, that historical research justifies, for the middle ages, the saying that *qualis in philosophia talis in theologia*, it invites us to complete it by another one: *qualis in theologia talis in philosophia*, which is neither less true nor less important. Indeed, these are two formulations of the same truth, which theologians themselves know very well. For if theology is the understanding of faith, we cannot isolate this understanding from the faith whose understanding it gives; nor can we isolate faith from the understanding which it is seeking. In brief, it is to its status as an instrument of theology itself that medieval philosophy owes its fecundity.

This lesson of history poses, in its turn, a number of doctrinal questions that the historian as such does not have the competence to resolve, but which he has a duty to ask, because their answer is not without importance for the future of scholasticism.[1]

If we give to the thirteenth century the title of the golden age of scholasticism, the reason no doubt is our conviction that this was the time when scholasticism reached its point of perfection and fully succeeded in its undertaking. And if it be true that *res eodem modo conservantur quo creantur*, it would seem that we cannot hope for such success in the future without proceeding in the same way as did the thirteenth-century scholastics. Now history is there to tell us, at this point, how the thirteenth-century theologians did their work.

Whatever excuses may be found for it, the most serious difficulty attending our modern dissociation of scholastic philosophy from its theology is that, by a resulting illusion of perspective, we begin to represent the work of the medieval theologians as having consisted in introducing, within a completely developed doctrine of faith, an also completely developed philosophy, which they borrowed in all its completeness from among the philosophers of their age. It is this illusion that has led to the often-repeated inference that redoing the work of the thirteenth century would consist, first of all, in our taking the philosophy and the sciences of our own age as a starting point, in order to rebuild a new scholasticism in harmony with the modern spirit and acceptable to our contemporaries. It seems to me that this amounts to nothing less than a misreading of history. The theologians of the thirteenth century did not begin with the philosophical sciences of their age in order to adapt theology to them; they rather began with faith in order to assume these philosophical sciences within faith by transforming them in its light. Dedicated as they were to the understanding of faith, our theologians accepted without criticism a great deal of ready-made philosophical and scientific knowledge that had no necessary relation to Christian revelation—and, be it noted, these are precisely the dead and antiquated parts of their work, which we have absolutely no reason to preserve. But if nothing is more transitory than positive science, nothing is less transitory than the Christian faith; and that is why, if the scholasticism of the thirteenth century should have to be redone, it would be necessary that faith, and not science, should have changed since the thirteenth century.

Even though it is my aim to be brief, I beg permission to stop a moment on this important point. For the illusions of perspective to which I have referred are not all on the same side. To those who request a new scholastic theology, founded on modern philosophy, there are others who reply that there is only one true philosophy, which is that of Aristotle, and that it is because scholastic theology is founded on this true philosophy that it itself is true. But neither Duns Scotus nor St. Thomas Aquinas *founded* their theologies on any philosophy, not even the philosophy of Aristotle. As theologians, they have made use of philosophy within the light of faith; and it is from this usage that philosophy has come forth transformed. What is of a metaphysical import in St. Thomas Aquinas and Duns Scotus is genuinely their own metaphysics. Each Aristotelian formula they take over and use receives from the notion of *esse* in St. Thomas Aquinas or from the notion of *ens infinitum* in Duns Scotus a meaning that Aristotle never knew, one that he would scarcely have understood and that only those who have inadequately penetrated it are willing to identify with the Aristotelian metaphysics of being. Consequently, to redo scholasticism *on the basis of* Kant or of Hegel

—this would be to wish to redo what had never been done. The decisive achievement of the masters of the middle ages was perhaps this, that, because they were theologians, they did not think *on the basis of* any science or *on the basis of* any philosophy. We are therefore interpreting history in a misleading way if we say that scholasticism tied the Christian faith to the ancient philosophy of Aristotle, and, consequently, that we are invited by its example to do the same thing with the philosophy of our age. What scholastic theology did was rather to create, in the human meaning of this word, a new metaphysics, whose truth, being independent of the state of science at any given historical moment, remains as permanent as the light of the faith within which it was born.

The future of scholasticism, then, will not consist in adapting the medieval metaphysics of being and its causes to the ceaseless variations in science and philosophy; its future will rather consist in integrating to it the positive acquisitions made by science and philosophy in order to correct and purify them. To proceed otherwise would be to place scholasticism in a situation violent to its nature. It would be both to suppress it and to lose, along with it, one of the greatest blessings that we owe to it. It is by bringing philosophy under its influence that medieval theology has liberated metaphysics from physics without enslaving it to itself. For the first time, theology severed the bonds which, even in Aristotle himself, still held first philosophy a captive on the earth of positive science; and theology did this by turning philosophy toward the heaven of faith. Metaphysics cannot lose itself in such a heaven, since it cannot reach it; but, nevertheless, it is by tending toward this heaven of faith that metaphysics achieves its own liberty and realizes its true equilibrium. Its future success will thus depend upon its remaining true to its own nature; and this consists in remaining intimately related to the understanding of faith.

The adventures of philosophy in the seventeenth century should be a lesson for us on this point. In spite of what has been said, the evil then affecting scholastic philosophy was not its ignorance of the new science; the evil was the illusion that the task before it was to defend the antiquated science of Aristotle against the new science. Actually, the task for scholastic philosophy then was to locate this new science in its proper place, under the light of those very metaphysical principles whose meaning it had forgotten. Our task today is the same. It is not indeed to build up a new metaphysics and a new scholastic theology every time positive science invents a new world. The men of our generation have been born in the scientific universe of Newton; they have reached maturity in the universe of Einstein; they are entering old age in the universe of undulatory physics and, with luck, hope to die in a fourth universe, as different from Einstein's as his was from Newton's. Is it going to be said that we should have built up three new metaphysics and three new scholastic theologies in order to keep pace with the evolution of positive science during our own lifetime? Was not it better for them to remain unborn than to be stillborn and straightway discarded? Our task today is to recapture the true spirit of medieval metaphysics, to grasp once more the genuine and profound meaning of its principles. I should add that scholasticism, covered over by more than five centuries of dust, is now experiencing its greatest evil—the ignorance of its own nature. To restore it to itself, let us listen to the counsel of history: scholastic philosophy must return to theology!

In saying this, I am not in the least contesting the distinction between faith and reason. Nor am I forgetting the formal distinction of objects, so dear to the dialecticians, between theology and philosophy. I am not speaking of philosophy in general, but of that kind of philosophy which we call "scholastic." I readily agree that, without paying attention to theology, it is possible to be a philosopher, but not a scholastic philosopher. The hackneyed objection that to philosophize as a theologian is not to philosophize at all forgets that a formal distinction of objects is not a real separation in the order of exercise. One even wonders at times whether this real separation is not responsible for the fact that, in certain minds, the notion of scholastic theology, no less than that of scholastic philosophy, has become obscured. If it were not obscured we should not have to stress the obvious fact that to exercise the human intellect within the transcendent light of faith means something else than to pretend to deduce philosophically demonstrated conclusions from an article of faith. The philosophy we call scholastic is not distinguished from other philosophies by its essence; it is rather distinguished from them as the best way of philosophizing. That is indeed how the encyclical *Aeterni Patris* has described scholastic philosophy, and with perfect reason: *Qui philosophiae studium cum obsequio fidei Christianae conjungunt, ii optime philosophantur*. To philosophize otherwise is assuredly to philosophize, but it is to philosophize less well. At any rate, it is no longer to philosophize as did the scholastics. There are certain fish that live only in warm water. To say that they will die in cold water is not to deny that they are fish. As for the fish that, as some insist at all costs, must be made to live in cold water in order to maintain the purity of their essences, they do not become true fish, but dead fish.

This is precisely what happened to metaphysics when, in order to liberate it from the theology that had formerly liberated it from Aristotelian physics, Descartes made it subservient to his own physics. Hence this paradoxical result, that, in our own days, the only real defenders of metaphysics as an autonomous science are found to be the scholastic theologians. Now, let us be careful to observe, these theologians do not hold that metaphysics is necessary to sacred doctrine. The word of God is sufficient unto itself without any metaphysics. But if you make good use of metaphysics in theology, you will get a better theology, and you also will get a better metaphysics. This, at least, is what happened in the thirteenth century, and the truth of yesterday points out that of tomorrow. It is by restoring the several scholastic philosophies to their natural places—namely, their natal theologies—that history will better and better succeed in understanding them as they were. *Non erubesco evangelium* is a saying that we must know how to pronounce in all domains, even including that of scholarship. And it also is by returning to its natural place that scholastic philosophy can have the hope, or rather the certitude, that it will once more bring forth flowers and fruit. Only a prophet would be able to say what is to be the shape of its future. But the historian can safely state by whom scholastic philosophy will be given a true life in the future. The true scholastic philosophers will always be theologians.

NOTES

1. It should already be clear that we do not here intend to propose, in any proper sense, a definition of the word "scholasticism." We have rather in mind a nominal definition, which is nothing more than a designation. We call "scholasticism" the manner of theologizing and philosophizing practiced by the great masters of the thirteenth and fourteenth centuries, such as St. Albert the Great, St. Bonaventure, St. Thomas Aquinas, or Duns Scotus. Even as a nominal definition, we do not propose it for currency. The point is that *that* is what we are talking about.

PART THREE

The Disciple of Christian Philosophy

The themes and lessons contained in the transformation of Greek philosophy by Christian thinkers have become associated with the name of Gilson ever since the famous "debate on Christian philosophy" over a quarter of a century ago. Gilson has repeatedly insisted that, while ancient Greece was the intellectual teacher of Christianity, the philosophy that Christian theologians created and expressed in the language of Plato and Aristotle was Christian in spirit, form, and content; so much so that there is a recognizable historical phenomenon called "Christian philosophy." The nature, horizons, and inspiration of that philosophy form the substance of the following pages.

10. Greek Philosophy and Christianity

The fourteen centuries of history whose development we have attempted to summarize* were dominated by two distinct influences, Greek philosophy and Christianity. Every time educated Christians came in contact with Greek philosophical sources, there was a blossoming of theological and philosophical speculation. Ancient Rome had produced no philosophy. The Ciceronian tradition, which never disappeared from the horizon during the middle ages, played an extremely important part in the history of Western civilization, and, through Petrarch, it became a decisive factor in bringing about the revival of classical humanism, but one does not see any philosophical doctrine whose origin could be traced back to any Roman writer. Cicero, Seneca, even Lucretius, have been busy popularizing ideas of Greek origin; they did not add anything important to their sources. The philosophical sterility of ancient Rome seems to be a fact. It accounts for this other fact, that the men of the middle ages never found in the Latin classics more than secondary sources of information incapable of initiating a new philosophical movement.

The ignorance of the Greek language, very general in the West after the fall of the Roman Empire, had for its result a severance of the Latins from the perennial source of Greek thought in the Western world. From the fourth century on, the role of the translators became extremely important. Practically every notable event in the history of Western thought in the middle ages is tied up with the presence of a man who had studied in Greece, or who knew Greek and had translated some Greek philosophical writings, or who had had access to such translations. Marius Victorinus translated Plotinus into Latin: we are indebted to him for making possible the doctrine of St. Augustine. Then nothing happened up to the time of Boethius, but Boethius translated the *Organon* of Aristotle

* That is, in the *History of Christian Philosophy in the Middle Ages*, of which this selection is the conclusion.

and he knew the Platonism of Alexandria; hence the whole history of medieval logic and even, owing to the theological opuscules of Boethius, a large section of the Latin theologico-philosophical speculation in the West up to the end of the twelfth century. Then again nothing happened until the Greek writings of Denys the Aeropagite exploded in the ninth-century Latin world. The immediate result was the *Division of Nature* by Scotus Erigena, a doctrinal synthesis to which nothing compares between the ninth and the twelfth centuries. Even the works of St. Anselm of Canterbury, whose dialectical genius is beyond discussion and whose philosophical gifts are evident, betray a certain metaphysical dryness probably owing to the fact that, apart from logic, his main source in philosophy was Augustine instead of being the Greek source of Augustine. After Anselm, the twelfth-century school of Chartres draws its inspiration from Chalcidius and other Platonic sources; Abélard feeds on the Greeks through Boethius; Bernard of Clairvaux opens the great tradition of Western speculative mysticism on account of his familiarity with the Greek theology of Gregory of Nyssa. Last, not the least, the arrival of Aristotle's encyclopedia at the end of the twelfth century, read either in itself or in its interpretations by Avicenna and Averroes, initiates the flowering of Christian speculation which we call scholasticism. The Philosopher *par excellence* was a Greek; the author of the *Elements of Theology* was a Greek; seen from this point of view, the philosophical speculation of the middle ages appears as a sort of appendix to the history of Greek philosophy.

But there is another side to the picture. Something happened to philosophy during the fourteen centuries which we call the middle ages. The easiest way to see what happened to it is to remember the general view of the world propagated by the last Greek philosophers and to compare it with the interpretation of the world common to the founders of modern philosophy; namely, Descartes, Malebranche, Leibniz, Spinoza, and Locke. In the seventeenth century, the commonly received philosophical notions of God, of the origin of the world, of the nature of man and of his destiny are strikingly different from those which the middle ages had inherited from the Greeks. Strict monotheism, an undisputed truth in the minds of all the metaphysicians of the thirteenth century, is only one of the points in case. In its content, the metaphysics of Descartes was much more a continuation of the metaphysics of the scholastics than of the Greeks. He himself was a Christian and it is no wonder that his philosophy continued, in a most original way, the tradition of the Christian theology of the middle ages. True, Descartes called it a philosophy, and it certainly was one, but the upshot of his *Meditations on Prime Philosophy* was to confirm by a new method all the main conclusions already established in metaphysics by Augustine, Anselm, Bonaventure, Thomas Aquinas, and Duns Scotus: the existence of one single God, infinite in being and in power, free creator of heaven and earth, conserving the world by his all-powerful will and acting as a Providence for man whose soul can be proved to be spiritual in nature. With Descartes, Malebranche, and Leibniz, the point of departure of modern philosophy coincides with the point of arrival of medieval theology. Even Spinoza cannot be fully accounted for without taking into account the speculation of the middle ages. To overlook what happened to philosophy in the thirteenth century is to deprive the history of Western thought of its continuity and, by the same token, its intelligibility.

This duality of nature explains the existence of two historical perspectives on the development of medieval speculation. Some historians prefer to follow its philosophical axis. The literary history of the progressive rediscovery of the Greek philosophical sources then becomes of paramount importance; from the end of the twelfth century on, Aristotle figures as the leading character in the play; Averroes and his followers then become, despite their occasional errors, the representatives of philosophy *qua* pure philosophy in the middle ages, or, at least, of the purely philosophical spirit from the thirteenth century up to the beginning of modern times. This is not only a perspective legitimate in itself, but one which answers an incontrovertible reality. It coincides with the very perspective adopted by the first modern philosophers on medieval speculation. It identifies it with Aristotelianism in its various medieval and more or less Christianized versions. It fully justifies the famous statement of O. Hamelin that Descartes comes immediately after the Greeks as though there had been nothing else in between. It is likewise tied up with an irreducible opposition to the notion of Christian philosophy in the past as well as in the present, with a corresponding tendency to make philosophy as independent from theology as possible and, consequently, to introduce into the theology of the scholastics a separation between rationally demonstrable conclusions and those whose premises, or at least one of them, rests upon faith.

A second perspective, no less historically justifiable, follows the axis of theology. It is the one which we have followed in this history, not on the strength of any preconceived ideas, but because of two facts. First, unless we consider the rediscovery of Greek philosophy as a philosophical creation of the medieval mind, all the original contributions made by the middle ages to the common treasure of philosophical knowledge have been made by theologians. Augustine, Denys, Anselm, Thomas Aquinas, Duns Scotus and Ockham have all been theologians; even when they wrote purely philosophical treatises, the deepest expression of their philosophical thought is found in their theological works; not one of them has ever imagined that there was no place for purely rational speculation in theology; in fact, their theologies are full of it, and to take medieval scholasticism just as it was should also be considered a historically justifiable perspective. True enough, it is an incomplete one, but no harm is done so long as this abstraction does not mistake itself for a separation in reality.

This second perspective has its drawbacks too. The fact that most modern theologians restrict the qualification of "theological" to conclusions among whose premises one at least is held as true by faith only, gives a paradoxical aspect to the history of doctrines which saw no difficulty in maintaining a position on strictly rational grounds and yet in considering it theological. It is not easy to persuade our contemporaries that they should look at medieval scholasticism from a medieval point of view; they may even have good reasons for refusing to do so, only these reasons cannot be historical ones. Now the only truth which history is supposed to look for is that of historical reality. Like every other truth, it has a right to be fully respected, and while no historian can be simple enough for confusing his own conclusions with historical truth itself, he himself cannot help stating it as he sees it. The progress of historical research and interpretation will finally put everything in its proper perspective, no honest effort will have been lost, and, since truth is one, there is nothing to lose and everything to gain in striving to respect it in all its orders and under all its aspects.

The philosophical appreciation of the results achieved by the Fathers of the Church and by scholastics does not fall under the competence of their historian. The least that a historian can say about this, however, is that apart from their ignorance of the facts, there is no excuse for those who describe the middle ages as a long period of philosophical stagnation. It might have been one. The Catholic Church could have condemned all philosophical speculation, including the very study of philosophy, as opposed to Christian faith. The Christian priests and monks could have been forbidden by the Church to indulge in such studies, to open schools and to teach doctrines that had been taught by pagans at a time when the gospel had not yet been preached to the Gentiles. The popes could have condemned all efforts to achieve any understanding of faith by means of philosophical speculation. Only no such thing happened during the middle ages; in fact, the very reverse took place between the times of Justin Martyr and those of Nicholas of Cues. It is not a good thing to judge fourteen centuries on the ground of their historical misrepresentation.

The intrinsic value of this Christian philosophy in the middle ages is a point for every philosopher to decide in the light of his own judgment. Most of them have their own opinion about it, but this opinion is not always founded upon a first-hand knowledge of the doctrines at stake. Now there is an excellent excuse, if not for judging what one does not sufficiently know, at least for not sufficiently knowing it. Life is short and the history of philosophy is growing longer every year. But if any Christian master felt the same indifference with respect to the history of scholasticism, he would be less easily excusable, because this is his own personal history or, at least, that of his own personal philosophical tradition. This tradition is not a dead thing; it is still alive and our own times bear witness to its enduring fecundity. There is no reason why this fecundity should come to an end. On the contrary, it can be expected to exhibit a new vitality every time it will re-establish contact with its authentic methods and its true principles, whose permanent truth is independent of time. The only object of the history of Christian philosophy, apart from being a history like all the others, is to facilitate access to the perennial sources of Christian speculation.

If, on the whole, this history has not completely misrepresented its object, it can be said that the treasure of Christian philosophy in the middle ages exhibits an amazing wealth of still incompletely exploited ideas. But even leaving them aside, this history should convey to its readers an invitation to establish personal contact with at least three main schools of thought which no Christian philosopher can afford to ignore. Augustine will introduce him to a metaphysical method based upon the data of personal introspection; Duns Scotus will introduce him to a metaphysical universe of essences; Thomas Aquinas will tell him what happens to such a universe when existence is added to essences as a further metaphysical dimension. Had they bequeathed to us nothing more than these three pure philosophical positions, the scholastics would still remain for all Christian philosophers the safest guides in their quest for a rationally valid interpretation of man and the world.

At this point our philosophical problem arises once more: how can a speculation be rational and philosophical if it is tied up with religious beliefs? Here again, history as such has no competence to answer the question. It knows, however, that far from sterilizing philosophical speculation, this alliance of two distinct orders of thought has given philosophy a new life and brought about positive philosophical results. The history of the influence of Christianity on the development of modern philosophy, quite independently of scholasticism and sometimes even in reaction against its methods, would be another field of investigation. From what little is already known of it, it appears that objectivity in judgment and freedom from settled intellectual prejudices are not the exclusive property of pagan philosophers, that reason is not always found at its best on the side of what is commonly called rationalism, and that, at any rate, the range of intelligibility is incomparably wider than that of reason. This is a lesson which only the frequentation of the true philosophical master minds can teach us. Why should we feel afraid of living in their company? No real master will ever invite us to listen to himself, but to the truth of what he says, such as we ourselves can see it in our own minds. In these matters, nothing can replace personal experience, and none can be more precious than this one if it is true to say, with Thomas Aquinas, that the "highest felicity of man consists in the speculation through which he is seeking the knowledge of truth."

11. What Is Christian Philosophy?

According to its etymology, the word "philosophy" means "the love of wisdom." As it used to be understood by the ancient Greeks, philosophy was less a doctrine or a knowledge than the pursuit of a certain doctrine or knowledge which, precisely, was wisdom. Each Greek philosopher entertained his own notion of wisdom; when several of them found themselves in general agreement about this notion, they were considered as constituting a philosophical school, such as that of Plato, of Aristotle and other ones. However deeply they might differ on secondary issues, all these schools agreed on the main characteristics of wisdom. They all considered it to be the supreme knowledge which, accessible only to men already possessed of the other sciences, enabled its owners to order and purify them, and to unify in its light the whole body of speculative and practical knowledge. Hence the now commonly received expression: the light of wisdom, and its traditional definition as the science of the first principles and of the first causes.

All love of wisdom so understood is philosophy. There are, therefore, a great many different ways of philosophizing, and many of them are unrelated to Christianity. This simply is a fact. The whole body of Greek philosophical speculation, from the fourth century B.C. to the beginning of the Christian era, came too soon to be able to see the world in the light of the Christian revelation. In our own day, a great many men choose to philosophize, as they say, in the light of natural reason alone, unaided by any sort of religious belief or revelation. The ancient Greeks had no choice, so that problem does not arise in so far as they are concerned; today we do have a choice, and there is for us a problem that deserves to be investigated.

A

The attitude of the early Christians was naturally different according to their individual differences in personal temperament, in intellectual formation, and in philosophical learning.

By and large, however, they seem to have agreed on three points.

First, Christianity was going to be their own philosophy, meaning thereby that, from that time onward, Christians would no longer have to worry about what, until then, the pagans had called philosophy. In other words, had he been asked the question: Have you a philosophy? a Christian would then have answered: I do have a philosophy indeed! Its name is Christianity.[1]

To this answer it was sometimes objected that philosophy and religion are two entirely different things, since philosophy is the quest of wisdom in the light of human reason alone, whereas religion, particularly Christianity, rests upon the acceptance by faith of a divinely revealed truth. But there was a remarkable answer to the objection. It was that, in point of fact, on all the points covered in common by philosophy and by revelation, rationality stood on the side of revelation much more than on that of philosophy. A single God, creator of heaven and earth, Ruler of the world and its Providence, a God Who made man in His own image and revealed to him, along with his last end, the way to attain it—where, in the splendid achievements of Greek philosophy, could one find a view of the world as clear and as perfectly satisfactory to the mind as the one revealed to men by Holy Scripture? Clearly, on all these problems, the teaching of revelation was incomparably more rational than the conclusions of reason.

A third characteristic of revealed truth further enhanced the already paradoxical nature of the second one. The conclusions of philosophy had been unsafe, mutually contradictory, and, even when they happened to hit the truth, always mixed with a measure of error. Moreover, this rather dubious learning was always the privilege of a small number of men living the leisurely life of scholars and endowed with the talent required to make good use of it. Not so with Christian revelation. God has spoken to all men, and He has done so in simple terms, so that all men can understand His words, provided only they be granted the grace of hearing them.

To sum up, since God Himself had spoken, what was thus revealed to mankind was certainly and completely true; it was more satisfying to reason than reason's own conclusions; and it was being offered to all men, irrespective of color, of race, of nation, as well as of social or economic conditions. No wonder, then, that Christians took to calling this revealed truth *their own philosophy;* by simply believing what God had said, they were finding themselves possessed of all that which they needed in the way of philosophical truth.

This memorable experience of the early Christians was not forgotten by their successors. Let us call it the notion of Christianity conceived as the philosophy of the Christians. Even today it represents a possible attitude; it is, in fact, the attitude of the great majority of Christians, who are not philosophers in the technical sense of the word, but who find in the Christian revelation a view of the world, of man, and of his destiny that gives full satisfaction to their reason. Today, as in the second century after Christ, the teaching of Catholic truth by missionaries provides men of all degrees of culture, or of the lack of it, with a perfect substitute for a philosophical view of the world. In the sixteenth century, the Catechism of the Council of Trent gave a name to revealed truth considered as fulfilling this particular function; the writers of the Catechism called it *Christian philosophy.* We still have a right to use the same expression, in the very same sense, provided we give it the same precise meaning.

B

The progressive constitution of the Christian theology in the middle ages brought about a new situation. What is now called scholastic theology has not been the work of any single man, and it has found several great exponents. Still, since we must single out one of them as representative of scholasticism in general, our best choice is St. Thomas Aquinas.

At the beginning of his great work *On the Truth of the Catholic Faith* (*Summa Contra Gentiles*),[2] the Master recalls the distinction between the two modes of truth about God, those that exceed the ability of the human reason (such as the Trinity), and those "which the natural reason also is able to reach. Such are that God exists, that He is one, and the like." In point of fact, Thomas adds, "such truths about God have been proved demonstratively by the philosophers, guided by the light of the natural reason" (I, 3, 2).

There is no difficulty in establishing the point that the truth about God that natural reason is not able to investigate is fittingly revealed to men and proposed to them as our object of belief. If the knowledge of such truth is necessary to man in view of salvation, and if God intends to make human salvation possible, there is no other way for such truth to become accessible to men than through the channel of divine revelation.

On the contrary, it is not immediately clear why God should have revealed to men the truth about Himself that is not beyond the reach of natural reason. Is it not at least superfluous to offer us as an object of belief what we are able to know?

Yet Thomas Aquinas enumerates a long series of reasons why even the truth about God that reason can investigate had to be revealed to men. The fourth chapter of Book I of the *Summa Contra Gentiles* is entirely devoted to the question. This chapter has been analyzed time and again, but even a careful analysis is bound to leave out a great deal of its content. Let us therefore recommend its careful reading[3] and content ourself with pointing out its significance for the problem under discussion.

In order to understand Thomas Aquinas on this point, one should remember that he is a theologian discussing this eminently theological problem: What was it fitting that God should reveal to men in view of their salvation? Related to our own problem, the question becomes: What would it mean for human salvation if, instead of revealing to us His existence, His unicity, and other such truths about Himself without whose knowledge no man can be saved, God had left the philosophers in charge of proving them demonstratively by the light of the natural reason?

The proper answer to this question is given to us in the spectacle of the philosophical teaching now distributed to students by countless good masters of philosophy, sometimes even by great philosophers, in modern colleges and universities. Some of them say there is no God; others say that there is a God but that His existence cannot be demonstrated; still others say there is a God and they can prove His existence, but their demonstrations fail to carry conviction, or else what they call God in no way resembles the object of our religious worship. There is no reason to wonder what would happen to our knowledge of God if it had been entrusted to the sole care of philosophy and the philosophers. We know it, we see it, and the answer is that philosophers have simply brought the problem to a chaotic condition.

Strangely enough, Thomas Aquinas himself placed more hope in philosophers than we do. The reason probably is that he had not seen anything like the condition of metaphysics in our own time. On the contrary, we rather seem to consider anybody as qualified to become a metaphysician, and the usual training required to this end, in modern philosophical factories, averages a duration of three to eight years.

This is a point on which Thomas Aquinas seems to have had misgivings. According to him, few men would possess the knowledge of God if the only source of such knowledge were philosophy. Some are not intellectually qualified for philosophical studies; others, because they are in business or in an office, lack the leisure of contemplative inquiry; above all, the knowledge of metaphysics presupposes a great deal of already acquired knowledge, which means much labor spent in study: "Now, those who wish to undergo such a labor for the mere love of knowledge are few"; in short, "if the only way open to us for the knowledge of God were solely that of reason, the human race would remain in the blackest shadows of ignorance" (I, 4, 3, and 4).

The attitude of Thomas Aquinas is simple. All men stand in need of salvation and, therefore, they need to know God's existence, His unicity, and the like; this knowledge is naturally acquired through the study of metaphysics, which "is the last part of philosophy to be learned" (I, 4, 3). Now, even among the few men who are able to learn philosophy, how many will live long enough to have time to become metaphysicians? All men need to know the existence of God from the earliest time of their lives. Unless we pretend that boys and girls seven years old are able to grasp metaphysical demonstrations, it must be conceded that rationally demonstrable conclusions had to be revealed by God in view of human salvation. The plain Thomistic truth of the case is that *all men,* without exception, must believe in the existence of God, and hold it true on faith, before being able to understand its demonstration. It also is that, were it necessary to hold such a truth on the strength of demonstration alone, very few could acquire it, and even these could not do so before a long time. Let us note the very words of Thomas Aquinas: very few men (*paucissimi*), and these only after a long time (*et hi etiam non nisi post longum tempus*).[4]

The *Summa Theologiae* assumes its full meaning in the light of these considerations. It contains an elementary exposition of all the truth revealed to men in view of their salvation. The part of that truth that is accessible to the light of natural reason is stated on the authority of revelation and accompanied by its philosophical demonstrations. In other words, that which either has actually been demonstrated by philosophers or, at least, can be demonstrated in a philosophical way, receives in the *Summa* the full benefit of rational demonstration.

We are not now concerned with the generous use that Thomas makes of philosophy in defining, explaining, and defending even that part of revealed truth that exceeds the reach of human reason. But the way he fulfilled the first part of his program is of primary importance for a correct understanding of the notion of Christian philosophy. True enough, Thomas himself never used the expression, but he left philosophy, particularly metaphysics, in a condition very different from that in which he had found it. After him, each and every revealed truth concerning God, if it was demonstrable to all, now was presenting itself along with its philosophical demonstration. Thomas himself would have been very much surprised to hear that, in giving philosophical demonstrations of philosophically demonstrable truths revealed by God to men, he was, although commenting upon the word of God, indulging in a non-theological activity. In the first place, it should be obvious that all which is found in the *Summa Theologiae* is theological; on the other hand, it is no less obvious that when a theologian deems it fit to give a rational demonstration, the only way for him to do so is to proceed as would any philosopher undertaking to do the same thing. From the time of Thomas Aquinas onward, there has existed a body of truth, revealed to men by God, but rationally demonstrable and, in the mind of the Angelic Doctor at least, philosophically demonstrated.

C

As has been said, Thomas Aquinas did not give this body of truth about God any special name. He had no need for any such name. To him all these philosophically demonstrated conclusions were part and parcel of Sacred Doctrine; the Doctor of revealed truth took them in stride; their existence simply raised no problem for the theologian.

The sixteenth century marked the beginning of a new era with respect to our problem, but the decisive turning point was reached with Descartes. In his *Discourse on Method*, the young reformer announced his intention to leave theology and revelation to theologians, who are in charge of leading us all to heaven, scholars and ignorant alike; as to himself, he would deal with problems related to the nature of things and deal with them in the light of natural reason alone. This regime of the separation of theology and philosophy, or of revelation and reason, was an attempt to return in Christian times to the pre-Christian position of the problem. This was an impossible thing to do, and, in point of fact, Descartes did not accomplish it. Himself a Catholic, he never seems to have wondered how it was that, philosophizing wholly apart from theology, he was spontaneously rediscovering the main conclusions about God and man already demonstrated by the theologians of the middle ages, particularly by Thomas Aquinas. At the same time, he was laying down the principles of his own mechanistic physics, but his way of doing so first supposed the demonstration of a God known from His creatures, Creator of heaven and earth, as well as of man, a strange being made of the substantial union of body and soul. Incidentally, since this soul is really distinct from its body, nothing prevents it from being immortal.

All these philosophical conclusions were established by Descartes in a most un-Thomistic way, but they all were Thomistic conclusions. Today, the *Discourse on the Method* still is on the *Index Prohibitorum Librorum*, but a great many Catholic professors of philosophy, while denouncing the philosophical errors of Descartes, in practice subscribe to his own notion of a philosophy separated from theology. To them, as to Descartes himself, where theology begins, philosophy comes to an end. If we philosophize, we cannot be theologizing at the same time. There are no available statistics, but were it possible to know how many priests, monks, or Catholic laymen in charge of teaching philosophy completely imitate the attitude of Descartes in this matter, it probably would appear that the author of the *Discourse* has carried the day.

The reason for this is apparent. Nearly all the philosophers who followed in the wake of Descartes[5] subscribed to the principle that philosophy has nothing to do with theology, or reason with revelation. Obviously, such was not the case with the philosophical speculation included in the theological works of the great scholastics. Consequently, if a scholastic theologian pretended to argue and to reach conclusions as a philosopher, his opponent would simply object that a scholastic master might well have a theology, but he certainly had no philosophy. The controversy was not a new one. Already in the middle ages, Averroes had reproached Avicenna with teaching revelation in philosophical garb; among the Latins, the Averroists had not only declared their intention to keep philosophy apart from revelation, they had fought, and suffered, to do what they had announced they would do. What was new after Descartes was the generalization of this attitude. This time, the representatives of medieval scholasticism realized that the new philosophical situation could not be ignored.

By and large, the sixteenth- and seventeenth-century scholastics followed the line of least resistance. To the objection: You have no philosophy of your own, their answer was: Yes, we do have a philosophy. In order to prove it, they simply extracted from the *Summae* and the Commentaries on Peter Lombard what of philosophical speculation their medieval predecessors had inserted within them. This philosophical material was set up and organized as an independent body of philosophical speculation to be taught as a philosophical introduction to the study of theology. The only alternative was to follow the example of the medieval Averroists; that is, to identify philosophy with Aristotle and to teach to the young Christians of the sixteenth century a revised version of Aristotelianism in which the worst discrepancies between his authentic doctrine and the Catholic faith were toned down and, wherever it was possible to do so, eliminated.

The consequences were to be damaging to the future of Christian thought. Instead of opposing the onslaught of Cartesianism with the deep metaphysics of Thomas Aquinas, an ever-present truth, the scholastics met it with school versions of the philosophy of Aristotle, and they did so at the very moment when the scientific basis of Aristotelianism, from biology to astronomy, was crumbling down under the impact of the new science. There was not even a battle. From that time onward, scholastic philosophy has survived under the form of textbooks, in which a philosophy using the language of Aristotle miraculously agrees with the conclusions of Catholic theology, from which, however, it is supposed to be specifically distinct.

Owing to this decision, Catholics and their schools could now boast of having a philosophy properly so called, separated from revelation and faith as every true philosophy should be, and fully qualified to claim a place of its own in the philosophical movement of the age. The only tie of this neo-scholastic philosophy with theology and revelation was its professed resolve never to contradict, in philosophical matters, the theological teaching of the Church. What happened to this neo-scholastic philosophy during the seventeenth and the eighteenth centuries is a matter of historical record. The purely negative pact of non-aggression, which was its only tie with the Sacred Doctrine, was not enough to prevent this school philosophy from absorbing strong doses of Descartes, Leibniz, Locke, Condillac, Victor Cousin, even Kant. In the thirteenth century, while philosophy was still part and parcel of theological speculation, the theologians had been the acknowledged leaders in the philosophical world; from the seventeenth century and onward, neo-scholasticism did little else than to contract temporary alliances with any form of philosophical thought that could be reconciled with the teachings of Revelation.

This is the reason that prompted some Italian theologians in the first half of the nineteenth century to advocate a return to the philosophical positions of St. Thomas Aquinas. Only, keeping in mind the desire of their contemporaries to have a philosophy of their own, these theologians called this philosophy a *philosophia christiana,* a Christian philosophy. This move culminated in the encyclical letter *Aeterni Patris* published on August 4, 1879, by Pope Leo XIII, "On the Restoration of Christian Philosophy in Schools."[6]

To the question: What is Christian philosophy? the shortest answer now is: If you read the encyclical letter *Aeterni Patris* you will find there the most highly authorized answer to your question. Reduced to its essentials, the answer is as follows.

In the first third of his encyclical Leo XIII recalls, along with the doctrinal function of the Church and the teaching office of the popes, the services rendered to theology by philosophy, but he does not forget to recall as well the benefits philosophy has always derived in the past from its close association with theology. In carefully weighted words, Leo XIII observes that "the human mind, being confined within certain limits, and these narrow enough, is exposed to many errors and is ignorant of many things . . . Those, therefore, who to the study of philosophy unite obedience to the Christian faith, are philosophizing in the best possible way; for the splendor of the divine truths, received into the mind, helps the understanding, and not only detracts in no wise from its dignity, but adds greatly to its nobility, keenness, and stability."[7]

Obviously we are here returning, under a new name, to the very same situation occupied by philosophy with respect to Christian faith from the time of St. Justin up to the Cartesian philosophical reformation. Nor is it only a question for philosophy not to disagree with faith; a positive influence of faith over the human reason is here advocated not only as the best safeguard against error but also as a remedy to human ignorance.

It is no wonder, then, that instead of sketching a system of Christian philosophy, Leo XIII devotes the middle section of his encyclical to a truly admirable history of what happened to philosophy during the many centuries of its association with faith in the doctrines of the early Apologists, the Fathers of the Church, and the scholastic Doctors. Clearly, what Leo XIII calls Christian philosophy cannot be reduced to the content of any single philosophy; it is neither a system nor even a doctrine. Rather, it is a way of philosophizing; namely, the attitude of those who "to the study of philosophy unite obedience to the Christian faith."[8] This philosophical method, or attitude—*philosophandi institutum*—is *Christian philosophy* itself.

It should now be clear that under the name of Christian philosophy Pope Leo XIII simply is sending us back to the method of handling philosophical problems traditional in the history of patristic and of scholastic theology; that is, to what the encyclical itself calls the "right use of that philosophy which the scholastic teachers have been accustomed carefully and prudently to make use of even in theological disputations."[9] The panegyric of the "philosophy" of St. Thomas that fills up the last third of *Aeterni Patris*, not to the exclusion of other Doctors, but praising it as the very model and idea of the Christian way of philosophizing, is enough to assure us of what Christian philosophy truly was in the mind of Pope Leo XIII. Before anything else, it was the investigation, by means of philosophy, of the saving truth revealed by God and accessible to the light of natural reason.[10]

D

Thus understood, Christian philosophy naturally centers around a core of problems perfectly summarized in the famous prayer of St. Augustine to God: "That I may know Thee, that I may know myself." Many modern philosophers would consider this as a sufficient reason to hold Christian philosophy as philosophically disqualified, but all that philosophers say is not necessarily true. On the contrary, Thomas Aquinas always insisted that, Christian or otherwise, all philosophy worthy of the name had in fact posited the knowledge of God as its last end. In this respect, Christian philosophy is like any other right-minded philosophy, with the only difference that it is better equipped than they to fulfill what has always been the common ambition of philosophical speculation.

This final orientation of Christian philosophy entails no *a priori* exclusion of any field of philosophical research. What can there be in the whole world that is irrelevant to the knowledge of God and man? Since the invisible of God is known from His creatures, there is no creature—that is to say, no thing—whose knowledge is unrelated to the knowledge of God; and since the world of knowledge is the work of man, it can be said of man that, in the last analysis, all his acquired knowledge is about himself. Leo XIII has stressed with great insistence the fact that thus to order all the sciences under the leadership of true philosophy is not to do away with them. On the contrary, "all studies ought to find hope of advancement and promise of assistance in this restoration of philosophic discipline which We have proposed."[11] In short, while the Christian way of philosophizing protects philosophical research against the risks of error and the evil of useless dispersion, it in no way deprives it of its necessary freedom of investigation.

A last benefit of the Christian attitude in philosophical matters is overlooked in our own days. This is the more curious as our contemporaries are acting in a way that makes it imperative for us to exploit it to the limit. In listing the reasons why God deemed it fitting to reveal to men some truths accessible to philosophical knowledge, Thomas Aquinas stressed the fact that many men die, if not young, at least years before reaching the age of philosophical maturity. As he himself saw it, philosophy was a lifetime pursuit, requiring a great liberty of mind, much intellectual leisure, and many years of work spent on the sciences whose knowledge is a necessary prerequisite to the study of natural theology. On the contrary, Thomas added, revelation and faith offer to human understanding the ready knowledge of the highest metaphysical truths under a form that makes them accessible to all.

Today the reverse seems to be considered true. Modern educators speak and act as if they thought that boys and girls are qualified students in metaphysics and, at the same time, they make a profession of teaching a philosophy which, careful as it is never to contradict the Christian revelation, is no less careful not to undergo its influence. The paradoxical nature of the situation scarcely needs to be stressed. In his *Summa Contra Gentiles*, a theological work so full of philosophy that it is often mistaken for a philosophical work, Thomas Aquinas makes no effort to conceal his indebtedness to revelation. Nay, he forcefully stresses the universality of the end pursued by God in presenting to men by way of faith the pure truth about Himself: "In this way, all men would easily be able to have a share in the knowledge of God, and this without uncertainty and error." In support of this conclusion, Thomas Aquinas quotes Isaiah, 56:13: "All thy children shall be taught of the Lord."[12] The younger the children, the more necessary it should seem to rely on the teaching of the Lord in order to make them share in the knowledge of God without uncertainty and error. On the contrary, to teach them a systematically non-Christian philosophy is to impose on them all the obligation of reaching in their youth a faultless metaphysical knowledge which, in the past, was the privilege of very few great philosophers, if any.

There would not be much point in explaining these things to non-Christian philosophers; but it is somewhat strange that such a philosophical attitude should be considered paradoxical, if not downright contradictory, by representatives of the Christian tradition. After all, it says only what Thomas Aquinas has done and it does no more than recommend a way of cultivating philosophy prescribed as the only safe one by Pope Leo XIII. The most serious obstacle to the acceptance of the method advocated—nay, prescribed—by Leo XIII to all Christian schools wherein philosophy is taught under any form is the extraordinary ignorance (in which so many Christians still live) of the philosophical principles of St. Thomas Aquinas. The name of the Common Doctor of the Church is frequently quoted; it is to be found on the title pages of many books and there have always been able interpreters of his doctrine; still, it too often happens that what is taught under the name of Thomism has little in common with the authentic philosophy of the saint. It has been our conviction that we must relearn the meaning of the notion of *being* proper to Thomas Aquinas and to follow it in its application to the main problems of Christian philosophy.

Unless we are mistaken, this notion is the master key to the metaphysics of the saint, and it is better to have at least striven to master it than, without it, to have covered a vast ground in a theology where it is everywhere present.

NOTES

1. See *The History of Christian Philosophy*, pp. 11–14 and pp. 554–555. The case of St. Justin is representative of several other ones.
2. This work will be quoted from its English translation by Prof. A. C. Pegis, a Doubleday Image Book, Garden City, N.Y., 1955, *Book One*: *God*. Following the division of the text adopted by Prof. Pegis, we shall quote, for instance: I, 3, 2, meaning *Summa Contra Gentiles*, Book I, chapter 3, par. 2.
3. *Summa Contra Gentiles*, I, 4; ed. cit., pp. 66–68.
4. *Quaestiones Disputatiae de Veritate*, q. 14, art. 10 Resp. According to Thomas Aquinas, *everybody* is held *explicitly* and *always* to believe that God is and that He aims at the good of man. These two notions are quoted by Thomas as those that every Christian must explicitly believe. This teaching rests upon the authority of the Apostle, Hebr. xi, 6. See *Qu. Disp. de Veritate*, q. 14, a. 11 Resp.: "Unde *quilibet* tenetur *explicite* credere et *omni tempore*, Deum esse et habere providentiam de rebus humanis." There is no reason to think that Thomas is here forgetting his other thesis, that one cannot know and believe one and the same thing at one and the same time (*Qu. Disp. de Veritate*, q. 14, a. 9, *Sed contra*); but very few men can acquire demonstrative knowledge of such truth and all the others are held, always and explicitly, to believe them as revealed of God. Cf. *In Boethium de Trinitate*, q. 3, a. 1.
5. Nearly all, not all, for indeed Malebranche was a clear case of Christian philosophy.
6. *The Church Speaks to the Modern World. The Social Teachings of Leo XIII*, a Doubleday Image Book, Garden City, N.Y., 1954, pp. 29–51. An apostolic letter published in 1880 refers to *Aeterni Patris* as to "Our Letter on the Restoring in Catholic Schools of the Christian Philosophy in the Spirit of St. Thomas Aquinas."
7. *Aeterni Patris*, ed. cit., p. 38. Cf. (p. 39) the quotation from the Vatican Council: "Faith frees and saves reason from error, and endows it with manifold knowledge."
8. "Quapropter qui philosophiae studium cum obsequio fidei christianae conjungunt ii optime philosophantur," *Aeterni Patris*, ed. cit., p. 52, note 4.
9. *Aeterni Patris*, ed. cit., p. 43.

10. The encyclical of 1879 goes even farther than this; it does not seem to consider philosophy as losing its specific character in helping theology to "assume the nature, form and genius of a true science." *Aeterni Patris*, ed. cit., p. 36. This aspect of the problem is left out as relevant to the notion of theology rather than to that of philosophy.
11. *Aeterni Patris*, ed. cit., p. 49.
12. *On the Truth of the Catholic Faith*, I, 4, 6, and 7.

12. God and Christian Philosophy

While the Greek philosophers were wondering what place to assign to their gods in a philosophically intelligible world, the Jews had already found the God who was to provide philosophy with an answer to its own question. Not a god imagined by poets or discovered by any thinker as an ultimate answer to his metaphysical problems, but one who had revealed Himself to the Jews, told them His name, and explained to them His nature, in so far at least as His nature can be understood by men.

The first character of the Jewish God was his unicity: "Hear, O Israel: the Lord our God is one Lord."[1] Impossible to achieve a more far-reaching revolution in fewer words or in a simpler way. When Moses made this statement, he was not formulating any metaphysical principle to be later supported by rational justification. Moses was simply speaking as an inspired prophet and defining for the benefit of the Jews what was henceforth to be the sole object of their worship. Yet, essentially religious as it was, this statement contained the seed of a momentous philosophical revolution, in this sense at least, that should any philosopher, speculating at any time about the first principle and cause of the world, hold the Jewish God to be the true God, he would be necessarily driven to identify his supreme philosophical cause with God. In other words, whereas the difficulty was, for a Greek philosopher, to fit a plurality of gods into a reality which he conceived as one, any follower of the Jewish God would know at once that, whatever the nature of reality itself may be said to be, its religious principle must of necessity coincide with its philosophical principle. Each of them being one, they are bound to be the same and to provide men with one and the same explanation of the world.

When the existence of this one true God was proclaimed by Moses to the Jews, they never thought for a moment that their Lord could be some thing. Obviously, their Lord was somebody. Besides, since he was the God of the Jews, they already knew Him; and they knew Him as the Lord God of their fathers, the God of Abraham, the God of Isaac, and the God of Jacob. Time and again, their God had proved to them that He was taking care of His people; their relations with Him had always been personal relations, that is, relations between persons and another person; the only thing they still wanted to know about Him was what to call Him. As a matter of fact, Moses himself did not know the name of the one God, but he knew that the Jews would ask him for it; and instead of engaging upon deep metaphysical meditations to discover the true name of God, he took a typically religious short cut. Moses simply asked God about His name, saying to Him: "Lo, I shall go to the children of Israel, and say to them: The God of your fathers hath sent me to you. If they should say to me: What is His name? What shall I say to them? God said to Moses: I AM WHO AM. He said: Thus shalt thou say to the children of Israel: HE WHO IS, hath sent me to you."[2] Hence the universally known name of the Jewish God–Yahweh, for Yahweh means "He Who is."

Here again historians of philosophy find themselves confronted with this to them always unpalatable fact: a non-philosophical statement which has since become an epoch-making statement in the history of philosophy. The Jewish genius was not a philosophical genius; it was a religious one. Just as the Greeks are our masters in philosophy, the Jews are our masters in religion. So long as the Jews kept their own religious revelation to themselves, nothing happened to philosophy. But owing to the preaching of the Gospel, the God of the Jews ceased to be the private God of an elect race and became the universal God of all men. Any Christian convert who was at all familiar with Greek philosophy was then bound to realize the metaphysical import of his new religious belief. His philosophical first principle had to be one with his religious first principle, and since the name of his God was "I am," any Christian philosopher had to posit "I am" as his first principle and supreme cause of all things, even in philosophy. To use our own modern terminology, let us say that a Christian's philosophy is "existential" in its own right.

This point was of such importance that even the earliest Christian thinkers did not fail to see it. When the first educated Greeks became converts to Christianity, the Olympian gods of Homer had already been discredited as mere mythical imaginings through the repeated criticism of the philosophers. But those very philosophers had no less completely discredited themselves by giving to the world the spectacle of their endless contradictions. Even those who were the greatest among them, taken at their very best, had never succeeded in correctly stating what they at least should have held to be the supreme cause of all things. Plato, for instance, had clearly seen that the ultimate philosophical explanation for all that which is should ultimately rest, not within those elements of reality that are always being generated and therefore never really are, but with something which, because it has no generation, truly is, or exists. Now, as has been pointed out by the unknown author of the *Hortatory Address to the Greeks* as early as the third century A.D., what Plato had said was almost exactly what the Christians themselves were saying, "saving only the difference of the article. For Moses said: *He Who is,* and Plato: *That which is.*" And it is quite true that "either of the expressions seems to apply to the existence of God."[3] If God is "He Who is," he also is "that which is," because to be somebody is also to be something. Yet the converse is not true, for to be somebody is much more than to be something.

We are here at the dividing line between Greek thought and Christian thought; that is to say, between Greek philosophy and Christian philosophy. Taken in itself, Christianity was not a philosophy. It was the essentially religious doctrine of the salvation of men through Christ. Christian philosophy arose at the juncture of Greek philosophy and of the Jewish-Christian religious revelation, Greek philosophy providing the technique for a rational explanation of the world, and the Jewish-Christian revelation providing religious beliefs of incalculable philosophical import. What is perhaps the key to the whole history of Christian philosophy and, in so far as modern philosophy bears the mark of Christian thought, to the history of modern philosophy itself is precisely the fact that, from the second century A.D. on, men have had to use a Greek philosophical technique in order to express ideas that had never entered the head of any Greek philosopher.

This was by no means an easy task. The Greeks had never gone farther than the natural theology of Plato and of Aristotle, not on account of intellectual weakness on their part, but, on the contrary, because both Plato and Aristotle had pushed their investigations almost as far as human reason alone can take us. By positing, as the supreme cause of all that which is, somebody who is, and of whom the very best that can be said is that "He is," Christian revelation was establishing existence as the deepest layer of reality as well as the supreme attribute of the divinity. Hence, in so far as the world itself was concerned, the entirely new philosophical problem of its very existence, and the still deeper one whose formula runs thus: What is it to exist? As J. B. Muller-Thym aptly remarks, where a Greek simply asks: What is nature? a Christian rather asks: What is being?[4]

The first epoch-making contact between Greek philosophical speculation and Christian religious belief took place when, already a convert to Christianity, the young Augustine began to read the works of some neo-Platonists, particularly the *Enneads* of Plotinus.[5] Augustine found there, not the pure philosophy of Plato, but an original synthesis of Plato, Aristotle, and the Stoics. Moreover, even where he borrowed from Plato, Plotinus had identified the Idea of Good, as described in the *Republic,* with that other puzzling principle, the One, which makes its late appearance in Plato's *Parmenides*. The very conclusion of this dialogue seems to have provided Plotinus with the keystone of his own metaphysical system: "Then were we to say in a word: if the one is not, nothing is, should we be right?—Most assuredly." And indeed, if the One is that without which nothing else could be, the existence of the whole world must of necessity depend upon some eternally subsisting Unity.

Let us then imagine, with Plotinus, a first principle whom we will call the One. Strictly speaking, he is unnamable because he cannot be described. Any attempt at expressing him must of necessity result in a judgment, and since a judgment is made up of several terms, we cannot say what the One is without turning his unity into some sort of multiplicity; that is, without destroying it. Let us say then that he is the One, not as a number that can enter the composition of other numbers, nor as a synthesis of other numbers, but as the self-subsisting unity whence all multiplicity follows without affecting in the least its absolute simplicity. From the fecundity of the One a second principle is born, inferior to the first, yet eternally subsisting like the One and, after him, the cause of all that comes after him. His name is the Intellect. Unlike the One, the Intellect is the self-subsisting knowledge of all that is intelligible. Since he himself is both the knowing subject and the known object, he is as near being the One as it is possible to be; yet since he is affected by the duality of subject and object inherent in all knowledge, he is not the One; consequently he is inferior to him.

Among the attributes which belong to the Intellect, two are of particular importance for a correct understanding of our historical problem. Conceived as an eternally subsisting cognition of all that which is intelligible, the Intellect of Plotinus is, by definition, the locus of all the Ideas. They are in him as a multiple intelligible unity; they are eternally sharing in the fecundity which he himself owes to the fecundity of the One; in short, the Intellect is big with all that multiplicity of individual and distinct beings which eternally flow from him. In this sense, he is a god and the father of all the other gods.

A second characteristic of the Intellect, much harder to grasp than the preceding one, is perhaps still more important. When can we say of anything: It is? As soon as, by an act of understanding, we apprehend it as distinct from something else. In other words, so long as nothing is actually understood, nothing is; which amounts to saying that being first appears in, by, and with this Intellect, who is the second principle in Plotinus' philosophy. These are the two supreme causes of the Plotinian universe: at the top, the One of Plato's *Parmenides;* immediately below him, and born of him, the self-thinking Thought of Aristotle, whom Plotinus calls the Nous, or Intellect, and whom he conceives as the locus of Plato's Ideas. Such also were the main data of the problem which Augustine boldly undertook to solve: how to express the God of Christianity in terms borrowed from the philosophy of Plotinus.

If we look at this problem as historians, and view it through fifteen centuries of history, our first impulse is to declare that such a problem was not susceptible of a satisfactory solution. Perhaps it was not. But we should remember that the creations of the human mind do not obey the analytical laws which preside over their historical explanations. What appears to us as a problem fraught with tremendous difficulties was never perceived by Augustine as a problem; the only thing he was ever aware of was its solution.

Generations after generations of historians have pondered over this extraordinary and, in a way, inexplicable phenomenon. Here is a young convert to Christianity who, for the first time in his life, reads the *Enneads* of Plotinus, and what he sees there at once is the Christian God Himself, with all his essential attributes. Who is the One, if not God the Father, the first person of the Christian Trinity? And who is the Nous, or Intellect, if not the second person of the Christian Trinity; that is, the Word, exactly as he appears at the beginning of the Gospel of St. John? "And therein I read, not indeed in the same words, but to the selfsame effect, enforced by many and divers reasons, that: In the beginning was the Word, and the Word was with God, and the Word was God. All things were made by Him; and without Him was not any thing made that was made."[6] In short, as soon as Augustine read the *Enneads*, he found there the three essentially Christian notions of God the Father, of God the Word, and of the creation.

That Augustine found them there is an incontrovertible fact. That they were not there is a hardly more controvertible fact. To go at once to the fundamental reason why they could not possibly be there, let us say that the world of Plotinus and the world of Christianity are strictly incomparable; no single point in the one can be matched with any single point in the other one, for the fundamental reason that their metaphysical structure is essentially different. Plotinus was living in the third century A.D.; yet his philosophical thought remained wholly foreign to Christianity. His world is a Greek philosophical world, made up of natures whose operations are strictly determined by their essences. Even the One of Plotinus, whom we can hardly refrain from designating as a He, exists and operates after the manner of an It. If we compare him to the rest, the One, or Good, is absolutely free, because all the rest depends upon him for its existence, whereas he himself, being the first principle, does not depend upon anything else. Taken in himself, on the contrary, the One is strictly determined by his own nature; not only the One is what he has to be, but he acts as he has to act on account of what he necessarily is. Hence the typically Greek aspect of the Plotinian universe as a natural, eternal, and necessary generation of all things by the One. Everything eternally flows from him as a radiation which he himself does not even know, because he is above thought, above being, above the duality of being and thought. In Plotinus' own words: "As to the unbegotten principle, who has nothing above him, who is eternally what he is, what reason might he have to think?"[7]

To Plotinus' question, let our answer be: No reason whatsoever; but let us immediately add that this alone is a sufficient reason why the god of Plotinus cannot possibly be the Christian God nor the world of Plotinus a Christian world. The Plotinian universe is typically Greek in this, that in it God is neither the supreme reality nor the ultimate principle of intelligibility. Hence this metaphysically momentous consequence, that the dividing line between the first cause and all the rest does not coincide in a philosophy of the One and in a philosophy of being. Since nothing can beget itself, what the One begets has to be other than the One; consequently, it must of necessity be multiple. This applies even to the Intellect, who is the highest Plotinian god. The Plotinian dividing line thus cuts off the One, who is the only unbegotten principle, from all the begotten multiplicity, that is to say, from all the rest. In all the rest are to be found the Intellect, who is the first god, followed by the supreme Soul, who is the second god, then all the other gods including the human souls. In other words, while there is a radical difference of nature between the One, or Good, and all that which, because it is not the One, is multiple, there are but differences of degrees between all that which is not the One, and yet is, or exists. We ourselves belong in the same metaphysical class as the Intellect and the supreme Soul; we are gods just as they are, begotten from the One just as they are, and inferior to them, in proportion to our respective degrees of multiplicity, as they themselves are inferior to the One.

Not so in a Christian metaphysics of being, where the supreme principle is a god whose true name is "He Who is." A pure act of existing, taken as such and without any limitation, necessarily is all that which it is possible to be. We cannot even say that such a god has knowledge, or love, or anything else; he is it in his own right, for the very reason that, were he not everything and anything that it is possible to be, he could be called "He Who is" but with some added qualification. If, as is part of Christian faith, such a god begets in virtue of his infinite fecundity, he must beget somebody else—that is, another person; but not something else—that is, another god. Otherwise, there would be two absolute acts of existing, each of which would include the totality of being, which is absurd. If, on the other hand, such a god actually is, or exists, his self-sufficiency is so perfect that there can be no necessity for anything else to exist. Nothing can be added to him; nothing can be subtracted from him; and since nothing can share in his being without at once being himself, "He Who is" can eternally enjoy the fullness of his own perfection, of his own beatitude, without needing to grant existence to anybody else, or to anything whatsoever.

Yet it is a fact that there is something which is not God. Men, for instance, are not such an eternal act of absolute existence. There are therefore some beings that are radically different from God at least in this that, unlike Him, they might not have existed, and still may, at a certain time, cease to exist. Thus to be, or exist, is not at all to be, or exist, as God Himself is, or exists. It is therefore not to be an inferior sort of god; rather, it is not to be a god at all. The only possible explanation for the presence of such finite and contingent beings is that they have been freely given existence by "Him Who is," and not as parcels of His own existence, which, because it is absolute and total, is also unique, but as finite and partial imitations of what He Himself eternally is in His own right. This act whereby "He Who is" causes to exist something that, of itself, is not, is what is called, in Christian philosophy, "creation." Whence there follows that whereas all that which the Christian God begets must of necessity share in the oneness of God, all that which does not share in His oneness must of necessity be not begotten but created.

Such is, in fact, the Christian world of St. Augustine. On the one side, God, one in the Trinity of a single, self-existing substance; on the other side, all that which, because it has but a received existence, is not God. Unlike the Plotinian dividing line which we have seen running between the One and all that is begotten by the One, the Christian dividing line runs between God, including His own begotten Word, and all that is created by God. As one among God's creatures, man finds himself therein excluded from the order of the divine. Between "Him Who is" and ourselves there is the infinite metaphysical chasm which separates the complete self-sufficiency of His own existence from the intrinsic lack of necessity of our own existence. Nothing can bridge such a chasm, save a free act of the divine will only. This is why, from the time of St. Augustine up to our own days, human reason has been up against the tremendously difficult task of reaching a transcendent God Whose pure act of existing is radically distinct from our own borrowed existence. How can man, who out of himself is not, living in a world of things which out of themselves are not, reach, by means of reason alone, "Him Who is"? Such is, to a Christian, the fundamental problem of natural theology.

In his effort to solve this problem, Augustine had nothing to help him but the philosophical technique of Plato in the revised edition of Plotinus. Here again, the philosophical eagerness of the Christian convert took him beyond the data of the problem straight to its solution. Interpreting Plato's doctrine of reminiscence, Plotinus had described dialectics as an effort of the human soul to rid itself of all material images so as to contemplate the intelligible Ideas in the light of the first Intellect, who is the supreme god. Was not this exactly what St. John himself had, if not philosophically established, at least clearly suggested in the first chapter of his gospel? When Plotinus and St. John thus met in the mind of Augustine, their combination was instantaneous. Reading the gospel into Plotinus' *Enneads*, he found there that the soul of man, though it "bears witness of the light," yet itself "is not that light; but the Word of God, being God, is that true light that lighteth every man that cometh into the world."[8] Why should not men use this constant presence of the divine light in their souls as an always open way to the Christian God?

This is precisely what Augustine did, or, at least, what he tried to do, for the task proved to be a much more difficult one than he himself had imagined. In inheriting the philosophical world of Plato, Augustine had fallen heir to Plato's man. Now, man, as Plato conceived him, was not the substantial unity of body and soul; he was essentially a soul. Instead of saying that man *has* a soul, we should therefore say that man *is* a particular soul; that is to say, an intelligent, intelligible, and eternally living substance, which, though it now happens to be conjoined to a body, has always existed before it and is ultimately destined to outlive it. In Plato's own words, man is "a soul using a body,"[9] but he is no more his body than a worker is the tools he uses or than any one of us is his own garments.

By accepting this definition of man, Augustine was putting himself in an exceedingly awkward philosophical position. In Plato's doctrine, and still more clearly in that of Plotinus, to be a purely intelligible, living, and immortal substance was exactly to be a god. Human souls, then, are just so many gods. When a man philosophizes and, discarding his body, focuses his mind upon intelligible truth, he simply behaves like a god who remembers to be a god. Rightly to philosophize, then, is nothing else, for each and every one of us, than to behave as becomes the god which each and every one of us actually is. True, we all are but individual Intelligences radiated by the supreme Intellect, and therefore by the One. For this very reason, just as we are by and in the One, we also know, and contemplate, by and in the light of the supreme Intellect who eternally emanates from the One. Yet, when all is said and done, we nevertheless are so many gods, lesser gods as we may be, patiently working our way back into the company of our fellow gods. Dialectics, as Plato and Plotinus understood it, was but the method which enables man to achieve a sort of philosophical salvation, by progressively raising him to the full awareness of his own divinity. A god may eventually forget himself but he cannot possibly stand in need of being saved.[10]

This is the fundamental reason why St. Augustine has found

it so hard to reach the Christian God by means of methods borrowed from Plato and Plotinus. To him, as to them, all that was immaterial, intelligible, and true was divine in its own right; but, whereas, in Plato's philosophy, man was naturally entitled to the possession of truth as a divinity is entitled to the possession of things divine, he could no longer appear as entitled to it in a Christian philosophy where, metaphysically speaking,[11] man in no way belongs in the divine order. Hence this important consequence, that man was bound to appear to Augustine as a creature endowed with something that was divine in its own right. If truth is divine, and if man is not a god, man should not be possessed of truth. In fact, however, man is; consequently, the only conceivable way for Augustine to account for the paradoxical presence of intelligible truth, which is divine, in man, who is not a god, was to consider man as knowing in the permanent light of a supremely intelligible and self-subsisting truth; that is, in the light of God.

Time and again, under a variety of different forms, Augustine has attempted the same demonstration of the existence of God as the only conceivable cause of the presence of truth in the human mind. His God is the intelligible sun whose light shines upon human reason and enables it to know truth; he is the inner master who teaches man from within; his eternal and unchangeable ideas are the supreme rules whose influence submits our reason to the necessity of divine truth. As demonstrations, the arguments of St. Augustine are very effective. Granting that truth is superhuman and divine in its own right, the bare fact that man knows truth conclusively proves the existence of God. But why should we grant Augustine that truth is a more than human object of knowledge? The only reason why he himself thought so was a merely accidental one. Augustine's implicit reasoning seems to have run as follows: Plato and Plotinus consider man as a god because man is possessed of truth; now man is emphatically not a god; hence man cannot possibly be possessed of truth. Taken in itself, such an argument is perfectly correct; it would even be a perfectly conclusive one if it were true to say that truth is too good a thing to be considered as naturally attainable by man.

What happened to St. Augustine is only too clear. An unsurpassed exponent of Christian wisdom, he never had the philosophy of his theology. The God of Augustine is the true Christian God, of Whose pure act of existing nothing better can be said than: He is; but when Augustine undertakes to describe existence in philosophical terms, he at once falls back upon the Greek identification of being with the notions of immateriality, intelligibility, immutability, and unity. Every such thing is divine; since truth is such, truth is divine. Immaterial, intelligible, and immutable, truth belongs in the order of that which truly is, or exists. Consequently, it belongs to God. Similarly the God of Augustine is the true creator of all things; but when it comes to defining creation, Augustine naturally understands it in accordance with his own notion of being. To create is to give being, and since to be is to be both intelligible and one, Augustine understands creation as the divine gift of that sort of existence which consists in rhythm, numbers, forms, beauty, order, and unity.[12] Like all Christians, but unlike the Greeks, Augustine has a quite clear notion of what it is to create something "out of nothing." It is to make it to be. What still remains Greek in Augustine's thought is his very notion of what it is to be. His ontology, or science of being, is an "essential" rather than an "existential" one. In other words, it exhibits a marked tendency to reduce the existence of a thing to its essence, and to answer the question: What is it for a thing to be? by saying: It is to be that which it is.

A most sensible answer indeed, but perhaps not the deepest conceivable one in philosophy, and certainly not a perfectly suitable one for a Christian philosopher speculating on a world created by the Christian God. For reasons which I will later try to make clear, it was not easy to go beyond St. Augustine, because the limit he had reached was the limit of Greek ontology itself, and therefore just about the very limit which the human mind can reach in matters of metaphysics. When, nine centuries after the death of St. Augustine, a new and decisive progress in natural theology was made, its occasional cause was the discovery of another Greek metaphysical universe by another Christian theologian. This time the metaphysical universe was that of Aristotle, and the name of the theologian was Thomas Aquinas.

"The religious side of Plato's thought," Gilbert Murray rightly says, "was not revealed in its full power till the time of Plotinus in the third century A.D.: that of Aristotle, one might say without undue paradox, not till its exposition by Aquinas in the thirteenth."[13] Let us add only this, that the "explanation" of Aristotle by Thomas Aquinas might perhaps be more justly called its metamorphosis in the light of Christian revelation. The self-thinking Thought of Aristotle has certainly become an essential element of the natural theology of St. Thomas Aquinas, but not without first undergoing the metaphysical transformation that turned him into the *Qui est*, or "He Who is" of the Old Testament.[14]

Why, St. Thomas asks, do we say that *Qui est* is the most proper name among all those that can be given to God? And his answer is because it signifies "to be": *ipsum esse*. But what is it to be? In answering this most difficult of all metaphysical questions, we must carefully distinguish between the meaning of two words which are both different and yet intimately related: *ens*, or "being," and *esse*, or "to be." To the question: What is being? the correct answer is: Being is that which is, or exists. If, for instance, we ask this same question with regard to God, the correct answer would be: The being of God is an infinite and boundless ocean of substance.[15] But *esse*, or "to be," is something else and much harder to grasp because it lies more deeply hidden in the metaphysical structure of reality. The word "being," as a noun, designates some substance; the word "to be"—or *esse*—is a verb, because it designates an act. To understand this is also to reach, beyond the level of essence, the deeper level of existence. For it is quite true to say that all that which is a substance must of necessity have also both an essence and an existence. In point of fact, such is the natural order followed by our rational knowledge: we first conceive certain beings, then we define their essences, and last we affirm their existences by means of a judgment. But the metaphysical order of reality is just the reverse of the order of human knowledge: what first comes into it is a certain act of existing which, because it is *this* particular act of existing, circumscribes at once a certain essence and causes a certain substance to come into being. In this deeper sense, "to be" is the primitive and fundamental act by virtue of which a certain being actually is, or exists. In St. Thomas' own words: *dictur esse ipse actus essentiae*[16]—"to be" is the very act whereby an essence is.

A world where "to be" is the act par excellence, the act of all acts, is also a world wherein, for each and every thing, existence is the original energy whence flows all that which deserves the name of being. Such an existential world can be accounted for by no other cause than a supremely existential God. The strange thing is that, historically speaking, things seem to have worked the other way around. Philosophers have not inferred the supreme existentiality of God from any previous knowledge of the existential nature of things; on the contrary, the self-revelation of the existentiality of God has helped philosophers toward the realization of the existential nature of things. In other words, philosophers were not able to reach, beyond essences, the existential energies which are their very causes, until the Jewish-Christian Revelation had taught them that "to be" was the proper name of the Supreme Being. The decisive progress achieved by metaphysics in the light of Christian faith has not been to realize that there must be a first being, cause of being in all things. The greatest among the Greeks already knew it. When, for instance, Aristotle was positing his first self-thinking Thought as the supreme being, he certainly conceived it as a pure act and as an infinitely powerful energy; still, his god was but the pure act of a Thought. This infinitely powerful actuality of a self-thinking principle most certainly deserves to be called a pure act, but it was a pure act in the order of knowing, not in that of existence. Now nothing can give what it has not. Because the supreme Thought of Aristotle was not "He Who is," it could not give existence: hence the world of Aristotle was not a created world. Because the supreme Thought of Aristotle was not the pure act of existing, its self-knowledge did not entail the knowledge of all being, both actual and possible: the god of Aristotle was not a providence; he did not even know a world which he did not make and which he could not possibly have made because he was the thought of a Thought, nor did he know the self-awareness of "Him Who is."

I would not like to minimize the philosophical indebtedness of Thomas Aquinas to Aristotle. He himself would not forgive me for making him guilty of such an ingratitude. As a philosopher, Thomas Aquinas was not a pupil of Moses, but of Aristotle, to whom he owed his method, his principles, up to even his all-important notion of the fundamental actuality of being. My only point is that a decisive metaphysical progress or, rather, a true metaphysical revolution was achieved when somebody began to translate all the problems concerning being from the language of essences into that of existences. From its earliest origins, metaphysics had always obscurely aimed at becoming existential; from the time of St. Thomas Aquinas it has always been so, and to such an extent that metaphysics has regularly lost its very existence every time it has lost its existentiality.

The metaphysics of Thomas Aquinas was, and it still remains, a climax in the history of natural theology. No wonder, then, that it was so soon followed by an anticlimax. Human reason feels at home in a world of things, whose essences and laws it can grasp and define in terms of concepts; but shy and ill at ease in a world of existences, because to exist is an act, not a thing. And we know it but too well. Every time a lecturer begins a sentence by saying: "As a matter of fact," you know at once that the man is at his wit's end. Granting that something is, he can tell you a great deal concerning that which it is; what he cannot do is to account for the very existence of the thing. How could he, if existence is a principle, and the innermost first principle of what the thing is? When dealing with facts as facts, or with things that happen as mere happenings, our *ultima ratio* always is and that's that. Obviously, to ask us to view the universe as a world of particular existential acts all related to a supreme and absolute Self-Existence is to stretch the power of our essentially conceptual reason almost to the breaking point. We know that we must do it, but we wonder if we can, because we are not sure that the thing can be done at all.

This, at least, is a point about which several among the successors of Thomas Aquinas have entertained grave doubts. Themselves Christian theologians, and sometimes very great ones, they had no hesitations concerning the true name of the true God. Their real difficulty was, granting that God is "He Who is," can such a God be attained by means of philosophical reason alone, unaided by Revelation? A perfectly relevant question indeed. After all, these theologians knew full well that philosophers had never thought of giving God such a a name until they had learned it from Moses, who himself had learned it from God. Hence the marked tendency, even in such a great metaphysician as Duns Scotus, to question the possibility of human reason's reaching, by means of philosophy alone, the absolutely existing and absolutely all-powerful Christian God.[17]

The reason for this hesitancy is simple. The human mind feels shy before a reality of which it can form no proper concept. Such, precisely, is existence. It is hard for us to realize that "I am" is an active verb. It is perhaps still more difficult for us to see that "it is" ultimately points out, not that which the thing is, but the primitive existential act which causes it both to be and to be precisely that which it is. He who begins to see this, however, also begins to grasp the very stuff our universe is made of. He even begins obscurely to perceive the supreme cause of such a world.

Why had the Greek mind spontaneously stopped at the notion of nature, or of essence, as at an ultimate explanation? Because, in our human experience, existence is always that of a particular essence. We directly know only individual and sensible existing things whose existence merely consists in being this and that individual thing. The existence of an oak tree obviously limits itself to being an oak tree or, rather, to being this one particular oak tree, and the same could be said of everything else. What does this mean, if not that the essence of any and every thing is not existence itself, but only one of the many possible sharings in existence? This fact is best expressed by the fundamental distinction of "being" and "what is" so clearly laid down by Thomas Aquinas. It does not mean that existence is distinct from essence as a thing from another thing. Once more, existence is not a thing, but the act that causes a thing both to be and to be what it is. This distinction merely expresses the fact that, in our human experience, there is no thing whose essence it is "to be," and not "to-be-a-certain-thing." The definition of no empirically given thing is existence; hence its essence is not existence, but existence must be conceived as distinct from it.

How, then, are we to account for the existence of a world made up of such things? You can take them all one after the other and ask yourself why each of them is, or exists; the essence of no one of them will ever yield the answer to your question. Since the nature of no one of them is "to be," the most exhaustive scientific knowledge of what they are will not so much as suggest the beginning of an answer to the question: Why are they? This world of ours is a world of change; physics, chemistry, biology can teach us the laws according to which change actually happens in it; what these sciences cannot teach us is why this world, taken together with its laws, its order, and its intelligibility, is, or exists. If the nature of no known thing is "to be," the nature of no known thing contains in itself the sufficient reason for its own existence. But it points to its sole conceivable cause. Beyond a world wherein "to be" is everywhere at hand, and where every nature can account for what other natures are but not for their common existence, there must be some cause whose very essence it is "to be." To posit such a being whose essence is a pure act of existing—that is, whose essence is not to be this and that, but "to be"—is also to posit the Christian God as the supreme cause of the universe. A most deeply hidden God, "He Who is" is also a most obvious God. By revealing to the metaphysician that they cannot account for their own existence, all things point to the fact that there is such a supreme cause wherein essence and existence coincide. Here at last, Thomas Aquinas and Augustine ultimately meet. Because his own existential metaphysics has succeeded in forcing its way through that crust of essences which is but the outer coating of reality, Thomas Aquinas can see the pure act of existing as one sees the presence of the cause in any one of its effects.

To reach this point was probably to reach the *ultima Thule* of the metaphysical world. St. Augustine had reached it on the strength of Christian faith, on the very day he had heard all things proclaim, in the language of the Bible: "We created not ourselves, but were created by Him who abideth for ever." To Augustine, however, "He who abideth for ever" essentially remained the self-existing "eternal Truth, true Love and loved

Eternity."[18] St. Thomas Aquinas has reached it on the strength of straight metaphysical knowledge, where he says that "all knowing beings implicitly know God in any and every thing that they know."[19] It was impossible to go farther, because human reason cannot go farther than the highest of all metaphysical principles. One might have expected at least this, that once in possession of so fundamental a truth, men would carefully preserve it. But they did not. Its loss almost immediately followed its discovery. How and why it has been lost is therefore the problem to which we now have to turn our attention.

NOTES

1. Deuteronomy 6:4.
2. Exodus 3:13–14.
3. *Hortatory Address to the Greeks*, chap. xxii, published among the works of Justin Martyr, in *The Ante-Nicene Fathers* (Buffalo, 1885), I, p. 272. Cf. E. Gilson, *L'Esprit de la philosophie médiévale* (Paris: J. Vrin, 1932), I, p. 227, n. 7.
4. J. B. Muller-Thym, *On the University of Being in Meister Eckhart of Hochheim* (New York: Sheed and Ward, 1939), p. 2.
5. For a good introduction to the many interpretations of this historical fact, see Charles Boyer, S.J., *La Formation de saint Augustin* (Paris: Beauchesne, 1920). An exactly opposite view is maintained by P. Alfaric, *L'Évolution intellectuelle de saint* Augustin (Paris: Nourry, 1918). The very nature of the problem entails psychological hypotheses which cannot be either historically demonstrated or historically refuted. I feel personally convinced that the views of C. Boyer on the question are fundamentally sound, but nobody should subscribe to them before carefully weighing the arguments set forward by Alfaric in support of his own interpretation.
6. St. Augustine, *Confessions*, Bk. VII, chap. ix, n. 13, trans. by the Rev. Marcus Dods, in "The Works of Aurelius Augustine" (Edinburgh, 1876), XIV, pp. 152–153.
7. Plotinus, *Enneads*, VI, 7, 37, in "Complete Works," trans. by Kenneth Sylvan Guthrie (Alpine, N.J.: Platonist Press), III, 762.
8. St. John, 1:7–9. Cf. St. Augustine, *op. cit.*, Bk. VII, chap. ix, n. 13, English trans., p. 154. The text of St. John directly applies to the problem of human salvation through Christ.
9. Plato, *Alcibiades*, 129e–130c. St. Augustine, *De Moribus ecclesiae*, Bk. I, chap. xxvii, p. 52; *Patrologia Latina*, Vol. XXXII,

col. 1332. Cf. E. Gilson, *Introduction à l'étude de saint Augustin* (Paris: J. Vrin, 1929), p. 55.

10. On this problem, see the extremely important analyses of Marcel de Corte, *Aristôte et Plotin* (Paris: Desclée de Brouwer, 1935), chap. iii, "La Purification plotinienne," pp. 177–227, and chap. vi, "La Dialectique de Plotin," pp. 229–290. These two essays are probably the deepest existing introductions to the method and spirit of the doctrine of Plotinus.

11. I beg to stress the words "metaphysically speaking," in order to make clear the radical difference there is between the order of metaphysics and the order of religion. As a Christian, any man can be "deified" through grace, because grace is a sharing in the life of God. Thus understood, grace is supernatural in its own right. So also is the whole sacramental order, as clearly appears from the well-known prayer of the Ordinary of the Mass, which I beg to quote in full because of its perfect clarity: "O God, who in creating human nature hast wonderfully dignified it, and still more wonderfully reformed it; grant, by the mystery of this Water and Wine, *we may be made partakers of His divine nature*, Who vouchsafed to become partaker of our human nature, namely, Jesus Christ, our Lord, Thy Son, Who with Thee livest and reignest, in the unity of the Holy Ghost, God, world without end. Amen." The man of Plato stood in no need of being made partaker of the divinity, because he himself was a god; hence, for Augustine, the necessity of stripping the man of Plato of what made him god; namely, his natural aptness to know truth. We will find Thomas Aquinas confronted with the contrary difficulty; namely, that of turning the eminently natural man of Aristotle into a being susceptible of deification.

12. On the metaphysical constituents of concrete existence, see Emmanuel Chapman, *Saint Augustine's Philosophy of Beauty* (New York: Sheed and Ward, 1939), chap. ii, pp. 13–44. The Platonic character of the Augustinian notion of creation has been stressed, and perhaps slightly overstressed, by A. Gardeil, *La Structure mystique de l'âme* (Paris: Gabalda, 1929), Appendix II, vol. II, 319–320. After rereading my own criticism of A. Gardeil's interpretation (in *Introduction à l'étude de saint Augustin*, p. 258, n. 8), I have reached the conclusion that what Gardeil had in mind when he wrote these pages was fundamentally true; yet I myself was not altogether wrong. Augustine had a clear idea of what it is to create, but he never reached a wholly existential notion of being.

13. Gilbert Murray, *Five Stages of Greek Religion* (New York: Columbia University Press, 1925), p. 17.

14. St. Thomas Aquinas, *Summa theologiae*, Pars I, q. 13, a. 11, *Sed contra*. On the Thomistic identification of God with Being, see E. Gilson, *The Spirit of Mediaeval Philosophy* (New York: Scribner's, 1936), chap. iii, pp. 42–63.

15. This formula is quoted from John Damascene by St. Thomas Aquinas, *op. cit.*, Pars I, q. 13, a. 11 Resp.
16. St. Thomas Aquinas, in I. *Sent.*, dist. 33, q. 1, a. 1, ad 1m. Cf. *Quaestiones disputatae: De Potentia*, qu. VII, a. 2, ad 9. This existential notion of being is discussed in E. Gilson, *Réalisme thomiste et critique de la connaissance* (Paris: Librairie Philosophique, J. Vrin, 1939), chap. viii, esp. pp. 220–222. For a general comparison between the God of Aristotle and the God of St. Thomas Aquinas, see the penetrating essay of Anton C. Pegis, *Saint Thomas and the Greeks* (Milwaukee: Marquette University Press, 1939). For a comparison between the God of Augustine and the God of Thomas Aquinas, see A. Gardeil, *La Structure de l'âme et l'expérience mystique* (Paris: Gabalda, 1927), Appendix II, vol. II, 313–325. The extreme simplicity of the notion of existence and the impossibility of our conceptualizing it have been stressed by J. Maritain, *Sept leçons sur l'Être* (1932–33) (Paris: Téqui, n.d.), pp. 98–99. These characteristics of "to be" probably account for the fact that many modern scientists consider the existence of a thing the most negligible of all its properties.
17. The existential character of being has been powerfully stressed by Duns Scotus; cf. Parthenius Minges, *I. Duns Scoti Doctrina philosophica et theologica* (Firenze: Quaracchi, 1930), I, pp. 14–17. What is peculiar to his own theology is a marked tendency to make the Christian God, taken *qua* Christian God, unknowable to natural reason unaided by faith. Moreover, it would prove interesting to investigate into the Scotist notion of created existence. According to him, "the essence and its existence in creatures are to each other as a quiddity to its mode" (*op. cit.*, pp. 16–17). The primacy of essence, which makes existence to be but one of its "accidents," appears in the doctrine of Duns Scotus as a remnant of the Platonism anterior to Thomas Aquinas. In a straight existential metaphysics, it would be much more correct to speak of the essence of an existence than to speak, with Duns Scotus, of the existence of an essence (*essentia et eius existentia*).
18. St. Augustine, *Confessions*, Bk. X, chap. x, n. 25, English trans., p. 227. Cf. Bk. VII, chap. x, n. 16, p. 158.
19. St. Thomas Aquinas, *Quaestiones disputatae de Veritate*, q. 22, a. 2, ad 1m. Similar statements will be found wherever Thomas Aquinas speaks about the natural and confused desire of all men for beatitude; for instance, *Summa Theologiae*, I, q. 2, a. 1, ad 1.

13. Science, Philosophy, and Religious Wisdom

I would feel quite at a loss to find an adequate expression of my gratitude if I did not remember that this is a meeting of Catholic philosophers and theologians, all of them fully aware of the meaning of the word "grace." As St. Augustine once said: when God crowns our merits, He crowns His own gifts. In the very same spirit, I beg to extend to you all my heartfelt thanks for reminding me tonight of my forty-five years of indebtedness to our common master St. Thomas Aquinas.* 'Tis him we are celebrating, not any one of his disciples. Let us therefore avail ourselves of this opportunity to extend to him the most fitting homage, which is to examine, as best we can, some concrete problem in the light of his own principles. This is what I now wish to do, with this reservation, however, that since I shall have to deal with twentieth-century science, St. Thomas himself should not be made responsible for my own application of his principles to a situation which he could not foresee. If there is any truth in what I am about to say, let the honor be his; if any error, let the responsibility be mine; my only desire is to tell you, in all sincerity, and under the form of an objective philosophical discussion, what I hold to be my greatest intellectual and spiritual debt to St. Thomas Aquinas.

My remarks will not be those of a scientist, but of a Christian philosopher fully aware of his shortcomings in the field of positive science. After assimilating the content of a score of books, a Greek philosopher could rightly boast of knowing the science of his own times. Nor were these books particularly hard to understand. Things began to change in the seventeenth century, which Whitehead has called the century of genius, when mathematics began to be considered as the true language of science. Yet, even Descartes, who was largely re-

* This paper was originally the Annual Association Address of the American Catholic Philosophical Association, given at the 1952 meeting.

sponsible for this evolution, did not hesitate to write a complete system of physics in one volume, after which he felt confident that, with time, he could dispose of the whole of biology in the same way. At the beginning of the nineteenth century, the existence of a scientist able to master the whole field of scientific knowledge had already become highly improbable. Such a man would have had to be a Newton and a Darwin rolled into one; a rather unlikely combination indeed. In our own times, the very progress of science has been attended by a still more acute specialization. A modern Academy of Sciences is a body of scientists, each of whom, although competent in some branches of his own field, lays no claim to have mastered contemporary science as a whole. Every one of us knows this from bitter experience. When we seek medical advice, we are often advised to consult a specialist. Naturally, this specialist will have a general knowledge of medicine, just as any scientist has a general knowledge of science, but there are many fields where neither one would venture to risk an opinion. Physicists who deal with physical theories often have to seek mathematical advice, and mathematicians themselves are constantly doing it within their own circle. Modern science has become much too big to lodge entirely in the brains of any one man.

Yet we cannot help worrying about what it says, not only because science is present in every one of the many gadgets we constantly use at home, but also, and still more, because it tells us what kind of world we are living in. From this point of view, it would be interesting to know, among those of us who are fifty years old, how many realize that they are living in their third universe? Any man who is forty-seven was born in the good old universe of Newton, ruled by a force of attraction causing absolute motions in an absolute space. In 1905, while asleep or thinking about something else, the same man entered the universe of Einstein, which was that of Relativity. This new scientific world was much more different from the world of Newton than the world of Newton was from the world of Ptolemy. From 1905 to 1927, we have been living in space-time; that is, in a universe in which what each of us considers as past, present, or future is all given at one time, and in which each observer determines in space-time his own space and his own time, and does it in his own way. Despite its revolutionary nature, the world of Einstein still retained an important feature of the Newtonian universe; namely, its unqualified recognition of scientific previsibility owing to the complete determination of physical phenomena. Now, this is precisely the reason why, today, other physicists find it natural to speak of the "old universe of Newton and Einstein," as though they were one and the same universe. For indeed, when in 1927 Heisenberg published for the first time his "relations of uncertitude," he was making possible the completion of what is now called "undulatory mechanics"; that is, of a physical universe so astoundingly new, even in comparison with that of Relativity, that Einstein himself still refuses unreservedly to accept it.

And no wonder! In this latest world of science, where the structure of matter is discontinuous, each element is a corpuscle associated with a wave, but their relation is such that, if we know the one, our knowledge of the other is affected by a certain coefficient of uncertitude. As a consequence, it is now considered impossible to situate with complete precision, in space and time, the elementary physical transformations which take place in the world. Now, for a phenomenon to escape the determinations of space and time is also to escape the determination of causality. In point of fact, the very identity of a material particle becomes questionable if we cannot know for sure where it is when we know when it is, and vice versa. In such a universe, there still are laws and, practically speaking, they remain just as safe as the classical ones, but their nature is no longer the same. Instead of resulting from strictly determined elementary phenomena, the laws of the new physics express a statistical average. There passes the dividing line between the ancient physics of Einstein and Newton on the one hand, and the new physics of Bohr, Heisenberg, and de Broglie on the other side; up to 1927, scientific previsibility was supposed to rest upon strict physical determinism; today, scientific previsibility results from the global probability arising from innumerable elementary indeterminations. Incidentally, this means that the strictly determined mechanical world of dialectical materialism, which Marxists still mistake for the world of science, died twenty-five years ago. They don't seem to know it yet.

This elementary survey of the history of science in the recent past was necessary to give a concrete meaning to the words "scientific knowledge." It is nothing like the exhaustive and self-satisfied knowledge of all things which some people imagine. On the contrary, we find ourselves, right now, in the very middle of another century of genius, probably far greater than the seventeenth century ever was; but, for this very reason, the universes of science now succeed one another with a curiously accelerated speed. Like the Patriarchs of the Old Testament, they seem to obey a law of diminishing longevity. The system of Ptolemy died fourteen centuries ago, which was a ripe old age; that of Copernicus, which replaced it, lasted almost three centuries; that of Einstein twenty-two years—that is, supposing that his world is dead, which Einstein himself stoutly refuses to concede. Naturally, these revolutions do not break up the continuity of the progress of physical science; each universe paves the way for its own successor which, in turn, is bound to maintain all that was true in the preceding one; yet, when all is said and done, the fact remains that, by reason of its accelerated progress, modern science is exhibiting an always decreasing stability.

There is a widely spread illusion that the stability of science is higher than that of metaphysics. The reverse is so true that most philosophical revolutions have been motivated by scientific ones. This is what happened to scholasticism in the early fifteenth century. The Aristotelian physics of forms and qualities was largely a philosophy of nature; but because the scholastics held it to be both a philosophy and a positive science, scholasticism became involved in the wholesale condemnation of Aristotle by the founders of modern physico-mathematics. Yet the most severe of its judges made the same mistake. When the new mechanics of Descartes died, which happened even before the time of Leibniz, his new metaphysics died together with it. The philosophy of Kant, whose table of categories had been made to fit the universe of Newton, has no longer any scientific universe to fit. The philosophy of Spencer, conceived at a time when the notion of biological evolution still had a precise scientific meaning, now remains as the arbitrary extrapolation of a law which no modern biologist would venture to formulate. Similar remarks could be made concerning the positivism of Auguste Comte: it rests entirely upon a so-called scientific law, the law of the three states, which has perished with the sociology of its inventor. Nearer to us, the parts of Bergson's philosophy that are already growing obsolete are precisely its biological and psychophysiological foundations. All philosophies perish by their science; all philosophies survive by the metaphysical truth which they contain. The constancy of the fact is such that it might almost be called a historical law.

This, however, should not induce us to believe that these repeated scientific revolutions are due to a sort of restlessness innate in the minds of modern scientists. The reverse is true. Inertia is not a property of matter only, it is also found in minds, only we call it intellectual conservatism, routine, or simply prejudice. When old intellectual positions ultimately give up, there are cogent reasons for their surrender. A scientific system lasts, in the minds of scientists, as long as one or several irreducible facts do not constrain them to change it. Even then they regularly begin by overhauling the old system in order to adapt it to these facts rather than to give up the old explanation for a new one. All these incredibly new notions, of which we philosophers are still far from having grasped the full philosophical import, are so many answers of the human understanding to the challenge of observable facts. Now what is most remarkable about this is another fact; namely, that the human understanding did find the answers. I am not here expressing a personal impression, which, not being a scientist, I am not qualified to express; I am merely reporting the personal experience of the greatest scientists of our own times. Confronted with their own amazing discoveries, they entertain no doubt about their truth, but they are beginning to wonder about their very possibility. "What is most incomprehensible about nature," Einstein says, "is its comprehensibility." As to Louis de Broglie, in one of the most remarkable chapters of his book *Physics and Microphysics*, he makes this almost identical remark: "What is most marvelous about the progress of science is that it has revealed to us a certain concordance between our thought and things, a certain possibility for us to grasp, through the resources of our intelligence and the rules of our reason, the deep-seated relations that obtain between phenomena. We do not wonder enough about the fact that some scientific knowledge is possible."

This remarkable statement clearly shows that nothing equals the ignorance of modern philosophers in matters of science, except the ignorance of modern scientists in matters of philosophy. For indeed, if the problem at stake is that of the possibility of science, it can truly be said that, ever since the times of Plato and Aristotle, philosophers have never ceased to worry about it. What must the nature of the world be, in order that matter itself be intelligible? And, if it is, what must the nature of the mind be, in order that the world be intelligible to it? Last, not least, how account for this reciprocal harmony which obtains between nature and reality, and without which science itself would not be possible, or rather, of which science is the most perfect expression?

One may well wonder, since scientists themselves are asking these questions, why they do not attempt to answer them; and still more why, when philosophers try to solve the problem, scientists do not pay much attention to their answers. The reason for this is simple. It is that the question of the possibility of science is not itself a scientific question. Any attempt to answer it in a scientific way results in a vicious circle, since a scientific demonstration of the possibility of science implies the existence of science, whose possibility it tries to demonstrate. We must therefore choose between two possible attitudes: either to content ourselves with accepting the intelligibility of the world as unintelligible, or else to resort to philosophical reasoning which, since it has to explain why scientific demonstration is possible, cannot itself be a scientific demonstration.

There might be a further reason for the reluctance of so many excellent minds to accept philosophical explanations in this matter. Since the problem is about the intelligibility of nature, its answer has to be sought beyond the order of nature. Now, according to the very etymology of the word, the philosophical knowledge of what lies beyond nature (in Greek, *physis*) is metaphysical by definition. Moreover, since the only way for us to account for the intelligibility of the world is to resort to a cause whose nature and operation made it to be, and to be intelligible, the answer to the problem must needs be found in the crowning part of metaphysics; that is, in that part of it which deals with the first principle in the highest cause. If there is such a cause, its name is God. In short, the only discipline that can answer this question is divinity, or theology. Now I quite agree that, to many scientists, philosophical or theological answers do not sound serious. But this is beside the point, for indeed it would not be serious to give metaphysical or theological answers to scientific questions; but the question asked by these scientists is not a scientific one; science never worries about its own possibility: were science not possible, it would not exist; that is all. What is now happening is that, on the basis of their scientific knowledge, some scientists are beginning to ask metaphysical and theological questions. And they are welcome to it, but if they do, they will have to look for metaphysical and theological answers.

This is the kind of answer which philosophers have been trying to find for more than twenty centuries in the West, and, in the East, for many more than twenty centuries. But if we go back far enough into the past, we shall observe another curious fact; namely, that when philosophers found answers to such questions as the origin and nature of the physical world, they did not create them out of nothing. They merely elaborated, in a rational way, solutions of the problem which had come to them through another channel than those of either science or philosophy; namely, religion. Religious knowledge is neither science nor philosophy, because it does not rest upon any kind of demonstration, but upon faith; it shines from on high, as a light that has nothing else to do than just to be, in order to be seen and to impart visibility to many other things. Because of its primitive evidence, it is called a revelation, and because, in its light, we understand the rest, we call it Wisdom. I know of no better description of it than a simple sentence of the Vedanta, which dates from about the fifth century before Christ: "That doctrine is not to be obtained by argument, but when it is declared by another, then, O dearest, it is easy to understand." Religious wisdom is that doctrine which is not to be obtained by argument, but which is easy to understand when it is declared by another, who is God.

Here again I am not offering any scientific argument, nor even a philosophical one, but I am quoting a fact, or, if you prefer, a human experience that is as old, if not as mankind, at least as that part of mankind which has left us a written expression of its beliefs. Not to lose ourselves in the endless field of past centuries, let us single out what has always appeared to me as the most striking exemplification of this experience; namely, the spreading of the Gospel among the peoples of Greco-Latin culture in the second century after Christ. It was, and in so far as I can see, it still remains an extraordinary phenomenon. Here was a civilized society which found at its disposal at least four or five scientific and philosophical interpretations of the universe; I am not now talking of mythologies, but of doctrines as purely rational as those of Plato, Aristotle, Democritus or Lucretius, Zeno or Epictetus. Of the men who were living in those times, it can be said that they had the pick of the best, since they could freely draw from any one of the systems which, still today, are considered in our universities a necessary introduction to the study of philosophy. Yet many of these men became Christians, and if we ask them why, they unanimously give the same answer. They all had read Holy Scripture, a book written in a rather barbaric language, whose crude statements were not supported by a single philosophical argument, and yet, to their deep surprise, they had found its doctrine infinitely more intelligent than that of any one of the philosophies they knew. Scripture was giving, to philosophical problems, non-philosophical answers that were deeper and more true than those given by philosophy itself. And it was all so simple! "In the beginning, God created heaven and earth." He created them out of nothing; and He could do it because, His name being He Who Is, or He Is, He was being itself; consequently, He could cause beings. But God was not only power, He was also wisdom. So He ordered His creation according to number, weight, and measure (Wisd. 11:21), and just as He had put wisdom in things, He likewise put it in the mind of man, when He created him to His own image. In my own turn, and after so many centuries, I feel like apologizing in concluding: this is why the world of nature is intelligible, and this is also the reason why the human mind is able to understand it. As Scripture says: God has poured wisdom out "upon all his works, and upon all flesh according to his gift" (Eccli. 1:10). Is this philosophy? Not a bit, but I beg to submit that no philosopher has ever said anything half as satisfactory on the question.

If there is any truth in what has just been said, the endlessly controverted problem of the relations between science and religion should not even arise. So long as they themselves don't ask religious questions, scientists will never be offered religious answers. Nor will these religious answers ever pretend to be scientific ones. Religious wisdom tells us that in the beginning God created heaven and earth, but it does not pretend to give us any scientific account of the progressive formation of the world. As Thomas Aquinas aptly says, precisely about this very text, there were things which Moses could not express to an ignorant people without using images which they could understand (*Sum. theol.*, I, 66, 1 ad 1m). Likewise, Scripture says that God has created all things in number, weight, and measure; and this again is a purely religious statement, but it is up to science, not to religion, to calculate these numbers, to weigh these weights, and to measure these measures. Science deals with nature *qua* nature, religious wisdom deals with nature *qua* work of God.

Such is the true reason why, far from keeping away from science, a truly religious mind should do its utmost to follow it in its progress, as the most perfect homage rendered by nature to its creator. "The heavens show forth the glory of God, and the firmament declares the work of his hands" (Ps. 18:1). This has never been more true than in our own day, at a time when astrophysics is beginning to reveal to us the prodigious dimensions of the world we are in. But there is something else which we could usefully remember: these words of Psalm 18 were already true at a time when men knew practically nothing about the nature of things in general, and when they were entirely wrong about what Scripture calls the firmament; they still are true, and much more evidently so, in our own century of scientific genius; and the same will become still more manifestly true when our own science of nature, an object of amazement to its creators themselves, will have been superseded by a more perfect one. This fact exemplifies more clearly than all I could say the difference there is between these two orders of knowledge: the words of science pass away; the words of Wisdom do not pass away.

Having to express by gratitude to our common Master, as well as to yourselves, I have thought that the best way for me to do it would be publicly to say what I consider the greatest lesson for which I feel indebted to St. Thomas Aquinas. May I add, for my modest part, that in the course of an already long life this truth has often been confirmed for me by personal experience? I have known many more cases of philosophers converted to scholastic philosophy by the Catholic faith than of philosophers converted to the Catholic faith by scholastic philosophy. I know that this is how it is; I feel infinitely grateful to St. Thomas Aquinas for having made me understand that this is how it should be. We cannot equal him in genius, and still less in holiness, but there is at least one way for us to prove his true disciples. It is, while exerting to their full limit the power of our intellects, to put our ultimate trust, for others as well as for ourselves, in Him in Whose light alone we shall see the Light.

PART FOUR

The Student of St. Thomas Aquinas

Gilson has been saying for years that St. Thomas was a theologian. He has also been saying that the philosophical notions of St. Thomas, and particularly "that sublime truth" that God is the pure act of being, are the true and lasting cornerstone of Christian philosophy. Moreover, Gilson has been at pains to insist that the philosophy of St. Thomas was a philosophy living *in* a theologian, in a man dedicating his intelligence to the study of the word of God. In this sense, St. Thomas the theologian contained within himself a philosophy serving his religious vocation. That philosophy has been for Gilson a high-water mark in history. Thomism is an authentic philosophy open to the existential dynamism of the universe around man and within man. It is a philosophy poised within the very mystery of existence, a philosophy whose intellectual radiance is the outward light of its internal spiritual fire.

14. The Christian Teacher

Man can choose only between two kinds of life, the active and the contemplative. What confers special dignity on the functions of the Doctor is that they imply both of these two kinds of life, properly subordinated the one to the other. The true function of the Doctor is to teach. Teaching (*doctrina*) consists in communicating to others a truth meditated beforehand.[1] It demands of necessity both the reflection of the contemplative in order to discover the truth, and the activity of the professor in order to communicate his findings to others. But the most remarkable thing about this complex activity is that there is an exact correspondence between the higher and the lower, between contemplation and action. According to our definition, then, the function of the Doctor is directed toward a twofold object, interior and exterior, depending upon whether it is a question of the truth which the Doctor meditates and contemplates within himself or of those whom he is teaching. Thus there are two sides to his life, the first of which is the better and which it is his task to regulate.

In the first place, it is clear that the activity of the Doctor is not superimposed artificially upon his contemplative life. Rather, it finds its source in his contemplation and is, so to speak, its outward manifestation. Teaching, as well as preaching to which it is allied, is certainly a work belonging to the active life, but it derives somehow or other from the very fullness of contemplation.[2] This is why it cannot be considered as an interruption of contemplation. When a person turns from his meditation on intelligible realities, the food of contemplation, in order to give himself to works good in themselves but purely exterior, he has to break with meditation. The distribution of alms and the entertaining of guests are excellent things, yet for all this, they exclude meditation properly so called. Teaching, on the contrary, is the outward expression of inward contemplation. If it is true that a soul truly free from temporal interests preserves something of this liberty, which it has acquired, in each of its exterior acts, certainly there is no place where this liberty can be more integrally preserved than in the act of teaching.[3] To combine thus the active and contemplative life is not, so to speak, a subtraction but an addition. Moreover, it is evident that here is most integrally to be realized that perfect balance between the two kinds of life, a balance which our present human condition demands that we seek.[4] To teach the truth which meditation reveals for us is to expand its contemplation without losing any of it, even increasing its better part.

From this derive several consequences which are important for determining the exact role St. Thomas was assuming as a Christian Doctor. The functions of this role struck him as particularly suited to the religious state of the monks[5] and especially of an order such as the Dominicans, who were at the same time teachers and contemplatives. St. Thomas never grew weary of defending against the attacks of seculars the legitimacy of the ideal to which he had consecrated his life, monastic poverty and the work of teaching. To those who would object to his right to live in absolute poverty, he cited the example of the ancient philosophers who sometimes renounced all riches in order to devote themselves more freely to the contemplation of truth. With how much more right may not he impose upon himself this renunciation, who wishes to follow not only wisdom, but Christ, according to the beautiful words of St. Jerome to the monk Rusticus: *Christum nudum nudus sequere*: "follow, naked, a naked Christ."[6] To those who question the legitimacy of assuming the honor or accepting the title of Master, St. Thomas replies sensibly that to be a Master is not to assume an honor but to accept a charge,[7] and that the title of Master is not something you give yourself but something you receive, and that it is next door to impossible to prevent people from giving it to you.[8] In reply to those who maintain that the real monk is bound to perform manual labor and that this is hardly compatible with meditation and teaching, St. Thomas makes a large number of distinctions in order to dispense with a manifestly subsidiary obligation like manual labor, and replace it by the *oral labor* of teaching or preaching.[9] Indeed, in his eyes, nothing is more legitimate than a religious order of contemplative and teaching monks.

For a member of such an order, it is highly desirable to aspire to the functions of the Doctor and to spend his life in fulfilling them. True enough, the office of Master is not without its dangers. A man might, for example, teach throughout his entire life out of vainglory, never so much as placing before himself the good of others as an end. Such a life consequently would be unworthy of a true religious. But one who is conscious of doing his teaching as a work of mercy and as true spiritual charity need experience no scruple in desiring to teach.

An objection constantly directed by seculars against the religious coming up for the title of Master was the difficulty of reconciling the monk's humility with this pretension to authority. St. Thomas answers this objection in terms which keep in mind the place of the Master in the University of Paris, and by carefully distinguishing between the candidate for a Master's chair and a candidate for a bishopric. To seek an episcopal see is to look for a dignity not yet actually possessed; but to be named for a Master's chair is not to receive a new dignity but only a chance to communicate one's knowledge to others. To confer a license on someone is not at all to endow him with learning but merely to give permission to teach it. A second difference between the two cases is that the learning required for holding a Master's chair is a perfection of the very individual who possesses it, while the pontifical power of the bishop actually increases his dignity by comparison with other men. A third difference is that it is pre-eminently divine grace which renders a man worthy to receive the episcopal honors, while it is learning which equips a man to teach.

Thus the basic difference between the two cases can escape no one: it is praiseworthy to desire one's own perfection and therefore also to desire learning and the teaching for which learning equips one; but it is wrong to desire power over others without knowing whether one has the grace necessary to wield it. On the contrary, the desire to teach—that is, to communicate to others the learning one possesses—is a desire to perform an act of charity. There is nothing more praiseworthy than to wish to have authorization to teach, provided that one is genuinely capable of doing so. Here again the case is clear-cut and definite. No one can know with certainty whether or not he possesses grace. God alone dispenses this. But anyone can know with certainty whether or not he possesses sufficient knowledge to have the right to teach.[10] It was with complete assurance of possessing the necessary learning, and out of love for the minds he wished to enlighten, that St. Thomas dedicated his whole life to the work of teaching. To contemplate truth by his intellect and to communicate it out of love, such is the life of the Doctor. It is an exalted human imitation of the very life of God.

We must be on our guard lest an equivocation hide from us the exact sense of St. Thomas's words. When he speaks of Doctor or Master, we are inclined to think first of the philosopher while he thinks first of the theologian. The master *par excellence* can only teach wisdom *par excellence*; that is, the kind of knowledge of divine things which is essentially theology. It is only in this sense that the office of Master can legitimately be the object of the ambition of a religious. It is this office that St. Thomas has in mind when he praises the life divided between teaching and the contemplation which inspires it. It is with this office in mind, too, that he enumerates the various gifts which the Doctor must possess:[11] a full knowledge of the divine things in which he must instruct others—it is faith that confers this; a power to persuade or to demonstrate in order to convince others of the truth—the gift of wisdom serves him here; an ability to develop his thought and to express it in a manner suitable for instructing others—here the gift of knowledge comes to his service.[12] Wisdom and knowledge are here directed primarily toward knowing divine things and employed to teach them, so that if there is a Doctor of philosophical truth in the complex personality of St. Thomas, it is only within the theologian that we can hope to find him.

In fact, his own definition of his role as a philosopher is that he is a philosopher in the service of a theologian. This abstract statement is inadequate because indefinite and many different theologies could use it in order to define their respective positions toward philosophy; yet it is a statement which must be considered at the very outset in its stark simplicity, with all the consequences it implies in the thought of St. Thomas, if we would avoid certain grave errors about the meaning of his doctrine.

St. Thomas considers that a religious may legitimately aspire to the title and to the functions of teacher. But in so far as he can only teach divine things, it is only in relation to the science of divine things that secular sciences can legitimately interest him. This is demanded by the very essence of the contemplative life, of which teaching is but the immediate prolongation into the order of the active life. In order to be the highest form of human life, contemplation must dwell upon the object whose knowledge is the end of this life. Such knowledge and contemplation will be perfect only in the future life and only then will they confer full beatitude upon us, whereas, being in this life but imperfect, they are likewise here accompanied by only a beginning of beatitude. Thus, the study of philosophy is both legitimate in itself and useful in view of this supreme contemplation. Indeed, we shall have occasion to point out that in man's present state, all his knowledge finds its base in the order of sensible things. It is therefore inevitably from a scientific and philosophical knowledge of the universe that the Doctor of Theology must set out to build up the science of its proper object—the word of God. But he need only strive to acquire this knowledge in the measure that it helps him to understand the word of God.[13] One can say, then, that although the study of philosophy and the sciences is useful to the Christian Doctor, it is not his own end.

What, then, do we call the philosophy of St. Thomas? As he had created it only for the sake of the service it renders Christian wisdom, he himself never separated it from this wisdom to give it a name. Probably he did not foresee that the day would come when scholars would go searching through his works to extract the elements of a philosophy from his theology. He never himself attempted such a synthesis. As a theologian, he felt no obligation to do so. But others have since done it, and it is therefore necessary now to find out in what sense it is legitimate to ascribe a philosophy to St. Thomas Aquinas.

NOTES

1. *Summma Theologiae*, II–II, q. 18, a. 3, ad 3.
2. *Sum. Theol.*, II–II, q. 188, a. 6.
3. *Sum. Theol.*, II–II, q. 182, 1, ad 3.
4. *Sum. Theol.*, II–II, q. 182, a. 4, ad 3.
5. *Sum. Theol.*, II–II, q. 186, a. 6.
6. *Sum. Theol.*, II–II, q. 186, a. 3, ad 3.
7. *Contra Impugnantes Dei Cultum et Religionem*, chap. II.
8. *Ibid.*
9. *Sum. Theol.*, II–II, q. 187, a. 3, ad 3; *Quaestiones Quodlibetales*, VII, aa. 17–18.
10. *Quodl.*, III, q. 4, a. 9, ad 3.
11. *Sum. Theol.*, I–II, q. 111, a. 4.
12. *Sum. Theol.*, II–II, q. 177, a. 1.
13. *Sum. Theol.*, II–II, q. 180, a. 4.

15. Haec Sublimis Veritas

It is hardly credible that the existential nature of the problem of the existence of God ever had to be discovered. It is even less credible that Christian theologians had to discover the existential nature of the Christian God. Was it not enough to open the Scriptures in order to discover it there? When Moses wished to know the name of God in order to reveal it to the Jewish people, he directly addressed God Himself and said to Him: "Lo! I go to the children of Israel, and I shall say to them: the God of your fathers sends me to you. If they ask me His name, what shall I say to them?" And God said to Moses: "I am Who am." And He added: "Thus will you reply to the children of Israel: *He Who is* sends me to you" (Exod. 3:13–14). Since God Himself called Himself *I am*, or *Who is*, as the name properly belonging to Him, how could Christians have ever been ignorant that their God was the supremely existing being?

We do not say that they did not know this. Indeed, everyone believed it, many struggled to understand it, and a certain number before St. Thomas carried the interpretation even to the level of metaphysics. Certainly the identification of God and Being is the common possession of Christian philosophers as Christian.[1] But the agreement of Christians upon this point did not prevent philosophers from being divided on the interpretation of the notion of being. Holy Scripture provides no treatise on metaphysics. The first Christians who wanted to think philosophically about the content of their faith had at their disposal only the philosophical techniques elaborated by the Greeks for altogether different ends. The history of Christian philosophy is in large measure that of a religion becoming progressively conscious of philosophical notions which as a religion it could, strictly speaking, do without. But she recognized more and more clearly that these notions were capable of defining the philosophy of those faithful who wished to have one. It is easy to understand how Christian thinkers had to struggle a long time in order to clarify the meaning of this basic text of Exodus. It was only gradually that a metaphysical interpretation was found. The mere inspection of the two distinct notions of being which turn up in the study of the problem of the existence of God is enough to show us this. History permits us to make a living analysis by comparing the essentialist interpretation of the text of Exodus, at which St. Augustine finally stopped, with the existential interpretation of the same text developed by St. Thomas Aquinas.

St. Augustine was so sure that the God of Exodus was Plato's being that he wondered how to explain the coincidence without admitting that Plato had somehow or other known Exodus: "But what makes me almost subscribe to the idea that Plato was not completely ignorant of the Old Testament is that when an angel conveys the words of God to the holy man Moses, who asks the name of the one who is ordering him to proceed to the deliverance of the Hebrew people, the reply is this: '*I am Who am; and you are to say to the children of Israel: it is He Who is who has sent me to you.*' As if, in comparison with him who truly is because he is immovable, he who has been made movable did not exist. Now Plato was intensely convinced of this and he took great care to say so."[2] Clearly, the Being of Exodus is here conceived as the immovable entity of Plato. Reading these lines, we are bound to suspect that the accord at which Augustine marvels conceals a little confusion.

Such, indeed, was St. Augustine's notion of God and being. "The first and highest being is that which is entirely immovable, and which can say by full right: '*I am Who am; and you will tell them, He Who is has sent me to you.*'"[3] But Augustine had a very deep sense of the difficulty of the problem, and he never, perhaps, expressed his final thought on this question better than in a homily on the Gospel of St. John. It is better to cite the entire text because we can sense in it both the depth of Augustine's Christian feeling and the Platonic limits of his notion of being.

"Nevertheless, pay good attention to the words spoken here by Our Lord, Jesus Christ: *if you do not believe that I am, you will die in your sins* (John 8:24). What is this: *si non credideritis quia ego sum? I am,* what? There is nothing added; and because there is nothing added, his word embarrasses us. We were waiting for him to say what he was, yet he did not say it. What did we think he was going to say? Perhaps, *if you do not believe that I am the* Christ; *if you do not believe that I am* the Son of God; *if you do not believe that I am* the Word of the Father; *if you do not believe that I am* the author of the world; *if you do not believe that I am* the former and reformer of man, his creator and recreator, he who made him and remade him; *if you do not believe that I am* that, *you will die in your sins.* This *I am,* he says he is, is embarrassing. For God also had said to Moses: *I am Who am.* Who can say rightly what is this *I am?* By his angel, God sent his servant Moses to deliver his people from Egypt (you have read what I am saying here, and you knew it, but I am recalling it to you); God was sending him trembling, reluctant but obedient. In order to find some excuse Moses said to God who, he knew, was speaking to him through the angel: if the people ask me, who then is the God who sent thee? What shall I reply? And the Lord said to him: *I am Who am;* then he repeated: *it is He Who is who has sent me to you.* Here, again, he did not say: *I am* God; or *I am* the maker of the world; or *I am* the creator of all things; or again, *I am* the propagator of this very people who must be liberated: but he only said this: *I am Who am;* then, *you will say to the children of Israel, He Who is.* He did not add: *He Who is* your God: *He Who is* the God of your fathers: but he only said this: *He Who is sent me to you.* Perhaps it was difficult for Moses, even as it is difficult for us too—and even more difficult for us—to understand these words: *I am Who am;* and, *He Who is has sent me to you.* Moreover, even if Moses understood them, how could they to whom God was sending him have understood them? God has then postponed what man could not understand and added what he could understand. This he added, indeed, when he said: *I am the God of Abraham, and the God of Isaac, and the God of Jacob* (Exod. 3:13–15). This, you can understand; but what thought can comprehend *I am?*"

Let us pause here briefly to greet in passing this first meeting, in God's own words, between the God of Abraham, of Isaac, and of Jacob and the God of the philosophers and scholars. Augustine knows very well that it is the same God. No more than the people of Israel can he hesitate over the identity of the living God of Scripture. But it is the *Qui est* that intrigues him, for God no more explained it to Moses than to Augustine or to us, as if, having revealed to men the truth that saves, He had reserved the understanding of it to the patient efforts of the metaphysicians. However, faithful to the teaching of the "interior master,"[4] Augustine is going to pray here to God Himself to enlighten him on the meaning of His words.

"I am going to speak, now, to Our Lord Jesus Christ. I am going to speak to Him and He will hear me. For I believe that He is present; I do not doubt it in the least, since He said: *Behold I am with you even to the consummation of the world* (Matt. 28:20). O Lord, our God, what have You said: *If you do not believe that I am?* Indeed, of all You have made, what is there that is not? The heavens, are they not? The earth, is it not? And the things that are on the earth and in the heavens, are they not? And the very man to whom You are speaking, is he not? If they are, if all these things You have made are, what then is being itself—*ipsum esse*—which You reserved for Yourself as something proper to You, and which You have not given to others, in order to be the only one to exist? Must we then understand: *I am Who am*, as if the rest were not? And how are we to understand the *If you do not believe that I am?* Those who understood it, then, were they not? Even if they were sinners they were men. What are we to do? Let being itself—*ipsum esse*—say what it is; let it speak it to the heart; let it say it within; let it speak it within; let the interior man understand it; let thought understand that to be truly is to be always in the same way."[5]

Nothing could be clearer than this statement: *vere esse est enim semper eodem modo esse* . . . To identify thus the true being (*vere esse*) which God is with "immovable being" is to assimilate the *Sum* of Exodus to the *ousia* of Platonism. Here we are again face to face with the same difficulty we had when it was a question of translating this term in the dialogues of

Plato. The Latin equivalent of *ousia* is *essentia*, and it seems, certainly, that Augustine identified in his mind the God of Abraham, of Isaac, and of Jacob with that alone which, being immovable, can be called *essentia* in all the fullness of the term. How would it be otherwise since to be is "to be immovable"? Hence this formal statement of the *De Trinitate:* "Perhaps it ought to be said that God alone is *essentia*. For He alone truly is, because He is immovable, and it is this He declared for Moses His servant when He said *I am Who am* and *you will tell them that it is He Who is Who has sent me to you* (Exod. 3:14)."[6] Hence the divine name of names, *Sum*, is best translated into philosophical language by the abstract term *essence*, which itself denotes the immutability of "*that which is.*"

We see here the source of that doctrine of divine *essentialitas* which was later through St. Anselm to influence so profoundly the theology of Richard of Saint-Victor, Alexander of Hales, and St. Bonaventure. To pass from this philosophical interpretation of the text of Exodus to the one St. Thomas was going to propose, it was necessary to bridge the gap between being of essence and being of existence. We have seen how St. Thomas' proofs for the existence of God have prepared that bridge. It remains only to recognize the proper nature of the God Whose existence they have demonstrated; that is, to recognize Him as the supreme act of being.

There is nothing more convincing in this regard than the order followed by the *Summa Theologiae*. Knowing that a thing is, one has only to ask in what way it is, in order to know what it is. Indeed, and we shall have to say why, we do not know what God is, but only what He is not. The only conceivable manner of circumscribing His nature is therefore to remove successively from our notion of Him all the modes of existing which cannot be His. Now it is remarkable that the first of the ways of being which St. Thomas eliminates as incompatible with the notion of God is composition. He does this by establishing at the outset that God is simple, not in the hope of giving us a positive concept of a simplicity like God's but to make us conceive of Him, at least negatively, as the being free from all composition whatsoever. What can we hope to find at the end of the analysis announced if not *being*, free from all that is not being? To progress toward this conclusion will be to do no more than to make evident a notion virtually included in the proofs for the existence of God.

In following St. Thomas' analysis it is well to fix the attention at least as much on the reasons for which all compositions are eliminated one after the other as on the nature itself of the compositions thus eliminated. Let us begin with the grossest among them, that of conceiving of God as a body. To eliminate body from the notion of God, it is enough to look again at the principal proofs of His existence. God is the first immovable mover; now no body moves unless it is moved; God is therefore not a body. God is the first being, and is therefore being in act, *par excellence*; now all body is continuous and, as such, divisible to infinity; all body is therefore divisible in potency; it is not being, in pure act; hence, it is not God. But existence has already been shown of God the most noble of beings; now the soul is more noble than the body; it is impossible therefore that God is a body.[7] Clearly, the principle dominating these various arguments is one and the same. In each case, it is a question of establishing that whatever is incompatible with the pure actuality of being is incompatible with the notion of God.[8]

According to this principle, we must deny that God is composed of matter and form, for matter is what is in potency, and since God is pure act, without any mixture of potency, it is impossible that He is composed of matter and form. This second conclusion immediately entails a third. According to our definition, essence is only substance as intelligible through the concept of its quiddity and susceptible of definition. Thus understood, essence expresses, before anything else, the form or nature of substance. It includes whatever falls under the definition of species, and only this. For example, the essence of man is *humanitas*, which notion covers everything by which man is man—a reasoning animal composed of soul and body. It is to be noted, however, that essence embraces only that part of the substance which all substances of the same species have in common and not what each substance possesses as an individual. It is of the essence of humanity that every man should have a body. But the notion of humanity does not include the very body, the members, the flesh, the particular bones belonging to the substance of a given man. All these individual determinations belong to the notion of man since no man can exist without them. Thus, man (*homo*) is said to designate the complete substance taken with all the specific and individual determinations which render it capable of existing, whereas humanity designates the essence or formal part of the substance, man. It is the element which defines man in general. From this analysis, it follows that in all substances composed of matter and form, substance and essence do not exactly coincide. Since there is more in the substance man than in the essence humanity, man and humanity are not wholly identical. Now we have said that God is not composed of matter and form. There cannot, then, be in Him any distinction between essence on the one hand and substance or nature on the other. We can say that man is man in virtue of his humanity but not that God is God in virtue of His deity. God (*Deus*) and deity (*deitas*) and anything else that can be attributed to God by way of predication are all one and the same thing.[9]

This last formula enables us to recognize at once the opponents whom St. Thomas had in mind in this discussion and at the same time to understand the exact meaning of his position. At the point of his analysis just reached, St. Thomas has not yet arrived at the order of existence, the ultimate term toward which he is tending. Thus far it is only a question of a notion of God which does not go beyond substantial being. What he is asking himself is simply whether on this level, which is not yet that of the act of being, it is possible to distinguish God's substance (what God is) from His essence (that by which He is). In this case, that by which God is God, is called His deity and the problem is reduced to asking whether God (*Deus*) is distinct from His *deitas* or identical with it.[10]

This thesis came from a Platonism different from St. Augustine's, that of Boethius. It is a rather curious fact that Plato's thought should have exercised so profound an influence on the thought of the middle ages which knew almost nothing of his works. But his thought reached the middle ages through several schools which he had directly or indirectly influenced. We have already met the Platonism of St. Augustine and its derivatives, and we shall be meeting the Platonism of Dionysius the Areopagite and its derivatives. But we must also take into account that of Alfarabi, Avicenna, and their disciples, as well as that which falls under examination here, the Platonism of Boethius, by no means the least important.

There have then been several forms of Platonism, not just one, behind medieval philosophies, and it is important to know how to distinguish them. But it is important also to remember that by their relationship to a common origin these various Platonisms have constantly tended to reinforce one another, to unite, and sometimes even to become confused. The Platonic current is like a river issuing from St. Augustine, being enlarged by the tributary from Boethius in the sixth century, from Dionysius, Scotus Erigena in the ninth century, from Avicenna and the *Book of Causes* in the twelfth century. Other less important tributaries like Hermes Trismegistus, Macrobius, and Apuleius, for example, can be cited, as well as the translation of the *Timaeus* by Chalcidius, with its commentary, the only fragment of Plato himself which was, if not known, at least used during the high middle ages. Thus St. Thomas found himself face to face with many allied forms of Platonism to which he had sometimes to adjust himself, which he had sometimes openly to combat, and against which he had always to be on guard.

In the case in question, the root common to the Platonism of Boethius and Augustine is the ontology which reduces existence to being and conceives of being as *essentia*. But this principle is developed differently by Boethius than by St. Augustine. Boethius seems to have begun with the celebrated remark made by Aristotle, as it were in passing, which was to give rise to such numerous commentaries: "What man is is different from that fact that he is" (II *Anal.*, II, 7, 92 b 10–11). This remark could have introduced, *à propos* a question of logic, the frequently discussed problem of the relation between essence and existence. Aristotle himself never raised the problem, for the simple reason that, as his faithful commentator Averroes very well saw, he never made the distinction between what substances are and the fact that they are. Aristotle is not saying in this passage that the essence of a substance is distinct from its existence, but simply that one cannot conclude from the mere definition of substance that it exists.

When in his turn Boethius took up the problem, he raised it to the plane of metaphysics. The very obscurity of his terse definitions tended to focus the attention of his commentators upon them. Boethius distinguished between *being* and *what is: diversum est esse et id quod est.* But his distinction between *esse* and *id quod est* does not mark a distinction between essence and actual existence. It designates, rather, the distinction between the thing itself that is (*id quod est*) and the form (*esse*) whereby it is that which it is. For this reason, the form (*esse*) of a substance is also called its *quo est*: that by which the substance is. Such a form is simple by definition; *ipsum esse nihil aliud praeter se habet admixtum;* on the contrary, the *quod est* only exists in so far as it is informed by the form that gives it being: *quod est, accepta essendi forma est atque consistit.*[11]

To comment on Boethius through Gilbert de la Porrée is certainly to explain *obscurum per obscurius*. However his modern commentators interpret Gilbert himself, they agree that, in his texts, "one must not translate *essentia* by essence. This term evokes, in its true meaning, a distinction, within being itself (essence and existence), which did not as yet exist in Latin thought. *Esse,* too, is taken as a form. *Esse* and *essentia* are in this sense equivalents. God's *essentia* is the *esse* of all being and, at the same time, form *par excellence.*"[12] Since it is here a question of a basic position, whether metaphysical or at least epistemological, it was to dominate even the problem raised by the notion of God. Indeed, Gilbert conceived God, the form of all being, as Himself defined by a form determining our notion of Him as God. Thought, therefore, would conceive of this *quod est,* which God is, as determined to being by the form *divinitas.* It is impossible to think that Gilbert conceived of God as composed of two really distinct elements, God (*Deus*) and divinity (*divinitas*), but he seems at least to have admitted that as far as we are concerned, God can only be conceived as a *quod est* informed by a *quo est,* which is His divinity. The influence of this doctrine has been considerable. Accepted or amended by some, condemned by others, it has left its traces even upon those who rejected it most energetically. This is hardly surprising, because philosophers frequently reject consequences whose principles they still accept. In order to set aside Gilbert's doctrine, it was necessary to pass beyond the realism of *essentia* to that of existence. In brief, it was necessary to bring about that philosophical reform which we associate with the name of St. Thomas Aquinas.

Put in terms of Thomistic philosophy, the distinction between *Deus* and *divinitas* was equivalent to conceiving of the divine being as a kind of substance determined to be such by an essence which would be the essence of divinity. It may be that this conclusion is practically inevitable so long as one seeks to circumscribe the divine being by the conceptual definition of an essence. Even if he affirms, as does Gilbert, that God is His divinity, whoever seeks to define such an essence can do so only by conceiving of God as being God by the very *divinitas* that He is. This is to reintroduce into Him, at least in what concerns thought, a distinction between potency and act, incompatible with the pure actuality of the divine being. In order to overcome this difficulty we must, with St. Thomas, pass beyond the identification of God's substance with his essence and posit the identity of his essence with His very act-of-being. What distinguishes his position from that of the followers of Gilbert is not that it gives testimony of a more lively sense of the divine simplicity. All Christian theologians know that God is absolutely simple; and they say so, but not in the same way. The lesson St. Thomas gives us here is that we cannot say this properly if we remain on the plane of substance and essence, which are objects of quidditative concepts. The divine simplicity is perfect because it is the simplicity of pure act. We cannot define it; we can only affirm it by an act of the judging faculty.

In order to understand the position of St. Thomas on this decisive point, we must first remember the privileged role he attributes to *esse* in the structure of the real. For him each thing has its own act-of-being. Let us say, rather, there is no real apart from distinct acts of existing, by virtue of each of which a distinct thing exists. We must, then, posit as a fundamental principle that everything is, in virtue of the act of existing proper to it: *unumquodque est per suum esse*. Since it is here a question of a principle, we can be certain that its scope extends even to God. It would perhaps be better to say that it is the very being of God which is at the basis of the principle. For God is, as the third proof for His existence shows, the necessary being. He is therefore an act of existing of such a kind that His existence is necessary. This is what is meant by being necessary *per se*. To posit God in this way is to affirm an act of existing which needs no cause of its own existence. Such would not be the case were His essence distinguished, in so far as it is, from His existence. If, indeed, the essence of God determined in any degree this act of existing, the latter would no longer be necessary. God is, therefore, the act-of-being that He is. Such is the meaning of the expression: *Deus est suum esse*.[13] Like whatever exists, God is by His own act-of-being; but, in His case alone, we have to say that *what* His being is is nothing else than that by which He exists; namely, the pure act of existing.

Any one of the proofs for the existence of God would lead to the same conclusion precisely because they all set out from contingent existences in order to reach the first *esse* which causes them. As St. Thomas himself says of this thesis: it can be shown in many ways. God is the first cause; He has therefore no cause; now God would have a cause if His essence were distinct from His existence, because then it would not be enough, in order to exist, to be what He is. It is therefore impossible that God's essence be anything other than His act-of-being.

We can begin, too, if it seems preferable, from the fact that God is act, free from any potency. Then the question is: What is most actual in all given reality? According to our analysis of the metaphysical structure of the concrete, the answer must be: The act-of-being, because to be is the actuality of all form, or nature. Actually to be good is to be a good being which exists. Humanity has actual reality only in an actually existing man. Let us suppose, therefore, that the essence of God were distinct from His existence. The divine act of existing would then be the act of the divine essence. This latter would therefore be, with regard to God's *esse*, as potency to act. Now God is pure act; therefore, His essence must be his very act-of-being.

It is possible also to proceed even more directly, starting

from God posited as being. To say that God's essence is not His *esse* would be to say that *what* God is has *esse* but is not itself *esse*. Now what has the act-of-being but is not the act-of-being is only by participation. Since, as we have just seen, God is His essence or His very nature,[14] He is not by participation. This is, moreover, what we mean when we call Him the first being. Thus God is His essence, and His essence is the act itself of being; He is, therefore, not only His essence but His act-of-being.[15]

Such is the God whom the five proofs of St. Thomas seek and finally attain by five different ways. The question here was incontestably a philosophical one. Historically located, this conclusion appears to be the result of an effort extending over several centuries to attain the very root of being, which was then to become identified with the act-of-being. Going beyond the Platonic ontology of essence and the Aristotelian ontology of substance, St. Thomas in one long stride also went beyond both the first substance of Aristotle and the God *essentia* of St. Augustine and his disciples. St. Thomas never says that God has no essence.[16] If we think of his many opportunities to say this, we must presume that he had good reasons for avoiding the expression. The simplest reason is probably that, since we know only beings whose essence is not their act-of-being, it is impossible for us to conceive of a being without essence. Also, in the case of God, we conceive less of an act-of-being without essence than of an essence which, by passing as it were to its limit, comes at length to be one with its own act-of-being.[17] Moreover, the case is similar with all the attributes of God in the doctrine of St. Thomas. Just as we do not say that God has no wisdom, but that His wisdom is His own being, so we do not say that He has no essence but that His essence is His act-of-being.[18] To grasp in one glance the extent of St. Thomas' reform on the plane of natural theology, we have only to measure the distance separating the God *essentia* of St. Augustine from the God of St. Thomas whose *essentia* is, as it were, absorbed by its *esse*.

However, this pure act-of-being which St. Thomas the philosopher met at the end of metaphysics, St. Thomas the theologian had met too in Holy Scripture. It was no longer the conclusion of rational dialectic but a revelation from God

Himself to all men that they might accept it by faith. There is no doubt that St. Thomas thought that God had revealed to men that His essence was to exist. St. Thomas is not lavish with epithets. Never did a philosopher yield less frequently to the temptation to wax eloquent. Here, however, seeing these two beams of light so converging that they fused into each other, he was unable to withhold a word of admiration for the overwhelming truth blazing forth from their point of fusion. He saluted this truth with a title exalting it above all others: "God's essence is therefore His act-of-being. Now this sublime truth (*hanc autem sublimem veritatem*) God taught to Moses when Moses asked what to reply if the children of Israel should ask His name. (Exod. 3:13). And the Lord replied: I am Who am. You may say this to the children of Israel: *He Who is* has sent me to you. Thus He showed that His proper name is *Who is*. Now every name is intended to signify the nature or essence of something. It remains then that the divine act-of-being itself (*ipsum divinum esse*) is the essence or nature of God."[19]

Let us note well that for St. Thomas this revelation of the identity of essence and existence in God was the equivalent of a revelation of the distinction between essence and existence in creatures. *Who is* signifies: He Whose essence is to exist; *Who is* is the proper name of God; consequently, the essence of anything that is not God is not to exist. We could, if we had to, make this simple inference by our reason. But we do not have to, the text is explicit: "It is impossible that the substance of any being other than the First Agent be its very act-of-being. Hence the name which Exodus (3:14) gives as the proper name of God, *Who is*. It belongs properly to Him alone that His substance be nothing other than His act-of-being."[20]

These positions have two principal consequences. First, Thomistic existentialism concerned not merely natural theology, but theology in the strict sense. It is here indeed a question of a literal interpretation of the word of God. To appreciate the importance of what is at stake we have only to compare St. Thomas' interpretation of the text with St. Augustine's. When St. Augustine read the name of God, he understood, "I am He Who never changes." St. Thomas reading the same words, understood them to mean "I am the pure act-of-being."

Whence, this second consequence, that no historian can consider St. Thomas' thinking to be a combination of distinct schools of thought. Neither the identity of essence and existence in God nor the distinction between essence and existence in creatures belongs to the *revelatum*, properly so called, since neither of these truths is beyond the range of natural reason considered as a judging faculty. Both are, nevertheless, for St. Thomas part of the revealable, and even of the revealable which has been revealed. Nowhere, perhaps, can we see more clearly how complex is the economy of revelation, the act by which God makes Himself known to man, in the teaching of St. Thomas. St. Thomas was far from believing or having others believe that God had at one time revealed to Moses the twenty-second chapter of Book II of the *Summa Contra Gentiles*. If anyone should think this, it is not St. Thomas who is naïve. God has given us His name; it suffices that man believe it lest any false god afterward seduce him. But the theology of the Christian Doctors is only revelation investigated by reason working in the light of faith. Time was necessary for reason to do its work. St. Augustine was on the right path; St. Thomas but followed the same road to its end. Everyone is free to imagine St. Thomas' genius as a living classification of the sciences. But those of us who do this will soon be at grips with this thorny problem: Is it St. Thomas the theologian who, reading in Exodus the identity of essence and existence in God, taught St. Thomas the philosopher the distinction between essence and existence in creatures? Or is it St. Thomas the philosopher who, pushing his analysis of the metaphysical structure of the concrete even as far as the distinction between essence and existence, taught St. Thomas the theologian that *He Who is* in Exodus means the *Act-of-Being?* St. Thomas himself as a philosopher thought of these two propositions as the two sides of one and the same metaphysical thesis. And from the day he understood them, he always thought of them as being in Holy Scripture. The word of God is too profound for human reason to exhaust its meaning. But it is always the same meaning of the same word which the reason of the Doctors of the Church ever pursues to depths more and more profound. The genius of St. Thomas is one and his work is one. One cannot separate, without destroying its perfect balance, what God has revealed to men from the meaning of what He has revealed.

This sublime truth is, for the historian at least, the key to the understanding of Thomism. His best interpreters have all seen this, and we need only repeat it after them. But each age repeats it in its own way, because new obstacles arise to obscure the meaning of the fundamental notion of existing. Today two distinct causes are moving concurrently in this direction. On the other hand, the permanent tendency of the human understanding to feed on quiddities inclines us to break up the unity of Thomism into a mosaic of essences. These, like the pieces in a jigsaw puzzle, are arranged side by side, powerless to communicate with one another. On the other hand, the progress of historical studies reveals for us in ever-increasing number the doctrinal sources on which St. Thomas drew in order to construct his work. So much is this so, that his work is apt to appear more and more as a mosaic of borrowed fragments of whose heteroclite nature he seems to have been unaware.

Thomism, indeed, can appear as the emptiest or fullest of philosophies, as the most inconsistent of eclecticisms or the luckiest stroke of drilling ever attempted through the thickness of concrete reality, according as it is interpreted as a logic of abstract being or a metaphysic of the act-of-being. We must, then, be neither scandalized nor disturbed when some find fullness and light where others find but obscurity and emptiness. St. Thomas' philosophical work is above all else the first discovery, through human reason, of the *Ultima Thule* of metaphysics. It is difficult to reach it and almost as difficult to stay there. This, however, is what we must try to do in following, even to its final consequences, this sublime truth —*hanc sublimem veritatem*—whose light illumines the whole of Thomism.

At the beginning of this quest, let us provide ourselves with this formula, the fullest and clearest of all those which Thomas himself has provided: "Being (*esse*) is used in two senses. In the first it denotes the act-of-being (*actum essendi*). In the second it denotes the composition of the proposition made by the mind in joining a predicate to a subject. If we take being in the first sense, we cannot know what God's being is (*non possumus scire esse Dei*), any more than we can know His essence. But we can know that the proposition we form about God in saying 'God is' is true; and we know this from His effects."[21]

NOTES

1. See E. Gilson, *Spirit of Mediaeval Philosophy*, chap. 3.
2. St. Augustine, *De Civitate Dei*, VIII, II; *Patrologia Latina*, vol. 41, col. 236.
3. *De Doctrina Christiana*, I, chap. 32, no. 35; *Pat. Lat.*, vol. 34, col. 32.
4. See E. Gilson, *Introduction à l'étude de saint Augustin* (Paris: Librairie Philosophique J. Vrin, 2nd ed., 1943), pp. 88–103.
5. St. Augustine, *In Joannis Evangelium*, tract XXVIII, chap. 8, no. 8–10; *Pat. Lat.*, vol. 35, col. 1678–1679.
6. St. Augustine, *De Trinitate*, VIII, chap. 5, no. 10; *Pat. Lat.*, vol. 42, col. 942.
7. *Summa Theologiae*, I, q. 3, a. 1.
8. *Summa Contra Gentiles*, I, chap. 18, ad *Adbuc, omne compositum*.
9. *Sum. Theol.*, I, q. 3, aa. 2–3; *Summa Contra Gentiles*, I, chap. 21.
10. *Sum. Theol.*, I, q. 3, a. 3, obj. 2.
11. Boethius, *De Hebdomadibus*; *Pat. Lat.*, vol. 64, col. 1311 B–C, 1331 B. For some bibliographical references, see my *Christian Philosophy of Saint Thomas Aquinas*, p. 455, notes 14–15.
12. M. H. Vicaire, "Les Porretains et l' avicennisme avant 1215" (*Revue des sciences philosophiques et théologigues*, vol. XXVI, 1937, pp. 449–482), p. 461.
13. St. Thomas Aquinas, *Summa Contra Gentiles*, I, chaps. 21–22.
14. See above, p. 236.
15. *Sum. Theol.*, I, q. 3, a. 4; *De Potentia*, q. VII, a. 2.
16. According to Father Sertillanges, "St. Thomas formally concedes in the *De Ente et Essentia* (chap. 6) that God has no essence." (*Le Christianisme et les philosophies*, I, 268.) But actually St. Thomas there says only: "Inveniuntur aliqui philosophi dicentes quod Deus non habet quidditatem vel essentiam, quia essentia sua non est aliud quam esse suum." St. Thomas explains here in what sense this expression would be true, but he does not seem himself to have used it. But in Avicenna we read: "Primus igitur non habet quidditatem." *Met.*, VII, 4, ed. Venice, 1508, fol. 99rb.

17. It is to be noted that it is the esse which absorbs the essence and not vice versa: "In Deo autem ipsum esse suum est sua quidditas: et ideo nomen quod sumitur ab esse proprie nominat ipsum, et est proprium nomen ejus: sicut proprium nomen hominis quod sumitur a quidditate sua." *In I Sent.*, d. 8, q. 1, a. 1, *Solutio*. God is, therefore, more properly called *Qui est* than *essentia*.
18. *De Potentia*, a. VII, a. 2, ad 1.
19. *Summa Contra Gentiles*, I, chap. 22.
20. *Summa Contra Gentiles*, II, chap. 52. The phrase is not absolutely perfect because it seems to indicate that God is composed of *Qui* and *est*. But it is by far the best because it is the simplest that a human understanding can conceive to designate God. The others, *Qui est unus, qui est bonus*, etc., add to the composition of *Qui* with *est* composition with a third term as well. Cf. *In I Sent.*, d. 8, q. 1, a. 2, ad 3 and ad 4. To say that it is the least imperfect does not mean that it is not proper to God. This name, *qui est*, is His *maxime proprium*; in this absolute sense it belongs to God alone (*Sum. Theol.*, I, q. 13, a. 11, *Sed Contra*); but it is still not a perfectly simple designation of the *Ipsum* esse. The terms composing it can still be attributed to creatures, since it is from them that our intellect has fashioned the terms.
21. *Sum. Theol.*, I, q. 3, a. 4, ad 2.

16. The Spirit of Thomism

Thus far we have been examining the more important philosophical problems dealt with by Thomas Aquinas. In discussing these problems we have attempted to show the bond which ties them together and gives continuity to their solutions. Perhaps it will be useful, here at the end of this study, to take a comprehensive look over our course and to pick out, as precisely as possible, what is constant in St. Thomas' philosophical outlook.*

One has no doubt perceived the unified character of a doctrine which provides a complete explanation of the universe and of man from the point of view of reason. This character is due to the fact that the texture of Thomism is made from a very small number of principles which continually penetrate one another. Perhaps, when all is said and done, all these principles are various aspects of one central notion, the notion of being. Human thought is satisfied only when it grasps an existence; but our intellection of a being is never limited itself to the sterile apprehension of something given. The apprehended being invites our intellect to explore it; it invites intellectual activity by the very multiplicity of aspects which it reveals. Inasmuch as a being is not distinguished from itself, it is one. In this sense we can say that *being* and *one* are coincident. No essence divides itself without losing at the same time its being and its unity. But since a being is by definition inseparable from itself, it lays the basis of the truth which can be affirmed about it. To say what is true is to say what is, and is to attribute to each thing the very being that it marks. Thus it is the being of a thing which founds its truth; and it is the truth of a thing which underlies the truth of thought.

We think the truth of a thing when we attribute to it the being that it is. It is thus that accord is established between

* The present selection forms the concluding chapter of *The Christian Philosophy of St. Thomas Aquinas.*

our thought and its object; and it is this accord which provides the basis for what is true in our knowledge just as the intimate accord which subsists between its object and the eternal thought which God has of it establishes the truth of the thing outside our thought. The line of the relationships of truth is therefore only one aspect of the line of the relationships of being.

We find exactly the same thing in the case of the good. Every being in so far as it is knowable is the basis of truth. But in so far as it is defined by a certain quantity of perfection, and consequently in so far as it is, it is desirable and presents itself to us as a good; and hence the movement to take possession of it which arises in us when we find ourselves in its presence. Thus the same being, without the addition of anything from outside, displays before us its unity, its truth, and its goodness. Whatever the relationship of identity which our thought can affirm in any one of the moments of the doctrinal synthesis, whatever the truth we set forth or good we desire, our thought always refers to being in order to establish its accord with itself, in order to assimilate its nature by way of knowledge or to enjoy its perfection through the will.

But Thomism is not a system if by this is meant a global explanation of the world deduced or constructed, in an idealistic manner, from *a priori* principles. The content of the notion whose content can be defined once and for all and set forth in an *a priori* way. There are many ways of being, and these ways must be ascertained. The one most immediately given to us is our own and that of corporeal things among which we pass our life. Each one of us "is," but in an incomplete and deficient manner. In the field of experience directly accessible to us we meet only substantial composites analogous to ourselves, forms engaged in matters by so indissoluble a bond that their very "engagement" defines these beings and that God's creative action, when it puts them into existence, directly produces the compounds of matter and form that constitute their beings. However imperfect such a being may be, it does possess perfection to the extent that it possesses being. We already find in it the transcendental relations of unity, truth, goodness, and beauty which are inseparable from it and which we have defined. But we note at the same time that, for some deep reason which we have still to determine, these relations are not fixed, closed, definite. Everything takes place —and experience verifies this—as though we had to struggle in order to establish these relationships instead of enjoying them peacefully. We are, and we are identical with ourselves, but not completely so. A sort of margin keeps us a little short of our definition. We do not fully realize human essence nor even the complete notion of our individuality. Hence, we are not involved in a simple manner of being, but in a permanent effort to maintain ourselves in being, to conserve ourselves, realize ourselves. It is just the same with all the sensible beings which we find around us. The world is under the constant impulse of forces, it is driven by various movements, it is forever becoming, like man himself ceaselessly passing from one state to another.

This universal becoming is normally expressed in terms of the distinction of potency and act, which extends to all given beings within our experience. These notions add nothing to the notion of being. Act always is being; potency always is possible being. Just as Aristotle had stated the universal extension of this principle without attempting to define it, St. Thomas readily uses it without explanation. It is a sort of postulate, a formula stating as a fact the definite modes of being given to us in experience. Any essence which does not completely realize its definition is act in the measure in which it does realize it, potency in the measure in which it does not, and privation in the measure in which it does not realize it. In so far as it is in act, it is the active principle which will release the motion of realization. It is from the actuality of form that all endeavors of this kind proceed; it is the source of motion, the reason of becoming; it is cause. Once more, it is the being in things which is the ultimate reason of all the natural processes we have been stating. It is being as such which communicates its form as efficient cause, which produces change as a moving cause, and assigns to it a reason for being produced as final cause. We are dealing, then, with beings which are ceaselessly moved by a fundamental need to preserve and complete themselves.

Now we cannot reflect upon an experience like this without noticing that it does not contain the adequate explanation of the facts it places before us. This world of becoming which is in motion in order to find itself, these heavenly spheres continually seeking themselves in the successive points of their orbits, these human souls which capture and assimilate being by their intellect, these substantial forms forever searching out new matter in which to realize themselves, do not contain in themselves the explanation of what they are. If such beings were self-explaining, they would be lacking nothing. Or, inversely, they would have to be lacking nothing before they could be self-explaining. But then they would no longer move in search of themselves; they would repose in the integrity of their own essence at length realized; they would cease to be what they now are.

It is, therefore, outside the world of potency and act, above becoming, and in a being which is totally what it is, that we must look for the sufficient reason of the universe. But this being reached by thought is obviously of a different nature than the being we observe, for if it were not different from the being which experience gives, there would be no advantage in positing it. Thus the world of becoming postulates a principle removed from becoming and placed entirely outside it.

But then a new problem arises. If the being we postulate from experience is radically different from the one given to us in experience, how can we know it through this experience and how will it help us to explain what we experience? Nothing can be deduced or inferred about a being from some other being which does not exist in the same sense as the first one does. Our thought would be quite inadequate to proceed to such a conclusion unless the reality in which we moved formed, by its hierarchical and analogical structure, a sort of ladder leading toward God.

It is precisely because every operation is the realization of an essence, and because every essence is a certain measure of being and perfection, that the universe reveals itself to us as a society made up of superiors and inferiors. The very definition of each essence ranks it immediately in its proper place in this hierarchy. To explain the operation of an individual thing, not only must we have the definition of this individual, but we must also have the definition of the essence which it embodies in a deficient manner. And the species itself is not enough because the individuals which embody the species are ceaselessly striving to realize themselves. Thus it becomes necessary either to renounce trying to account for this operation or else to seek for its explanation at a higher level, in a superior grade of perfection.

From here on, the universe appears essentially a hierarchy and the philosophical problem is to indicate its exact arrangement and to place each class of beings in its proper grade. To do this, one principle of universal value must always be kept in mind: that the greater or less can be appraised and classified only in relation to the maximum, the relative in relation to the absolute. Between God Who is Being, pure and simple, and complete nothingness, there come near God pure intelligences known as angels and near nothingness material forms. Between angels and material nature come human creatures on the borderline between spirits and bodies. Thus the angels reduce the infinite gap separating man from God and man fills in the gap between angels and matter.

Each of these degrees has its own mode of operation since each being operates according as it is in act and as its degree of actuality merges with its degree of perfection. The orderly and arranged hierarchy of beings is thus made complete by the orderly and arranged hierarchy of their operations, and in such a way that the bottom of the higher degree invariably comes into close contact with the top of the lower. Thus the principle of continuity gives precision and determination to the principle of perfection. Actually, both of these principles but express the higher law governing the communication of being. There is no being save the divine being in which all creatures participate; and creatures differ from one another only by reason of their greater or lesser degree of participation in the divine being.[1] Their perfection must, accordingly, be measured by the distance separating them from God. It is in thus differentiating themselves from one another that they arrange themselves into a hierarchy.

If this is true, it is analogy alone which enables our intelligence to arrive at a transcendent God from sensible things. It is analogy, too, which alone permits us to say that the universe has its existence from a transcendental principle and yet is neither confused with it nor added to it. The similarity of the analogue has, of course, to be explained, and it can be explained only by means of what the analogue imitates: "For being (*ens*) is not said of many equivocally, but analogically, and thus must be reduced to unity."[2] But at the same time that it possesses enough of its model's being to require it as its cause, it possesses it in such a manner that the being of this cause does not become involved in that of the thing caused. And because the word "being" signifies two different modes of existence when applied to God and to creatures, no problem of addition or subtraction can arise. The being of creatures is only an image, an imitation of the divine being. Even as reflections appear about a flame, increasing, decreasing, and disappearing, without the substance of the flame being affected, so the likenesses freely created by the divine substance owe all their being to this substance. They subsist only through it, yet borrow nothing from its *per se* mode of being, a mode very different from their own. They neither add to it nor subtract from it even in the least degree.

These two principles, analogy and hierarchy, enable us to explain the creature through a transcendent Creator. They also permit us to maintain relations between them and to extend bonds between them which become the constitutive principles of created essences and the laws which serve to explain them. Whatever physics or natural philosophy ultimately shows to be the nature of things, it has necessarily to remain subordinate to a metaphysics of being. If creatures are similitudes in what concerns their basic origin, then it is to be expected that analogy will serve to explain the universe just as it explains creation. To account for the operation of a being, we shall always have to show that its operation is based, beyond its essence, in its act-of-being. And to give account of this essence will always be to show that a definite degree of participation in being, corresponding exactly to what this essence is, ought to have a place in our universe. But why was such a determined similitude required by a universe like ours? It is because the similitudes of any model can be essentially different only if they are more or less perfect. A finite system of images of an infinite being must have all the real degrees of likeness which can appear within the bounds assigned to the system by the free will of the Creator. The metaphysical explanation of a physical phenomenon must always be concerned with putting an essence in its place in a hierarchy.

This sense of hierarchy shows the profound influence of the Pseudo-Dionysius on the thought of St. Thomas. There is no denying this influence; and it explains why some have wished to rank the author of the *Summa Theologiae* among the disciples of Plotinus. Only when we strictly limit its range does such a thesis become acceptable. The Areopagite furnishes the framework of the hierarchy. He firmly implants in thought the need for a hierarchy. He makes it impossible not to consider the universe as a hierarchy. But he left for St. Thomas the task of completing it; and even though Dionysius assigns the various grades in the hierarchy, he does not know the law which governs their arrangement and distribution.

But is it true to say that St. Thomas thought of the content of this universal hierarchy in a neo-Platonic spirit? If we except with numerous reservations the case of pure spirits, it is quite apparent that the answer is no. The God of St. Thomas the Christian is the same as St. Augustine's. That St. Augustine was under neo-Platonic influence does not mean that his God could be confused with the God of Plotinus. Between Plotinian speculation and the theology of the Fathers of the Church there stands Jehovah, the personal God, Who acts by intelligence and will, and Who freely places outside Himself that real universe which His Wisdom chose from an infinity of possible universes. Between this freely created universe and God the Creator there is an impassable abyss and no other continuity than the continuity of order. Properly speaking, the world is an ordered discontinuity. Must we not see that we are here far removed from neo-Platonic philosophy? To make of St. Thomas a Plotinian, or even a neo-Platonizer, is to confuse him with the adversaries he resisted so energetically.

The distance between the two philosophers is no less noticeable when we move from God to man. We said that St. Thomas' God was not the God of Plotinus but the Christian God of Augustine. Neither is St. Thomas' man the man of Plotinus. The opposition is particularly sharp right at the heart of the problem: in the relation between soul and body, and in the doctrine of knowledge which results from this. In Platonism there is the affirming of the extreme independence and almost complete aseity of the soul; this allows for Platonic reminiscence and even for the momentary return to the One through the ecstatic union. But in Thomism there is a most energetic affirming of the physical nature of the soul and vigilant care to close all paths which might lead to a doctrine of direct intuition of the intelligible in order to leave open no other road than that of sense knowledge. Platonism locates mystical knowledge in the natural prolongation of human knowledge; in Thomism, mystical knowledge is added to and co-ordinated with natural knowledge, but is not a continuation of it. All we know about God is what our reason teaches us about Him after reflecting upon the evidence of the senses. If we want to find a neo-Platonic doctrine of knowledge in the middle ages, we will have to look elsewhere than in St. Thomas.

This becomes clearer when we put aside the consideration of this particular problem and examine directly the Thomistic hierarchy of the universe. We have had a great deal to say about God and His creative power, about the angels and their functions, about man and his operations. We have considered, one after the other, all creatures endowed with intellect, and the First Intelligence itself. What we have seen is that the nature and compass of the many kinds of knowledge it has been given to us to acquire have varied very considerably according to the greater or less perfection of the reality which was its object. One who wishes to extract a clear notion of the spirit of Thomistic philosophy must first examine the ladder of being, and then inspect the values which locate each order of knowledge in its proper degree.

What is knowing? It is apprehending what is. There is no other perfect knowledge. Now it is immediately apparent that all knowledge, properly so called, of the higher degrees in the universal hierarchy is relentlessly refused us. We know that God and pure intelligences exist, but we do not know what they are. There is no doubting, however, that the awareness of a deficiency in our knowledge of God leaves us with a burning desire for higher and more complete knowledge. Nor can it be doubted that, if knowing consists in grasping the essence of the object known, God, angels, and, generally speaking, anything of the purely intelligible order are by definition beyond the grasp of our intellect. This is why, instead of having an intuition of the Divine Essence, we have but a vast number of concepts which, taken together, are a confused sort of imitation of what would have been a true notion of the Divine Essence. When all that we have been able to say about such a subject is put together, the result is a collection of negations or analogies, nothing more.

Where, then, does human knowledge find itself at home? When is it in the presence of its own object? Only at that point where it comes into contact with the sensible. And although it does not here totally penetrate the real, because the individual as such implies or presupposes matter and is therefore beyond expression, still reason is in control of the field in which it is working. In order to describe man—that is, the human composite—to describe the animal and its operations, the heavenly bodies and their powers, mixed bodies or the elements, rational knowledge remains proportioned to the order or rank of the objects it is exploring. Although its content is incomplete, it is nevertheless positive. What is original and truly profound in Thomism is not an attempt either to establish science more solidly or to extend it. St. Thomas places the proper object of the human intellect in the sensible order, but he does not consider the study of this order to be the highest function of the knowing faculty. The proper object of the intellect is the quiddity of the sensible, but its proper function is to make the sensible intelligible.[3] From the particular object on which its light falls it draws something universal. It can do this because this particular object carries the divine image naturally impressed upon it as the mark of its origin. The intellect is, in the proper sense of the term, born and made for the universal. Hence its straining toward that object which is by definition vigorously inaccessible, the Divine Being. Here reason knows very little, but what little it knows surpasses in dignity and value any other kind of certitude.[4]

All great philosophies, and St. Thomas' is no exception, present a different front according to the particular needs of the age which turns to them. It is hardly surprising, then, that, in a time like ours when so many minds are seeking to re-establish between philosophy and concrete reality bonds which idealism has broken, Thomists of different varieties should be insisting upon the notion of the act-of-being in his philosophy. The fact that they have reached analogous conclusions quite independently of one another makes their convergence still more significant. Restricting ourselves to recent statements, we can find any number of remarks like the following: The proper object of the intelligence is being, "not only *essential* or quidditative but existential." Or again: The entire thought of St. Thomas "seeks existence itself, though not, as in the case with practical philosophy, to produce it, but to know it."[5] Or again: "Thomistic philosophy is an existential philosophy." Mr. Maritain, the author of these statements, explains them at length in a special section of his *A Digression on Existence and Philosophy*.

When Maritain speaks in this way about St. Thomas, he is trying to make us understand that all human knowledge, including the metaphysician's, begins from sense knowledge and ultimately returns to it "not in order to know their essence. It (i.e., metaphysics) does so to know how they exist, for this too metaphysics should know, to attain their mode of existence, and then to conceive by analogy the existence of that which exists immaterially, which is purely spiritual."[6]

This is a lesson of the greatest importance. The only trouble is that the various statements of it are so compact that they tend to obscure its full significance. To insist on the existential character of Thomism in the above sense is to resist the very natural tendency of the human mind to remain on the level of abstraction. The very art of teaching fosters this tendency. How is anyone to teach without explaining, simplifying, abstracting? We tend to keep both ourselves and others on this level of conceptual abstraction which is so satisfying to the mind. First we disentangle essences from concrete reality; then we hold back the moment when we must again blend these essences into the unity of the concrete. We are afraid that we may fall back into the confusion from which we set out and which it is the very object of analysis to remove. Some hold back this moment so long that they never allow it to arrive. In this case, philosophy is reduced to making cuts into the real, following the cleavage plane of essences, as if knowing from what essences the real is composed were the same as knowing existing reality. This reality is only directly apprehended by us in and through sensible knowledge, and this is why our judgments attain their object only when, directly or indirectly, they are resolved into it: "In other words the *res sensibilis visibilis*, the visible object of sense, is the touchstone of every judgment, *ex qua debemus de aliis judicare*, by which we must judge of everything else, because it is the touchstone of existence."[7]

Lest the metaphysician forget this principle, or rather, lest he be unaware of the point of view which it imposes on him, he should immerse himself in existence, enter ever more deeply into it "by means of as keen a sensitive (or aesthetic) perception as possible, and also by his experience of suffering and of existential conflicts, in order that, away up in the third heaven of the natural intelligence, he may devour the intelligible substance of things." After this comes the almost inevitable remark: "Need we add that the professor who is only a professor, who is withdrawn from existence, who has become insensible to this third degree of abstraction, is the direct opposite of the true metaphysician? Thomistic metaphysic is called *scholastic*, from the name of its most bitter trial. Scholarly pedagogy is its particular enemy. It must ceaselessly combat and subdue the professorial adversary attacking from within."[8]

It could hardly be put better. But just let us see what happens when we neglect to push judgments beyond abstract essences to the actually existing concrete. St. Thomas has noted that the properties of the essence are not the same when it is taken abstractly in itself as when taken in the state of concrete actualization in a really existing being. In fact he explains himself so explicitly on this point that we might as well let him speak for himself.

"Whatever be the object considered in the abstract, we can truly say that it contains no foreign element; that is, nothing outside and beyond its essence. It is in this way that we speak of *humanity* and *whiteness* and everything else of this kind. The reason for this is that *humanity* is then designated as that by which something is a man, and *whiteness* as that by which something is white. Now, formally speaking, a thing is a man only by something pertaining to the formal reason of man. Similarly, a thing is only formally white by what pertains to the formal reason of whiteness. This is why abstractions like these can include nothing foreign to themselves. It is quite different in the case of something signified concretely. Indeed, *man* signifies something possessing humanity, and white, something that has whiteness. Now the fact that man has humanity or whiteness does not prevent him from having something else which does not depend on the formal reason of humanity or whiteness. It is enough that it be not opposed to it. This is why *man* and *white* can have something more than humanity and whiteness. Moreover, it is for this reason that *whiteness* and *humanity* may be called parts of something, but are not predicated of concrete beings themselves, because a part is never predicated of the whole of which it is a part."[9]

If we apply these observations to philosophy, we shall see how, in the approach to problems, perspectives vary according to whether we avoid or face them. The philosopher begins with the experience common to everyone. And he ought in the end to return to this same common experience in so far as it is this which he set out to explain. The only way to succeed is to begin with an analysis, pushed as far as possible, of the various elements included in the factual data which go to make up this experience. Here we have as first task the breaking up of the concrete into its intelligible elements. Whatever we find out has to be separated into its parts and each part isolated from the others. This can be done only by means of a distinct concept for each element. A necessary condition in thus distinguishing any concept is that it contain everything its definition includes, and nothing else. This is why every abstract essence is distinguished from the others as its concept is from theirs, and is only distinguished from them in that it excludes them. *Humanity* is that by which a man is a man, and it is that exclusively. So far is *humanity* from including *whiteness*, that there are men who are not white. Inversely, *whiteness* is that by which what is white is white. This does not include *humanity*. There can be an incredible number of white beings none of them men. Thus our inquiry into the real leads us to break down the confusion of the concrete into an enormous number of intelligible essences each quite distinct in so far as it cannot be reduced to the others.

Does philosophy consist in these abstract essences taken in the state of abstraction in which we are right now considering them? To say Yes is to become involved in a philosophy of the quiddity. We mean by this not simply a philosophy that calls upon quiddities, for this necessity is co-essential to all human knowledge, but a philosophy whose notion of the real reduces it to the essence, or quiddity. History shows us many such philosophies. Indeed their very classifications are innumberable, but there is no need to go into them here. This attitude concerns us primarily in that it expresses a natural tendency of the reason to think by "clear and distinct ideas," and consequently to reject as obscure and confused whatever does not allow itself to be included within the limits of purely quidditative notions. From this point of view, the "simple natures" on which Descartes worked are no different from the essences of the tree of Porphyry which he denounced as sterile.

Let us go farther. Whatever method we invoke, and even if we begin by admitting that the concept cannot be the ultimate object of philosophy, we end up in actual fact with a philosophy of the quiddities whenever we fail to carry research beyond the level of abstract notions. A simple glance at the history of the various philosophies leads to this same conclusion. Restricting ourselves to Thomistic philosophy, we have to choose between locating its ultimate object in the grasping of the essences out of which the concrete real is made up, in which case our highest mode of knowing is a sort of intellectual intuition of pure essences, or assigning to Thomistic philosophy as its ultimate term rational knowledge of the concrete real through the essences engaged in the metaphysical texture of that concrete real.

Whatever we may think, there can be no doubting that the thought of St. Thomas, in first intention, turned toward knowledge of the existing concrete given in sensible experience and of the first causes of this existing concrete whether they be sensible or not. The whole philosophy we have been studying, from metaphysics to moral philosophy, bears testimony of this. This is why it is and remains philosophy in the proper sense and not, in the widely spread pejorative sense of the term, a "scholasticism." Every philosophy engenders its own scholastic presentation, its own school-doctrine, its own scholasticism. But the terms "philosophy" and "scholasticism" designate specifically distinct facts. Every philosophy worthy of the name starts out from the real and returns thereto. Every scholasticism starts from a philosophy and returns thereto. Philosophy degenerates into scholasticism the moment when, instead of taking the existing concrete as object of its reflections in order to study it deeply, penetrate it, throw more and more light upon it, it applies itself rather to the statements which it is supposed to explain, as if these statements themselves and not what they shed light on were the reality itself.

To fall into this error is to become quite incapable of understanding even the history of philosophy. Because understanding a philosophy is not merely reading what it says in one place in terms of what it says in another; it is reading it at each moment in terms of what it is actually speaking about. An error like this is far more harmful to philosophy itself than to the history of philosophy. St. Thomas' teaching has degenerated into scholasticism whenever and wherever it has been cut off from the real, the only object on which its illuminating rays can properly be focused. This is not a reason for believing that Thomism is a scholasticism, for its object is not Thomism but the world, man, and God, attained as existing beings in their very existence. It is therefore true that in this first sense the philosophy of St. Thomas is existential in the fullest sense of the word.

Beyond this first sense, there is another far more radical one which commands our attention even more imperatively. In this case, however, the very expression "existential philosophy," which is so inviting in itself, lends itself to so many misunderstandings that we stand in dread of the birth and spread of new "scholastic" controversies if, that is, certain necessary precautions are not taken. It is a rather modern expression; and although it has arisen out of problems as old as Western thought, it can hardly be applied to the doctrine of St. Thomas without giving the impression of striving to rejuvenate it from without by fitting it up in modern dress. To attempt something like this is hardly wise. It even has the effect of aligning Thomism with philosophies which in certain fundamental points are its direct contrary. To speak of "existential philosophy" today brings immediately to mind such names as Kierkegaard, Heidegger, Jaspers, and so on. In these we find divergent tendencies. No Thomism conscious of what it really is itself could under any circumstances fully align itself with any of them. To do so would only lay it open to the charge of seeking artificial rejuvenation, of postponing its threatening dissolution by laying claim to a title generally conceded to recent philosophies still full of vitality. The whole undertaking would be undignified and profitless to all parties concerned and could only lead to misunderstandings which it would take generations to remove.

The first and most serious of these misunderstandings would be to give the impression that Thomism was *one more* existential philosophy; whereas what really ought to be the issue at stake is whether or not these philosophies to which Thomism is being likened have really any right to be called existential philosophies at all. Assuredly these are philosophies very much concerned with existence. But they really only deal with it as an object of a possible phenomenology of human existence, as though the primacy of existence signified chiefly that primacy of ethics which Kierkegaard so strongly insisted upon. If we look here for a philosophy that passes beyond the phenomenological and establishes the act-of-being as the keystone of metaphysics, we shall look in vain. But this is just what St. Thomas has done. As philosophy of the act-of-being, Thomism is not *another* existential philosophy, it is the only one. All those phenomenologies which are on the hunt for an ontology seem unconsciously to be moving in its direction as though driven on by the natural desire of their own justification.

What characterizes Thomism is the decision to locate actual existence in the heart of the real as an act of transcending any kind of quidditative concept and, at the same time, avoiding the double error of remaining dumb before its transcendence or of denaturing it in objectifying it. The only means of speaking about the act-of-being is to grasp it in a concept, and the concept which directly expresses it is the concept of being. Being is *that which is*; that is, *that which has the act-of-being*. It is quite impossible to come to the act-of-being by an intellectual intuition which grasps it directly, and grasps nothing more. To think is to conceive. But the proper object of a concept is always an essence, or something presenting itself to thought as an essence; in brief, an object. The act-of-being, however, is an act. It can be grasped only by or in the essence whose act it is. A pure *est* is unthinkable; but an *id quod est* can be thought. But every *id quod est* is first a being. And because there is no concept anterior to this, being is the first principle of knowledge. It is so in itself; it is so in the philosophy of St. Thomas. Such a philosophy has every claim to be called a "philosophy of being."

If it is true that even the possibility of philosophy is tied up with the use of the quidditative concept, it is also true that the name which correctly designates a philosophy is drawn from the concept its first principle is based on. This cannot be the act-of-being because, taken in itself, the act-of-being is not the object of a quidditative concept. It must, then, inevitably be being. To call Thomism an existential philosophy does not call into question the legitimacy of its traditional title, but only confirms it. Since existence can be conceived only in the concept of being, Thomism is always a philosophy of being, even though called existential.

It seems proper to make this point because the abstract notion of being is, by its very definition, ambivalent. In a "that which is" (*id quod est*), or a "having being" (*esse habens*), we can spontaneously emphasize either the *id quod* and the *habens* or the *esse* and the *est*. Not only can we do this, but we actually do so, and usually it is the "that which" (*id quod*) and the "having" (*habens*) which we emphasize because they place before us the "thing" which exists; that is, being as the object of the quidditative concept.

This natural tendency to abstract and to confine ourselves to the abstract concept is so strong that it has been responsible for the appearance of several forms of Thomism in which *esse*—that is, the very act-of-being—seems to have no effective role to play. By yielding to this natural tendency, we abstract from *esse* and make Thomism a philosophy of the *id quod.* In order to rectify this situation, it is just as well to qualify Thomism as an "existential philosophy." To recall in this way the full meaning of *ens* in St. Thomas' language is to guard against impoverishing both *ens* itself and the philosophy whose first principle it is. It is to forget that the concept signified by *ens* implies direct reference to existence: *nam ens dicitur quasi esse habens.*[10]

It might be argued that a new expression like this is superfluous, because everyone is quite aware of what it is meant to express. This may be so. But it is not enough that everyone know it. Everyone must think it as well, and it is perhaps harder to do this than might be suspected. The history of the distinction between essence and existence and the endless controversies to which the same distinction is giving rise in our own day show that there is a very real difficulty. The very controversy itself is revealing. It shows how easy it is to substitute the abstract concept of existence for the concrete notion of the act-of-being, to "essentialize" the act-of-being, to make an act into the object of a simple concept. The temptation to do this is so strong that scholars began to do it in the first generation after St. Thomas. So far as we can tell from research done up to the present, Giles of Rome is the starting point of the controversies over essence and existence. Now it has often been noted that this resolute defender of the distinction spontaneously expressed himself as though essence were one thing, existence another. Whether he consciously went so far as to reify the act-of-being has not been adequately demonstrated. But for our purposes it is quite enough merely to observe that his language betrays a marked tendency to conceive of *esse* as though it were a thing, and consequently to conceive the distinction between essence and existence as between two things. Indeed, he actually writes: "Existence and essence are two things."[11] Many other professed Thomists since his time have expressed themselves in identical terms. But little is to be gained by making this distinction if existence itself is taken as an essence. To call Thomism an "existential philosophy" serves to focus attention on this very important point.

But we have still to come to the chief justification of the expression "existential" as applied to Thomistic philosophy.

It is not enough to say of all being that its concept connotes its *esse,* and that this *esse* must be taken as an act. It must also be said that this *esse* is the act of the same being whose concept connotes it. In every *esse habens* the *esse* is the act of the *habens* which possesses it, and the effect of this act upon what receives it is precisely this—to make a being of it.

If we accept this thesis in all its force and with all its ontological implications we come immediately to that well-known Thomistic position: *nomen ens imponitur ab ipso esse.*[12] So we might as well say that the act-of-being is the very core of being since being draws everything, even its name, from the act-of-being. What characterizes Thomistic ontology thus understood is not so much the distinction between essence and existence as the primacy of the act-of-being, not over and above being, but within it. To say that Thomistic philosophy is "existential" is to stress more forcibly than usual that a philosophy of being thus conceived is first of all a philosophy of the act-of-being.

There would be no advantage in making a great to-do about the act-of-being to the point of forgetting about the reality of the essence or even in allowing oneself to belittle its importance. Essences are the intelligible stuff of the world. Hence ever since Socrates, Plato, and Aristotle, philosophy has been one long hunt for essences. But the great question is to know whether we will bring home the game dead or alive. An essence is dead when it is deposited in the understanding as a quiddity, without preserving its contact with the act-of-being. It is certainly a lot easier to handle dead essences. Reason surrounds them from all sides through the definitions she can give them. The mind knows what each of them contains, is assured that none of them either is or can be anything other than it is, and is secure against surprise from any quarter. One can, without fear, deduce *a priori* the properties of essences and even calculate beforehand all their possible combinations.

But a philosophy of the act-of-being cannot be satisfied by such methods. It wants to know which, among all the possible combinations of these essences, has actually been realized. This will very probably lead it to assert that many real combinations of essences are the very ones which would have been regarded as rather unlikely or perhaps even judged *a priori* to be impossible. No doubt living essences find in their own acts of existing a fertility and invention quite beyond the powers of the bare definitions of their concepts. Neither essence nor existence has any meaning apart from the other. Taken separately, they are but two abstractions. The only finite reality which the understanding can fruitfully explore is concrete being itself, the original, unique, and, in the case of man, unpredictable and free actualization of an inexhaustible essence by its own act-of-being.

It is rather difficult to find in St. Thomas a single concrete problem whose solution is not ultimately based on this principle. He is primarily a theologian; and it is in constructing his theology with such striking technical originality that he best proves his fertility of mind. Wherever his philosophy touches his theology there is to be seen that new light with which the act-of-being illumines all it touches. Sometimes, when St. Thomas brings up problems and notions not central to his real interests, he allows them to stand like hardened essences in the margin, as it were, of his work. He neither takes the time to rejuvenate them by bringing them into contact with the act-of-being, nor appears to feel the need for doing so. But had he undertaken to do something like this, his philosophy would still remain with its face turned to the future. It will always be thus because the principle to which he makes his appeal is the fertile energy of an act rather than the fixed expression of a concept. A universe like this will never stop surrendering its secret unless someday it ceases to be.

This is because it is an ordered plurality of real essences perfected by their acts-of-being. Such must perforce be the case, since this universe is made up of beings, and since a being is "something having an act-of-being." Each being has its own proper act-of-being, distinct from that of every other: *habet enim res unaquaeque in seipsa esse proprium ab omnibus aliis rebus distinctum.*[13] Let us go further: it is by this act-of-being which it has that it is a being, because it is by it that it is–*unumquodque est per suum esse.*[14] And if we can say, as it is often said, that a being's acting proceeds from its act-of-being–*operatio sequitur esse*–it is not merely in the sense of "like being like operation," but also and especially because the acting of a being is only the unfolding in time of the first act-of-being which makes it to be. It is this way that we get a notion of the efficient cause which is in agreement with the immediate certitudes of common sense and confers on them that metaphysical profundity which they lack by nature. There are many who feel that the efficient cause extends right to the very existence of its effect. And it is here precisely that they find complete justification: *causa importat influxum quemdam in esse causati.*[15]

God is the only being to which this formula, which is valid for others, cannot as such be applied. Of Him it cannot be said that He is *by* His act-of-being, He is His act-of-being. Since we can only think in terms of being, and since we can only grasp a being as an essence, we have to say that God has an essence. But we must hasten to add that what in Him serves as an essence is His act-of-being: *In Deo non est aliud essentia vel quidditas quam suum esse.*[16] The act-of-being is the act of acts; it is the primary energy of a being and from it all operations proceed (*operatio sequitur esse*). Since God is very *Esse,* the operation belonging to Him and only to Him is the producing of acts-of-being. To produce an act-of-being is what we call creating. Creating is, therefore, action proper to God: *Ergo creatio est propria Dei actio.*[17] And as it is as Act-of-Being that He alone has the power to create, the act-of-being is His proper effect: *esse est ejus proprius effectus.*[18]

The linking of these fundamental notions is rigidly necessary. As God is by essence the Act-of-Being itself, the created act-of-being must be His proper effect: *Cum Deus sit ipsum esse per suam essentiam, oportet quod esse creatum sit proprius effectus ejus.*[19] Once this conclusion has been reached, it becomes in its turn the principle of a long line of consequences, for every effect resembles its cause, and that by which the effect is most profoundly indebted to its cause is that by which it resembles it most. If therefore being is created, its primary resemblance to God lies in its own act-of-being: *omne ens, in quantum habet esse, est Ei simile.*[20]

From this we see right away that it is the act-of-being in each being that is most intimate, most profound and metaphysically primary. Hence the necessity, in an ontology which does not stop at the level of abstract essence, of pushing right to the existential root of every being in order to arrive at the very principle of its unity: *unumquodque secundum idem habet esse et individuationem.*[21]

Such is, in a particular way, the solution of the problem of the metaphysical structure of the human being. Where the essence of the body and the essence of the soul are taken separately, there can be no return to that concrete unity which a man is. The unity of a man is first of all the unity of his soul, which is really only the unity of his own *esse*. It is the same act-of-being which has issued forth from the divine *Esse*, which passes through the soul, which animates the body, and which penetrates even the tiniest cells of that body. When all is said and done, this is why, although the soul is a substance, its union with the body is not accidental: "It does not follow that the body is united with it accidentally because the selfsame act-of-being that belongs to the soul is conferred on the body."[22]

Thus that knowing being, man, is bound to God by its deepest ontological root, and has to look no farther for the entrance to the paths which will lead it to the knowledge of its cause. If it pursues its metaphysical analysis far enough, any being whatsoever will place it in the presence of God. God is in everything as its cause. His action affects it in its very act-of-being. Hence it is at the heart of what it is that God is actually present: *Oportet quod Deus sit in omnibus rebus, et intime.*[23] To prove God is to reclimb by reason from any finite act-of-being whatsoever, to the pure Act-of-Being which causes it. Here the knowledge of man reaches its ultimate terminus. When God has been established as the supreme Act-of-Being, philosophy ends and mystical theology begins. More simply put, reason asserts that what it knows depends in its very root upon the God it does not know: *cum Deo quasi ignoto conjungimur.*[24] To understand St. Thomas in this way is not at all to de-essentialize his philosophy. It is rather to restore real essence to it, to re-establish it in its full right. Essence is far more than the quiddity which satisfies reason; it is that by which, and in which, being has existence: *quidditatis nomen sumitur ex hoc quod diffinitionem sig-*

nificat; sed essentia dicitur secundum quod per eam et in ea ens habet esse.[25] There is nothing further to be said. But it is worth repeating, because the human mind is so constituted that anyone is quite capable of forgetting it.

It has been rightly insisted that we must distinguish whatever separates *problem* from *mystery,* and upon the need for the metaphysician to pass beyond the first plane into the second. But neither is to be sacrificed for the sake of the other. When philosophy abandons the problem in order to immerse itself in the mystery, it ceases to be philosophy and becomes mysticism. Whether we like it or not, problems are the very stuff out of which philosophy is fashioned. To think is to know by concepts. Yet as soon as we begin to interpret the real in terms of quidditative concepts we are involved in the order of problems. We are here face to face with the inescapable, and even those who tend most strongly to escape from it must perforce recognize it. "What cannot be problematized cannot be examined nor objectified, and this by definition."[26] If philosophizing is a kind of examining of the real, philosophy can deal with the real only to the extent that the real can be problematized. The philosopher can get to God only by way of the problem of His existence, which the problem of His nature follows hard upon. He is then confronted with the problem of God's action and of God's government in the world. There are as many problems as there are mysteries, and they are met not only when philosophy talks about God. Man's science is alive with mysteries, as knowledge and liberty so eloquently testify.

Nor does mystery dwell only in the world of matter. Reason has for centuries been challenged by such obscure facts as efficient causality and the presence of quality. To give up the problematizing of mysteries would be to give up philosophizing. This is not the way to seek the solution of the crisis confronting philosophy today. But if we must not abandon problems, neither ought we to abandon mystery. The real danger begins where problems are confronted by the mystery and pretend to be self-sufficient and to lay claim to an autonomy that they do not actually possess. The moment a philosophy makes this mistake it is victimized by its own combinations of abstract concepts and enters a game that will never end. In fact it enters the realm of the antinomies of pure reason. Kant was not wrong when he said that escape from the antinomies was impossible. We need only add that the philosophic reason has every invitation not to enter, because such a reason ought not to be a discussion of pure problems or a flight from mystery; it ought to be a perpetually renewed effort to treat every problem as though it were bound up in a mystery or to problematize mystery by examining it with the help of concepts.

There is, to be sure, a mystery that can be called the object *par excellence* of philosophy, since metaphysics presupposes it; namely, the act-of-being. The philosophy of St. Thomas locates this mystery in the heart of the real and so insures itself against the risk, so fatal to metaphysical thought, of growing sterile in the very purity of abstraction. To a certain point, Aristotle had already walked in this way. His reformation had been to give philosophy an object that was, not the ideal essence conceived by thought, but real being as it is and as it behaves. With Aristotle, *ousia*, reality, is no longer the Idea, it is substance that merits the title. In order to measure the scope of this revolution, we have only to compare the solutions to the problem of the first principle of all things proposed by Aristotle and Plato. When Plato takes up the problem, he sets out from an analysis of the real which disengages the intelligible element from it and then proceeds back from one intelligible condition to another until he comes to the first. It is the Good in itself; an Idea, that is, an hypostasized abstraction. Aristotle sets out from the concrete substance given in sensible experience; that is, he sets out from the existent. Then, contrary to Plato, he begins by bringing into evidence the active principle of its being and of its operations. Then he proceeds back from one ontological condition to another until he comes to the first condition. It is Pure Act that thus becomes the highest reality because it alone fully deserves the name of being—that on which everything else depends because everything else imitates it in an eternally recommenced effort to imitate in time its immovable actuality.

The distinctive work of St. Thomas was to push into the interior of being itself. He pushed back as far as the secret principle that establishes, not the actuality of being as substance, but the actuality of being as being. To the age-old question (even Aristotle referred to it as old), What is being? St. Thomas replied: It is that which has the act of existing. An ontology such as this loses nothing of the intelligible reality accessible to man under the form of concepts. Like that of Aristotle, it never grows tired of analyzing, classifying, defining, but it always remembers that, in what is most intimate within it, the real object it is struggling to define is beyond definition. It is not an abstraction; it is not even a thing; it is not even merely the formal act which makes it to be such-and-such a thing; it is the act that posits it as a real being in existence, by actualizing the very form that makes it intelligible.

A philosophy like this is at grips with the secret energy that causes its object. It finds in the meaning of its limitation the principle of its very fertility. It will never believe that it has come to the end of its inquiry because its end is beyond what it can enclose within the limits of a concept. In the case of Thomism, we are not dealing with a philosophy that turns its back on existence and consequently cannot see it. Rather we have to do with a philosophy that faces existence and never stops looking at it. Of course, we cannot see existence, but we know it is there and we can at least posit it, by an act of judgment, as the hidden root of what we can see and attempt to define. This is also why Thomistic ontology refuses to be limited to what the human mind knew about being in the thirteenth century. It even refuses to allow itself to be halted by what we know about it in the twentieth. It invites us to look beyond present-day science toward that primitive energy from which both knowing subject and object known arise.

If all beings "are" in virtue of their own act-of-being, each one of them breaks through the enclosing frame of its own definition. Better, perhaps, it has no proper definition: *individuum est ineffabile.* Yes, the individual is ineffable, but because it is too big rather than because it is too little, St. Thomas' universe is peopled with living essences sprung from a source as secret and rich as their very life. His world, by a filiation more profound than so many superficial dissimilarities might indicate, projects into Pascal's world rather than into Descartes'. In Pascal's world, the imagination is more likely to grow weary of producing concepts than nature to tire of providing them. There "all things hide a mystery; all things are veils hiding God."[27] Is not this what St. Thomas had already said with a simplicity no less striking than Pascal's: God is in all things, and that intimately—*Deus est in omnibus rebus, et intime?* For of such a universe two things can be said at the same time. Everything in it possesses its own act-of-being, distinct from that of all others. Yet, deep within each of them there lies hidden the same Act-of-Being, which is God.

If we want to recapture the true meaning of Thomism we have to go beyond the tightly woven fabric of its philosophical doctrines into its soul or spirit. What lies back of the ideas is a deep religious life, the interior warmth of a soul in search of God. There have in the recent past been prolonged and subtle disputes as to whether, according to St. Thomas, men experience a natural desire for their supernatural end. Theologians must ultimately decide such questions. They have to reach some kind of agreement about expressions and formulas which concern God's transcendence and still do not allow man to be separated from Him. The historian can at least say that St. Thomas leaves questions only partially settled, like the projecting stones of an unfinished wall awaiting the hand of a second builder. The very gaps in St. Thomas' work suggest that nature awaits the finishing touches of grace.

At the basis of this philosophy, as at the basis of all Christian philosophy, there is a deep awareness of wretchedness and need for a comforter who can be only God: "Natural reason tells man that he is subject to a higher being because of the defects he discerns in himself, defects for which he requires help and direction from some higher being. Whatever this being may be, it is commonly spoken of as God."[28] This is the natural feeling which grace excites in the Christian soul and which the perfection of charity brings to fulfillment when this soul is the soul of a saint. The burning desire of God which in a John of the Cross overflows into lyric poems is here transcribed into the language of pure ideas. Their impersonal formulation must not make us forget that they are nourished on the desire for God and that their end is the satisfaction of this desire.

There is no point in seeking, as some appear to do, an interior life underlying Thomism which is specifically and essentially different from Thomism itself. We ought not to think that the learned arrangement of the *Summa Theologiae* and the unbroken advance of reason constructing stone by stone this mighty edifice was for St. Thomas but the fruit of a superficial activity beneath which there moved deeper, richer, and more religious thinking. The interior life of St. Thomas, in so far as the hidden stirrings of so powerful a personality can be revealed, seems to have been just what it should have been to be expressed in such a doctrine. Nothing could be more desirable, nothing more indicative of an ardent will than his demonstrations fashioned from clearly defined ideas, presented in perfectly precise statements, and placed in a carefully balanced arrangement. Only a complete giving of himself can explain his mastery of expression and organization of philosophic ideas. Thus his *Summa Theologiae*, with its abstract clarity, its impersonal transparency, crystallizes before our very eyes and for all eternity his interior life. If we would recapture the deep and intense spirit of this interior life, there is nothing more useful than to reassemble for ourselves, but in terms of the order he gave them, the various elements that go to make up his remarkable *Summa*. We should study its internal structure and strive to arouse in ourselves the conviction of its necessity. Only that will to understand, shared between ourselves and St. Thomas the philosopher, will serve to make us see that this tremendous work is but the outward glow of an invisible fire, and that there is to be found behind the order of its ideas that powerful impulse which gathered them together.

Only thus does Thomism appear in all its beauty. It is a philosophy which creates excitement by means of pure ideas, and does so by sheer faith in the value of proofs and denials based on reason. This will become more evident to those who are disturbed by the very real difficulties encountered in the beginning, if they consider what St. Thomas' spirituality really was. If it were true that his philosophy were inspired by one spirit, his spirituality by another, the difference would become apparent by comparing his manner of thinking with his manner of praying. But a study of the prayers of St.

Thomas which have been preserved, and which are so satisfying that the Church has placed them in the Roman breviary, shows that they are not characterized by the note of rapture or emotion or spiritual relish common enough in many forms of prayer. St. Thomas' fervor is completely expressed in the loving petitioning of God for what He should be asked for, and in becoming manner. His phrases tend to be rather rigid because the rhythms are so balanced and regular. But his fervor is genuine, deep, and readily recognizable and reflects the careful rhythms of his thought: "I pray Thee, that this holy Communion may be to me, not guilt for punishment, but a saving intercession for pardon. Let it be to me an armor of faith and a shield of good-will. Let it be to me a casting out of vices; a driving away of all evil desires and fleshly lusts; an increase of charity, patience, humility, obedience, and all virtues; a firm defense against the plots of all my enemies, both seen and unseen; a perfect quieting of all motions of sin, both in my flesh and in my spirit; a firm cleaving unto Thee, the only and true God, and a happy ending of my life."[29] Spirituality like this is more eager for light than for taste. The rhythm of his phrases, the pleasing sonority of his Latin words never modifies the perfect order of his ideas. But the discriminating taste can always perceive, beneath the balanced cadence of his expression, a religious emotion that is almost poetic.

Indeed, because he serves reason so lovingly, St. Thomas actually becomes a poet, and, if we believe a disinterested judge, the greatest Latin poet of the middle ages. Now it is remarkable that the lofty beauty of the works attributed to this poet of the Eucharist depend almost entirely on the aptness and concentration of his expressions. Poems like the *Oro te devote* and *Ecce panis angelorum* can almost be called little theological treatises and they have supplied generations of faithful Christians with inspiration and devotion. Perhaps the most distinctive of all his poems is the *Pange lingua* which inspired Rémy de Gourmont to say, in words matching, almost, the flawless beauty of the style he was attempting to describe: "The inspiration of St. Thomas is fired by an unwavering genius, a genius at once strong, sure, confident, and exact. What he wants to say, he speaks out boldly, and in words so resounding that doubt grows fearful and takes to flight."[30]

> *Pange lingua gloriosi corporis mysterium*
> *Sanguinisque pretiosi quem in mundi pretium*
> *Fructus ventris generosi Rex effudit gentium.*
>
> *Nobis datus, nobis natus ex intacta Virgine*
> *Et in mundo conversatus, sparso verbi semine*
> *Sui moras incolatus miro clausit ordine.*

And so we pass from St. Thomas' philosophy to his prayer, and from his prayer to his poetry without becoming aware of any change of context. And indeed there is no change! His philosophy is as rich in beauty as his poetry is laden with thought. Of both *Summa Theologiae* and *Pange lingua* we can say that his is an unwavering genius, strong, sure, confident, and exact. What he wants to say, he speaks out boldly and with a firmness of thought that doubt itself grows fearful and takes to flight.

Nowhere else, perhaps, does so demanding a reason respond to the call of so religious a heart. St. Thomas considered man as marvelously equipped for the knowledge of phenomena; but he did not think that the most adequate human knowledge was the most useful and the most beautiful to which man could aspire. He locates man's reason among sensible things as in its proper domain; but in equipping it for the exploration and conquest of this kingdom, he invites it to prefer another which is not merely the kingdom of man but that of the children of God. Such is the thought of St. Thomas. If we grant that a philosophy is not to be defined in terms of the elements it borrows but in terms of the spirit that quickens it, we shall see in Thomism neither Plotinianism nor Aristotelianism but, above all, Christianity. It is a philosophy that set out to express in rational language the total destiny of the Christian man. But, while constantly reminding him that here below he travels the paths of exile along which there is no light and no horizon, yet it has never ceased to guide his steps toward those distant peaks from which can be seen, far off in the mists, the borders of the Promised Land.

NOTES

1. *Summa Theologiae*, I, q. 44, a. 1.
2. *Summa Contra Gentiles*, II, chap. 15.
3. *Sum. Theol.*, II–II, q. 180, a. 5, ad 1; *De Venitate*, q. XIII, a. 3.
4. *Summa Contra Gentiles*, I, chap. 5, ad *Apparet*.
5. Jacques Maritain, *A Preface to Metaphysics* (*Seven Lessons on Being*) (London: Sheed and Ward, 1943), pp. 21, 24. The lectures published in this volume date from 1932 to 1933.
6. *Op. cit.*, p. 23.
7. *Ibid.*
8. *Op. cit.*, p. 24.
9. *In Boet. de Hebdomadibus*, chap. II; *Opuscula Omnia*, ed. P. Mandonnet (Paris: P. Lethielleux, 1927), vol. I, pp. 173–174.
10. *In XII Metaphysicorum*, lectio 1, ed. Cathala, no. 2419.
11. Giles of Rome, *Theoremata de Esse et Essentia*, ed. E. Hocedez (Louvain, 1930), p. 127, line 12. On the interpretation of this expression, see the Introduction to this work, pp. 54–56. As Father Hocedez puts it, the distinction *inter rem et rem*, taken literally, amounts to making the distinction between essence and existence a distinction between essence and essence (p. 55).
12. *In IV Metaph.*, lect. 2, ed. Cathala, no. 558.
13. *Summa Contra Gentiles*, I, chap. 14, ad *Est autem*.
14. *Op. cit.*, I, chap. 22, ad *Item, unumquodque*; cf. *op. cit.*, II, chap. 53.
15. *In IV Metaph.*, lect. 1, ed. Cathala, no. 751. On the doctrine, see J. de Finance, *Etre et agir dans la philosophie de saint Thomas* (Paris: G. Beauchesne, 1945).
16. *Summa Contra Gentiles*, I, chap. 21, ad *Ex his autem*.
17. *Ibid.*, ad *Adhuc, effectus*.
18. *Op. cit.*, II, chap. 22, ad *Item, omnis virtus*.
19. *Sum. Theol.*, I, q. 8, a. 1.
20. *Summa Contra Gentiles*, II, chap. 22, ad *Nullo autem*; cf. II, chap. 53.
21. *Quaest. Disp. de Anima*, a. 1, ad 2.
22. *Ibid.*, ad 2.
23. *Sum. Theol.*, I, q. 8, a. 1.
24. *Summa Contra Gentiles*, III, chap. 49.
25. *De Ente et Essentia*, chap. I.
26. Gabriel Marcel, *Etre et avoir* (Paris: Aubier, 1935), p. 183.
27. Pascal, *Pensées et opuscules*, ed. L. Brunschvicg (ninth ed., Paris: Librairie Hachette, 1920), p. 215.
28. St. Thomas Aquinas, *Sum. Theol.*, II–II, q. 85, a. 1.

29. It is interesting to compare this prayer with the prayer attributed to St. Bonaventure which immediately follows it in the breviary. The contrast is striking.
30. R. de Gourmont, *Le latin mystique* (Paris: Les Editions Crès, 1922), pp. 273–274, 275. All texts dealing with the spirituality of St. Thomas are brought together by Father Sertillanges in his *Prières de saint Thomas d' Aquin* (Paris: Art Catholique, 1920).

PART FIVE

The Christian Teacher

As an educator, Gilson has been an uncompromising disciple and defender of the high calling of the Christian teacher. The work of such a teacher touches something divine at two moments: in the activity of teaching and in the mind of the student. In a world in which we have but one Master, the teacher is a servant of truth; in a world in which the intellect is a participation of divine light, the teacher is taking part in a divine work: the growth of the human person in the sight of God. Such a high estimation of teaching explains Gilson's critical views on the teaching of philosophy today, his opposition to mediocrity whenever he has found it in Catholic education, and his entire unwillingness to downgrade intelligence or learning in the name of democracy.

17. Thomas Aquinas and Our Colleagues

I wish first to apologize for the somewhat cryptic title of this lecture.* The only justification it ever had in my mind was that I could not find a better one, and, after all, what it says is exactly what I have in mind to say. I do think I have a message from Thomas Aquinas for our colleagues, and his feast day is a good day on which to deliver it. Yet, before beginning to say what it is, I beg to introduce two remarks concerning my personal intentions in this matter.

First of all, although I consider Thomas Aquinas my spiritual father and my guide, I would not, in any way, make him responsible for my own conclusions. In the first part of this lecture, I shall do my utmost to let him deliver his own message in his own words; to the extent that a historian can make sure of the meaning of another man's word, I shall try to report some statements made by Thomas Aquinas in the thirteenth century, and to elucidate their meaning. In the second part, I shall attempt to answer the questions raised by these texts. But, and this is my second preliminary remark, my tentative answer will in no way engage the responsibility of Thomas Aquinas. Given the basic nature of the problem at stake, if what Thomas has said about it was true in the thirteenth century, it is still true in the twentieth. But when it comes to applying this standing truth to our own times, there is no point in consulting the complete works of Thomas Aquinas, the answer is simply not there. We are on our own. Such is the reason why I wish to make it clear that my tentative conclusion will be given under my sole responsibility.

I. WHAT IS THE PROBLEM?

I found myself unexpectedly confronted with it about the end of 1951. A Catholic institution invited me to give a lecture on this precise question: What is the place of philosophy

* Given as an Aquinas Lecture at the Aquinas Foundation at Princeton University, March 7, 1953.

in the curriculum of a liberal arts college? My first reaction was that I did not know. I knew that all Catholic colleges make it a point to teach philosophy to their pupils, and that the deeper their affection for Thomas Aquinas is, the more convinced they feel that every boy and girl should be given a chance to learn something about his doctrine. And, indeed, why not? I could not find in this charming invitation any problem to tackle. Naturally it is always possible to say: Children, do remember that philosophy is the love of Wisdom, which is better than strength since a wise man is better than a strong man, etc. But to preach is one thing and to teach is another. So I would not have given this project another thought were it not for the fact that, vaguely ashamed of my complete lack of opinion on the subject, I made the careless move of consulting Thomas Aquinas about it. Naturally, I did not ask him how to teach philosophy in a twentieth-century American college; I just asked him: Dear St. Thomas, how do you think that we should teach philosophy in general? I got an answer, and I have been worrying about it ever since. For my own peace of mind, I would prefer not to have heard of it.

While writing his commentaries on the *Ethics* of Aristotle, Thomas chanced upon the passage of Book I, Chapter 2, where the Philosopher, who also was a seasoned professor, asks himself to whom political philosophy should be taught. His answer is: Not to young men, anyway. Everybody is a good judge of what he knows well. Now political philosophy deals with problems of which a young man has no experience; how then could he form correct judgments about matters of which he knows nothing? This sounds somewhat strange to our ears. One does not imagine a professor of political philosophy, nor, for that matter, of what they call political science, dismissing his class with this simple remark: you are still too young to form correct judgments in matters in which the political life of the city is involved; please go home, or study something else in the meanwhile; in a few years, when you have acquired some political experience, you will be welcome to share in this adult entertainment.

This would not be prudent advice. Apart from the fact that professors of political philosophy themselves seldom have any political experience, except reading their daily newspaper, it is insulting to tell modern young men that there is any teaching whatsoever which they are not fit to receive. This is plain mental cruelty. The proper thing to say is that, precisely because they have not yet been corrupted by political life, young men have a perfectly open mind about it. To make full measure, it might even be a good rhetorical precaution to add that, since we enjoy the privilege of living in democratic societies, in which any citizen is as good as any other citizen, young men and women should not hesitate to speak up in such matters. The responsibility of the common political good is theirs, and since they will soon have a right to vote, who has any right to tell them that they are not fit auditors in political philosophy?

I am not suggesting that such advice would not be a sound one to give; my only point is that this is not at all what Aristotle said. And, as if to make things still worse, the Philosopher adds one more reason in favor of his opinion. Political philosophy, he says, is not a speculative science; it is a practical one: its end is not cognition, but action. When I ask myself a question concerning the aim and purpose of political life, my ultimate interest is in knowing what I myself should do about it. Now, precisely because political matters are practical ones, their discussion requires a dispassionate judgment. This again is not a view popular in our own times. In my own country, at least, there is a new school of thought, and even of art, which makes it a point that in order to be genuine, thought and art should be, as they say, "engaged." Now, engaged thinking is passionate thinking. But Aristotle was a curious man. He wanted us to embark in politics in order to know what it is and then, on reaching the age of philosophical reflection, to disembark in order to judge in a dispassionate way this passionately acquired experience. Young men, Aristotle thought, simply are not of age to perform this difficult trick. They are not lacking the passions which are required in view of action; on the contrary, they are so full of them that they cannot forget them when the time for philosophical speculation is ripe. Now, please, do not tell me that Aristotle is an out-of-date philosopher whose personal opinions are of no importance to us. As a matter of fact, *qua* opinions, they are of no importance whatsoever; only, this time, he was talking about facts. What is the age for those absolute and passionate political convictions that are proof against any kind of abstract reasoning? Twenty, twenty-five, and occasionally longer if they survive in the minds of ineffectual dreamers who sincerely believe, because they themselves never act, that real political life is the concrete duplicate of some abstract political philosophy. Youth is the time when man should be passionate, because it is the right age for action and self-sacrifice; all that Aristotle says is that, precisely because youth is the proper time for action, it is not the proper time for speculation.

And what does Thomas Aquinas say to this? He simply goes a little farther. Aristotle had been mainly concerned with political philosophy. By a very neat trick, Thomas elicits from Aristotle this much wider conclusion: "Aristotle concludes what he intended to prove; namely, that a young man is no fit auditor in politics, *nor in the whole of Ethics*, which is included under politics." Now, if it be true that we should not teach our students any ethics, the situation becomes rather embarrassing for our colleagues. Looking at the problem in the light of my own experience, which is limited but extends to a few countries, I would say that even if universities and colleges were to drop the teaching of all the parts of philosophy but one, the surviving one would be ethics. The reasons for this are obvious, and are not primarily concerned with philosophical speculation. Where totalitarian states take an active interest in promoting some sort of ethical orthodoxy, they see to it that it be taught. In democratic countries, the teaching of ethics is looked upon as a kind of substitute for the teaching of a religion which universities cannot teach. It helps to keep law and order. But Thomas Aquinas had something different in mind; namely, moral *philosophy*, which is a pure intellectual speculation about the rules of moral action. Ultimately, ethics is about actions, but its proper function is to tell us, in the light of objective and dispassionate reason, what our ethical decisions should be even in the heat of passionate action. To this attitude, the spontaneous reaction of youth is that Aristotle was a pedant. Away with Aristotle, they say; if that old man does not understand that we are full of passions because we are full of life, we don't want to attend his lectures anyway. Yes, but then there is no problem, because this is precisely the reason why Aristotle and Thomas Aquinas are refusing to teach them ethics. Youth is the proper time in which to be given a proper moral training, which is a very different thing from speculating about moral philosophy. What Thomas Aquinas says is both precise and simple: "Moral science teaches men to follow reason and to keep away from the things to which they feel attracted by the passions of their souls, such as concupiscence, anger, and the like." Because young people are normally passionate, there is no use in asking them to discuss moral problems in a dispassionate way. Let them wait a few years. Time and age will do their work. Those boys and girls will calm down. Later on, if they still feel like studying philosophy, Thomas Aquinas will be delighted to teach them ethics.

Since I would not like to attribute to Thomas a theory of my own, even on the basis of what he says, I beg to add one more remark he expressly made about this problem. A ready objection to his conclusion was that there are quite a few old boys whose morality is not noticeably less shaky in their old age than it was at the time of their youth. The fact that a man is old is therefore no reason why we should teach him ethics. To which Thomas rejoins that, indeed, it is not. However advanced in years he may be, if a man has not outgrown the passions of his youth, he still does not qualify as a student in moral philosophy. But, and this is the point I wish to stress, the reverse is *not* true. Even if he has reached in his youth the moral maturity of a riper age, a young man still does not qualify for this study. The reason for this is simple. Moral philosophy is speculation in view of moral action. However morally mature he may be, a young man lacks the intellectual maturity required for philosophical speculation in those matters. In Thomas Aquinas's own terms: "Just as he who is young in years does not measure up to the end of this science, inasmuch as it aims to know, so also he who is young in conduct falls short of that end of this science inasmuch as it aims to act."[1] If we were looking for a loophole, let us face the fact that Thomas Aquinas has carefully stopped the last one. What he is telling our colleagues is simply that, as professors of ethics and of political philosophy, they can have no young students.

Nor is this all. The last quoted sentence of Thomas contains a rather disturbing element. Let us consider it more closely. If a morally mature young man is still lacking *intellectual* maturity simply because he is young, our conclusion should extend far beyond the orders of ethics and of political philosophy. He should also be immature with regard to other things. As a matter of fact, Thomas says, he is. In another passage of the same Commentary on the *Nicomachean Ethics* of Aristotle, he fondly develops a remark made by the Philosopher to the effect that boys can become mathematicians, but not physicists, and still less metaphysicians. Mathematics is abstract enough to be simple; yet, at least in its beginning, it remains close enough to concrete reality to offer an object accessible to the mind. If he is gifted for this kind of study, a boy can learn mathematics very rapidly. In point of fact, the history of the sciences abounds in precocious mathematical geniuses. In physics, Thomas goes on to say, things are already different. Natural science requires a lot of experience and, in turn, experience requires a lot of time. Now time, by definition, is what youth has not yet got. There is therefore little hope for us to turn our students into physicists, and, for still another reason quite different from the preceding one, there is no hope at all that we may succeed in turning them into metaphysicians.

The object of metaphysics is a pure intelligible. True enough, all our cognitions have to be about something intelligible, otherwise they would not be cognitions at all, but metaphysics is different from the other types of knowledge in this, that its object should be grasped beyond both sense knowledge and imagination. Absolutely speaking, this is a psychological impossibility. The intellect of the metaphysician is like any other human intellect: it draws its data from sense perception and never thinks without images; but, precisely, metaphysical speculation requires a special effort to reach, within or above reality, elements that can be neither perceived nor imagined. In this case, instead of being a help, sensations and images are a hindrance. Now, Thomas says, "the young can easily grasp what falls under imagination, but when it comes to what escapes both sense and imagination, their mind does not attain it, partly because their intellect has not yet been trained for that kind of reflection, and partly because of many changes in their nature." What does Thomas mean by these many changes in their nature (*propter plurimas mutationes naturae*)? He does not say. Up to now, although you certainly realized that I was commenting upon his own Commentary on Aristotle, I feel fairly certain that I have not betrayed his thought. This time, on the contrary, I am forced to take a chance. I therefore make bold to suggest that, according to Thomas Aquinas, metaphysical thinking presupposes a physiological maturity which the body of man does not reach before a certain age. Without entering the practically infinite field of psychological considerations, I beg to suggest that, when he spoke of changes taking place in the *nature* of man, Thomas Aquinas had something like that in mind. Most certainly, because he said it so often, he thought that the passions of youth are an impediment even in abstract metaphysical thinking, but I think he saw farther than this, and here is my reason for thinking he did.

In reading Thomas' explanation, one may feel tempted to get rid of his conclusion by the normal reaction of the reader who does not like what he reads: Thomas does not really mean it. I am afraid that he does. Thomas is simply restating a truth which Aristotle had seen more than sixteen centuries before him. And Aristotle had seen it, not because he was a philosopher, but because he was a seasoned professor of philosophy. To sum it up in his own words, his personal experience was that, when it comes to metaphysical propositions, "young people do not understand, they just talk" (*Nic. Eth.*, VI, 8, 1142a 19–20). They do not understand because, not being able to grasp the abstract meaning of the terms, they cannot assent to the meaning of the propositions they form. Here again, if we were looking for a loophole, let us face the fact that Thomas Aquinas is carefully stopping the last one. We might prefer to make him say: Young people cannot be metaphysicians, but let us teach them metaphysics now, they will understand it later. His precise point is that what cannot be understood cannot be taught at all. These boys, Thomas says, do not have in their minds what is in their mouth: *non attingunt mente, licet dicant ore.*[2] Translated into plain language, this means that young students in metaphysics can only be taught to repeat words which they cannot understand. A well-known class of birds can perform the same trick; only, what these birds are taught is usually more fun than metaphysics.

II

Before such texts, two reactions are possible. First, we may decide to pay no attention to them. I hasten to say that this is the sound social attitude, and I could not advise you too strongly to adopt it. When taken seriously, philosophical conclusions mean trouble. Philosophy is about ideas, and ideas are revolutionary by essence for the simple reason that concrete reality is not made up of ideas; it is a confused mixture out of which we extract pure ideas, none of which is to be found there in its purity. All great revolutions are carried on through the strength of some idea: Liberty, Equality, Fraternity, Race, Class, and so on indefinitely, and they all make havoc of reality. Yet, without these pure Ideas, reality would not make sense and we must attempt to order it in their light. We must at least face ideas, and face them honestly, fearlessly, without either blindly expecting that things can be made integrally conformable to them, or still more blindly refusing to see them in the hope that, if they are not seen, they will not set forth their necessary consequences. Fortunately for us, the problem at stake has nothing to do with the future of human societies at large. Thomas Aquinas is simply confronting us with a proposition whose practical consequences would only affect our colleagues, the professors of philosophy. Should we continue to teach young students metaphysics and ethics?

Let me first answer a question you certainly have in mind: What do I call "young"? When I said "the young," or "young men," I was trying a literal rendering of the Latin word *juvenis* used by Thomas Aquinas in his Commentary. Naturally, the question arises: What did he himself have in mind when he was using this word? What age is Thomas thinking of when he says *juvenis?* A first indication comes to us from his Commentary on the *Book of Causes* in which, describing the course of studies followed by the philosophers of old, Thomas tells us that they wisely allotted the later part of their lives to the study of metaphysics and ethics. This text,[3] and it is an incontrovertible one, cannot be made to mean that, to Thomas Aquinas, a youth was a fifteen-year-old boy. Even at twenty, a man has not yet reached the later part of his life. According to the English thirteenth-century Franciscan, Roger Bacon, youth (*juventus*) came to an end after, let us say, thirty years of age.[4] If this were true, our colleagues should expect a sharp drop in the enrollment of their students in metaphysics, political philosophy, and ethics. All boys under thirty should be turned out of our colleges and universities and invited to put in a new application after reaching their thirty-first year. As I do not wish to complicate the problem more than is strictly necessary, I shall refrain from asking Bacon and Thomas Aquinas what we should do with girls. We all agree that thirty-year-old girls are still very far from the end of their youth; my point is that Thomas never foresaw a time when teen-agers would be taught metaphysics and ethics. I am well aware of the fact that we are no longer in the thirteenth century, but one of Thomas' objections to the teaching of metaphysics to young people was that such studies "transcend imagination and require a robust intellect."[5] Granting that, unlike their medieval sisters, modern girls find it easy to transcend imagination, Thomas would still maintain that they should wait for the end of their youth before tackling metaphysics and ethics. According to his own computation, which is not the same as that of Roger Bacon, adolescence ends at twenty-five; youth (*juventus*) ends at fifty; old age (*senectus*) ends at seventy, after which comes senility (*senium*), which lasts, Thomas calmly says, up to the end. Thomas has certainly anticipated by seven centuries the modern definition of youth so far as womanhood is concerned, but regarding our problem, this means that, for men and women, philosophical life begins at fifty. Incidentally, this is the third writing of Thomas Aquinas I have quoted in this lecture,[6] and they all agree: 1) young people are not fit to study metaphysics; 2) youth ends at fifty; 3) the ancient philosophers used to allot the later part of their lives to the study of metaphysics. I do not consider this a particularly important part of his doctrine; my only point is that, having said this, he stuck to it.[7]

You may well wonder why we should make a fuss about a few old texts. I am not saying anybody else should, but I must confess that I do because what they say agrees with my own experience. I distinctly remember a young man of twenty passionately interested in metaphysical problems, but fully aware of the fact that he could not understand the metaphysicians. He thought it wise to bide his time and to teach the history of philosophy in order to learn philosophy before teaching it. Many years later, he began to realize that the history of philosophy requires identically the same intellectual maturity as philosophy itself, because unless you are something of a philosopher, you may well report what philosophers have said, you cannot understand it. Their words are in your mouth, Thomas would say, their ideas are not in your mind. He then began to understand why Henri Bergson was living in constant fear of his future historians. Just as art critics say what they think about what artists do, so historians of philosophy say what they understand of what philosophers think. In both cases, it seldom amounts to much.

With those of our colleagues who think there is no problem, however, I shall have no quarrel. My only quarrel is with myself. *If* what Thomas says is true, what right did I have to teach philosophy at an age when I could not understand it? And what right have I to teach it, even now, to boys and girls who are still far from being of philosophical age?

To this question, my first defense reaction is to ask Thomas: "How did you do it yourself?" For indeed, when he wrote all this, Thomas could not ignore the fact that his whole life was flatly contradicting his words. When he died, in 1274, Thomas was forty-nine years old, just one year short of the proper age he himself requires from a student in metaphysics. According to his own computation, he never reached the end of his youth. Yet he left us the thirty-four volumes of his complete works in the Fretté edition, and nobody could say that they are not crammed with metaphysics and ethics. But there is more. When he wrote his epoch-making treatise *On Being and Essence*, in 1256, Thomas was thirty-one years old, which is nearly twenty years too young to understand metaphysics; at that age, he had no right to make any metaphysical discovery; only he did. When he began to learn metaphysics under Albert the Great, in 1245, Thomas was twenty years old; Albert should have sent him back to his convent and told him to stay there for thirty more years before daring to approach metaphysical problems. It would have been too bad because, thirty years later, the old professor was still alive, but the pupil was dead. My own question to Thomas Aquinas is: How do you reconcile your own doctrine with your own life? Why should we hesitate to teach philosophy, beyond logic, to students who are twenty years old, since this was exactly your age when you yourself learned it?

Thomas Aquinas never answered this question because he himself never asked it. But the very fact that the question never occurred to his mind is an important element of the answer. Had he placed himself in the grossly inconsistent position we just described, he would have noticed it. Any man writing, when he is thirty-five or forty, a metaphysical treatise in which he says that nobody should study metaphysics until he is fifty, would perceive the discrepancy between what he says and what he does. It takes no metaphysical genius to notice it. My own suggestion is that the reason why Thomas Aquinas did not feel the contradiction was that, in his mind, there was none. But the explanation of why a contradiction may not have existed in Thomas' own mind could well sound scandalous to many modern ears. Today, if we tell a theologian that he is not a philosopher, he feels insulted; had we told Thomas Aquinas he was a philosopher, he would have felt insulted. To tell the whole truth, I do not think he would have understood the meaning of the proposition.

Returning for a moment to strictly historical ground, let us observe that, in the thirteenth century, the word "philosopher" had a very precise meaning. Its first connotation was "a pagan." From this point of view, we should have today a very great number of philosophers; only, most of them are perhaps too young to philosophize. Young pagans may be very intelligent; some of them may eventually become very great philosophers, but so long as they are young, they have nothing to philosophize about: they have not yet reached the age when natural reason alone, unaided by religious faith, is prepared, if not to ask metaphysical questions, at least modestly to accept their answers. In the thirteenth century, however, the situation was different. All those who were interested in philosophy were Christians; in fact, all those who were teaching it were either monks, or priests, or, at least, clerics. And they were not interested in philosophy because they wanted to become philosophers, but rather, at least in most cases, because they wanted to become theologians. True enough, many of them were anxious to use philosophy in their theology, but the masters had a name for those who philosophized in theology; they called such a man a *philosophans* (one who philosophizes); they would not call him a "philosopher" (*philosophus*). Now while Thomas Aquinas said that young men were not qualified to study metaphysics, including natural theology, he certainly never said, nor thought, that young people should not study revealed theology, including what of metaphysics and ethics it may contain. He could not perceive any contradiction between what he had written and what he had done, because the two questions were entirely different. He had written that a man with no religion, or, at least, with no religious revelation, if his ultimate goal were to become a philosopher, had better wait for the later part of his life before handling metaphysical problems. Himself a young Christian, and already a monk, Thomas had studied philosophy in view of becoming a theologian in his thirties, and not at all a "philosopher" such as Plato or Aristotle. Two questions, two answers. Do you intend to become a metaphysician? Then you can hardly begin too late. Do you want to become a theologian? Then you cannot begin too soon.

What does this mean for our own problem? So far as I can see, what makes the difference between the two cases is the presence or absence of a religious revelation. Now, obviously, no religious revelation can teach us any metaphysics, nor even, to the extent that it is a speculative science known in the light of natural reason, ethics. God commands or forbids, He is no professor of ethics. God tells us about Himself; He does not give us metaphysical demonstrations of what He says. Then how can revelation help the philosopher? Not by giving him ready-made conclusions which he has only to demonstrate. First, because revelation teaches many conclusions about God which no metaphysics can demonstrate; secondly, because, even when it can be demonstrated by natural reason, its demonstration does not make a revealed truth more certain to the theologian than it was before. Still more obviously, it would not do for a Christian to deduce by natural reasoning the consequences following from an article of faith and to call it philosophy. Then what is the difference between philosophizing in the light of revelation and philosophizing in the light of natural reason alone?

To this extremely complex problem, and without pretending to solve it, I beg to suggest at least where I would look for the beginning of an answer. I would look for it in an order of facts that are little known and are all related to the natural history of the human intellect. How is it, for instance, that practically all the great philosophers wrote their ethics after writing their metaphysics? And how is it that many men become interested in theological or merely religious problems at just about the age assigned by Thomas and Aristotle to metaphysical maturity? I need not tell you that I don't know. The reason for these facts probably lies somewhere in those many changes which, Thomas says, take place in the natures of young people. If we could account for it by merely saying that people become metaphysicians and moralists because they are getting senile, the question would be greatly simplified. But it is not so. Senility hardly accounts for the fact that Kant had to wait up to the age of fifty-seven before he could establish metaphysics as a science, and only then, having published the *Critique of Pure Reason*, to publish the *Critique of Practical Reason* when he was sixty-five years old. There is indeed a metaphysical age, then an ethical one, and neither one is precocious. But if he is a Christian, a young man of twenty finds himself in an entirely different situation, and I would like, by way of conclusion, to say where I see the difference.

The main reason of Thomas Aquinas against an early teaching of metaphysics was the exceedingly abstract nature of its object. Religion cannot change it, but religion provides an exceedingly concrete approach to certain notions which the metaphysician considers in an abstract way. To take only one example, I do not consider it easy to interest a class of undergraduates in the metaphysical notion of "pure act"; but if you can tell them that what you call pure act is another name for

God, then they will realize that you are talking about something they already know, and not about a mere word. If, moreover, the teaching of religious knowledge has already given them at least the beginnings of a theological training, then your students will find it most natural to use the light of their reason in order to understand something of what God has told us about Himself, or to investigate the why of His commandments with respect to moral conduct. All the concreteness conferred by religion upon the abstract object of metaphysical speculation, all the moral maturity of a young man, or woman, long trained to the complexity of ethical problems, can be considered so many favorable conditions for the earlier ripening of aptness to philosophical speculation. In the thirteenth century, philosophy was taught in such a religious atmosphere; it really was a preamble to theology, just as certain philosophically demonstrable propositions were held to be preambles to Christian faith. This, I submit, is the reason why what applied to philosophers did not apply to himself, to his own masters, nor to his fellow students, in the mind of Thomas Aquinas. Unless we re-create around our teaching of philosophy a like religious atmosphere, I fail to see how we can avoid the objections raised by Thomas Aquinas against the college teaching of metaphysics and ethics.

I know full well that this conclusion is open to countless objections directed against it from all sides. It would take a long time to list them and a still longer time to answer them; but you have nothing to fear, I am not going to do it. I am not even going to do anything to prevent them. I only beg those who might feel like opposing this conclusion not to argue against what was not said.

There are two things which I did emphatically not say. The first one is that philosophy should be taught everywhere in the way I said. There are a great many non-Christian teaching institutions, and my problem was not to tell them what to do with the difficulty. At any rate, they have a full right to solve it in their own way and by their own means. One solution I have been taught, more than forty years ago, by a master with whom I never agreed but whose memory I dearly cherish, was that there were no such things as metaphysics or ethics. To him, metaphysics was so dead that there was no point in refuting it; as to ethics, the very notion of a *science* about what one *ought to* do was to him a contradiction in terms. To the question: What should one do? he once wrote: There is no answer. If this be true, my problem does not arise; nothing of what I said applies and that is the end of it. On the contrary, for those who still believe in the usefulness of teaching ethics to the millions, many problems arise, and I would be the last not to consider them seriously. Only these were not today my problem. I only asked: If what Thomas Aquinas has said is true, and if he has done what he has done, what should we do?

The second thing I emphatically did not say is that the correct answer to the problem is to substitute in our liberal arts colleges the teaching of theology for the teaching of philosophy. Even if we wanted to, we could not possibly do it. In the thirteenth century it took much longer to make a theologian than to make a philosopher. However we may conceive it, the teaching of our liberal arts colleges cannot be calculated to turn out yearly crops of philosophers and still less of theologians. But there is a great deal of straight rational speculation concerning God, human nature, and morality included in the theology of St. Thomas Aquinas. On this precise point, my sole conclusion has been to the effect that, if we wish to introduce Christian students to metaphysics and ethics, to teach them the relevant parts of his theology will be to provide them with the best short cut to some understanding of these disciplines. It may well be that, even within these limits, the conclusion does not prove satisfactory. Then one should not waste any time on refuting it. The only useful thing to do would be to find another answer to the problem raised by the texts of Thomas Aquinas.

Where there is neither metaphysics nor ethics, there is, as I said, no problem. Where there is a theology, there still should be no problem, but for the opposite reason. In Catholic teaching institutions whose proper mission it is to prepare future theologians, no hesitation should be possible. The method in use in the golden age of Scholasticism is just as valid today as it ever was. To such schools I would unhesitatingly say: If you want to teach your students both metaphysics and ethics, teach them straight theology, provided only it be theology as Thomas Aquinas himself understood it. But universal agreement cannot be said to obtain on this point.

Even among Thomists, many seem to imagine that according to Thomas Aquinas a theological conclusion is always deduced, directly or indirectly, from some premise held as true by faith in the light of revelation. Assuredly, all such conclusions are essentially theological and it is of such conclusions that theology is essentially made. But it is enough to open the *Summa Theologiae* in order to make sure that, as Thomas himself understood it, theology contains many other ones. The demonstration of the existence of God, to quote only one of them, is a purely rational argument: it appeals to no revealed truth; yet this purely rational conclusion, in both concepts and method, is a theological conclusion. All that is in the *Sum of Theology* is theological, including the philosophical demonstrations assumed by the theologian in view of his theological end.

What a liberation it would be for all those vitally interested in such problems if the authentically Thomistic notion of theology were restored by our theologians themselves in its purity! Philosophy has no more to lose from being assumed by theology than nature has from being informed by grace. Should not philosophy aspire, on the contrary, to that metamorphosis as to its higher destiny? "Since grace does not destroy nature," Thomas says, "but perfects it, natural reason should minister to faith as the natural perfection of the will ministers to charity."[8] Why should a theologian worry about losing philosophy, since he now has it transformed into theology, and no less rational than before, but more true, and consequently rational in a better way?

Thomas Aquinas was well aware of the objection. There have always been men to wonder at what they considered the strange speculative mixture of philosophy and theology they found in the *Summa Theologiae*. Still today, many excellent minds feel inclined to put some order in the whole thing, and, the better to avoid misunderstandings, they sort out in the *Summa* what is philosophy and what is theology. There is no harm in doing so. But if anybody imagines that by taking theology out of the *Summa* and putting it in another book it becomes philosophy, I am afraid he is deceiving himself. At any rate, he sees a mixture where there is none. If there were a mixture, Thomas says, the nature of theology would be altered by that of philosophy, and inversely. Then indeed would we have, on the one hand, the adulterated theology so heartily hated by the Reformers and, on the other, the adulterated philosophy which nobody wants to have, neither the philosophers nor the theologians. But what happens, Thomas Aquinas adds, is something entirely different; since one of the two elements passes into the nature of the other one, there is no mixture because only a single thing is left. Then he concludes: "Consequently, those who use philosophical documents in Sacred Scripture and put them at the service of faith do not mix water with wine, but rather, they change water into wine."[9] How could we say the same thing more clearly? But even if we could, what good would it do?[10] There is no reason why those who prefer water should drink wine. Let them drink their water in peace. Only, they should not advertise it as the wine of Thomas Aquinas.

NOTES

1. We beg to stress this point because the text of Thomas Aquinas is sometimes misconstrued as an attenuation of his usual position. Thomas grants that even an old man can still be too young to study ethics, if, not having mastered his passions, he remains without qualification for this kind of study. Thomas has never said that, if he has already mastered his passions, a young man (*juvenis*) is qualified to study ethics. Morally mature, he still remains intellectually immature. He is ready for moral action, not for moral speculation: "Quia sicut juvenis aetate deficit a fine hujus scientiae qui est cognitio, ita et ille qui juvenis est moribus deficit a fine qui est actio." Thomas Aquinas, *In Ethic.*, I, lect. 3; ed. R. M. Spiazzi, O.P., Marietti (Romae, 1949), nos. 38–40, pp. 10–11.
2. "Juvenes sapientialia quidem, scilicet metaphysicalia, non credunt, idest non attingunt mente, licet dicant ore." Thomas Aquinas, *In Ethic.*, VI, lect. 7; nos. 1209–1211, pp. 330–331. In this sentence, the Latin words *non credunt* stand for the Greek words *ou pisteuousin* (Aristotle, *Eth. Nic.*, VI, 9, 1142a 19–20). The meaning of *credunt* is clear. Since young men cannot grasp the meaning of the metaphysical terms, they cannot assent to the propositions made up by these terms. The consequence is that there can be no metaphysical truth in their

intellects; that is, no metaphysics at all. Aristotle still more bluntly says: "They do not assent, they only talk." This decision cannot be overruled on the strength of merely dialectical arguments. If what Aristotle says is true, and if we take it as understood by Thomas Aquinas, the reason why metaphysics should not be taught to young minds lies in the very nature of the intellect. Incidentally, this disposes of the objection that if a premature teaching of metaphysics does no good it cannot do any harm. Any experienced teacher will remember at once more than one case of a young student blaming on metaphysical truth his own failure to grasp it. An acquired distaste for philosophy is sometimes the only visible fruit of its untimely teaching. The religious consequences of such failures are no fitting subject for philosophical consideration.

3. "Hence it is that the intention of the philosophers aimed principally at this, that through whatever they considered in things, they might arrive at the knowledge of the prime causes. That is why they placed the science concerned with the first causes last, and allotted the last part of their lives to its consideration. For first they began with logic, which teaches the method of the sciences. Secondly, they went to mathematics, which even boys are capable of learning. Thirdly, they took up the philosophy of nature, which requires time because of the experience needed to acquire it. Fourthly, they turned to moral philosophy, of which young people are not suitable students. Finally, they arrived at divine science, whose object is the first causes of things." Thomas Aquinas, *In Lib. de Causis*, lect. I (*Opuscula*, ed. P. Mandonnet, O.P., I, p. 195).
4. Roger Bacon, *Compendium studii theologiae*, ed. Brewer, *Opera inedita*, p. 412.
5. Thomas Aquinas, *In Nic. Ethic.*, VI, lect. 7, Spiazzi ed., n. 1211, p. 331.
6. Thomas Aquinas, *In IV Sent.*, d. 40, *explanatio textus*.
7. Without entering problems beyond the competence of the philosopher, we beg to observe that, though a man can be too young to be a student in ethics, he never is too young to be a saint. Likewise, even though he is too young to be a metaphysician, he may not be too young to be a theologian. True enough, a theologian needs to know metaphysics, but the study of metaphysics in view of, or in connection with, theology is another case than that of the philosophers whose course of studies has been described by Aristotle and Thomas Aquinas. That this was the thought of Thomas Aquinas is evident from what he wrote *In Ethic.*, VI, lect. 7, I, 2; Pirotta, no. 38: young men cannot study metaphysics or theology (*sapientialia et divina*). Obviously, he never intended to say that no men under fifty should study revealed theology. He never imagined that priests should "allot the last part of their lives to its consideration." The theology he had in mind was the "natural

theology" of the pagan philosophers, not the philosophical reflection of Christian intellects already familiar with the *divina* in virtue of their Christian education. In dealing with this problem, we should remember its connection with the following fundamental positions of St. Thomas.

One of the reasons why God has revealed to men truths that are knowable in the light of natural reason is that the knowledge of these truths—for instance, the existence of God, creation, the immortality of the soul, etc.—are necessary for salvation. Even young boys and girls need to be saved. Since nobody knows how long he is going to live, nobody can say what is the last part of his life; so that nobody can afford to wait in order to allot it to the study of metaphysics. This is precisely the reason why, after reminding us that philosophical truth, on account of its profundity, can be grasped only by the intellect after a long training, Thomas adds that God has instructed us "to hold by faith even those truths which human reason is able to investigate." In *Contra Gentiles,* I, chap. 4, the paragraph "Secundum inconveniens est . . ." entirely rests upon the reasons developed in the commentaries on Aristotle. Without revelation, young men could not discover such truths by reason alone, because their soul *non est apta ad tam altae veritatis cognitionem.* The point we are enforcing is that the apparently casual remarks of Thomas Aquinas in his commentaries are part and parcel of his theology. They support his second argument for the necessity (given the divine will to save man) of a supernatural revelation even in matters accessible to the natural light of reason. So far as we can see, there are only two ways to justify a different pedagogy: either to prove that Aristotle was wrong in his appreciation of the metaphysical aptitudes of young minds, or to prove that human nature no longer is what it was in the thirteenth century. Our personal inability to see how this could be done does not prove that it is impossible; but to take its possibility for granted is not enough to justify a pedagogy so hard to reconcile with some authentic philosophical and theological positions of St. Thomas Aquinas. There is something at least paradoxical in teaching straight philosophical metaphysics and ethics *ad mentem Divi Thomae Aquinatis* to students whom Thomas Aquinas himself considered unfit to receive such a teaching.

8. Thomas Aquinas, *Summa Theologiae,* I, q. 1, a. 8; transl. A. C. Pegis, New York, 1948. The problem of the nature, object, and unity of theology according to St. Thomas Aquinas has recently become the object of an animated controversy among theologians. In expressing his personal preference for a certain interpretation of the doctrine, a philosopher cannot intend to solve a problem that falls entirely under the jurisdiction of the theologians. A good introduction to the question is found in F. Van Ackeren, S.J., *Sacra Doctrina. The Subject of*

the *First Question of the Summa Theologica of Saint Thomas Aquinas* (Romae: Catholic Book Agency, 1952).

9. Thomas Aquinas, *In Boethii de Trinitate*, q. II, a. 3, ad 5.
10. It is always untimely to question the wisdom of current practice. One of the most frequent answers to such questions is: Then what do you suggest we should do? My only answer to this is: We should put our heads together and consider the problem. What are we doing? And should we continue to act in the same way? No single man should consider himself qualified to tell others what they should do in matters of such importance. Besides, the problem might well be susceptible of different solutions according to cases, circumstances, and ends in sight. A minimum of historical reflection might throw some light on the problem. The reason why modern liberal arts colleges and universities are teaching metaphysics to young men and women is that, in the sixteenth century, the Jesuits decided to do so. And they had an excellent reason to enter upon that way. They were the first to meet the new demand for the Christian education, not of future monks, nor of future priests, but of future laymen whose lives would be spent in some temporal vocation. The reason why they decided that philosophy should be taught in colleges is stated in full in their *Ratio Studiorum* of 1599: "The liberal arts and the sciences of nature prepare the mind for the study of theology; they help to acquire a perfect knowledge of it as well as to put it to good use; moreover, they work toward the same goal as theology. Let the professors teach these arts as diligently as they possibly can, but always with a heartfelt desire to find in them the honor and the glory of God. In short, let professors prepare their pupils, especially our own men, for the study of theology, and inspire their minds with the strongest desire to know their creator." This was a clear-cut proposition. Nor can we help thinking that St. Thomas Aquinas would have unreservedly subscribed to it, the more so as, in the *Ratio Studiorum* of 1586, it had been foreseen that all professors of philosophy should be theologians; otherwise, the document says, "they would not be safe in their conclusions, nor in their demonstrations, nor even in their language . . . ; they could hardly solve the arguments of unbelievers . . . ; nor would they handle philosophy in such a way that it might be of assistance to theology." The question at issue is whether we should continue, against the repeated warnings of St. Thomas Aquinas and the example of the Society of Jesus, to teach young men and women metaphysics and ethics in a purely philosophical spirit and for a purely philosophical end.

18. The Eminence of Teaching

Two years ago, on April 30, 1951, the Catholic world was celebrating the third centenary of the birth of St. John Baptist de la Salle, and even outside the Church many men open to the significance of his work joined in the celebration. No homage could have been more general or better deserved. It is not my intention to celebrate the sanctity of de la Salle, but I have reason to begin this lecture by mentioning his name. For were I asked to cite what appears to me as one of the higher moments in his spiritual life, I would recall an episode which even his historians sometimes forget, unless they veil it in order not to hurt our modern feelings.

We are in 1681. At that date, de la Salle has already done a great deal to foster the work of popular education. In 1679 he had already rented a house next door to his own in Rheims, and he had provided the masters of his schools with what they needed to live, including the daily food supplied to them from his own kitchen. Yet, for reasons he could not clearly discern, things were not working according to his desire, so he consulted another saintly priest, Father Barré, who had founded several poor schools in Rouen, and he asked him for advice about what he should do. Father Barré's answer was a simple one: "Do you really want to form your teachers to piety and to make them love their work on account of the good they can do? Take them into your own house and live in their company."

Seen from a distance and with modern eyes, this piece of advice does not appear particularly terrible. Since he was already supporting the masters in the house next door, why should this holy man have hesitated to welcome them into his own home? After all, he would have saved the rent of a house. Yet Father Barré was confronting de la Salle with the hardest decision he ever had to make during the course of his life. And do you know why? Because he was being asked to take *teachers* in his own home! He himself belonged, if not to high nobility, at least to the best society of his native city; schoolteachers, on the contrary, were simply nobody; no gentleman could be expected to live with such people in his own house without raising a sort of social scandal. De la Salle knew it well, first from his own personal feelings, for he was a man of his time, but also from the feelings of his family, which was sure to consider itself publicly insulted by such a decision. He made it, however, not without a severe internal struggle, and the result was a twofold one.

On the human side, his family considered him crazy and all his younger brothers and sisters were taken away from the schools he was conducting, as if he were incompetent to care for them. This was to remain in his memory as one of the deepest sorrows of his life. On the supernatural side, his sacrifice was rewarded a hundredfold, for it became the source of the prodigious development of popular education by the Brothers of the Christian Schools. How could I forget this episode? I am indebted to it for my first Christian education.

In recalling it, however, I fully realize that this is not a wholly democratic story. It is full of social class prejudice which we are supposed to have long overgrown. But have we, at least as completely as we like to imagine? Socially speaking, I hope I can truly say yes. But I am not certain that many men have ever stopped to consider what kind of work it is to teach. I am not even certain that all teachers think of asking themselves the question. We teach because, at the time of our youth, for reasons that even then were not too clear to ourselves and that we have partly forgotten, we decided that we would be teachers. Others are teaching by religious obedience and chiefly as a way of serving the Church. Still others just found themselves engaged in the work of teaching, as much by chance as of their own will; and since they once began to teach, they continue to do it. When it is not saintly, all this is at least natural, sensible, and above any reproach, but it will certainly not do any harm for us to ask ourselves: What do we do when we teach?

This is by no means an easy question to answer, unless, of course, we content ourselves with a nominal definition of teaching activity in general. Incidentally, this is what common sense would do. To teach, any sensible man would say, is to give lessons at school or elsewhere, in or on any subject. It is to cause a person to do something—for instance, to read and write—by instruction and training. But if you had desired to hear a sensible man, you would not have invited a philosopher. The true philosopher's business is precisely to ask questions which common sense considers settled, and, let us add, rightly so. Should it be resolved that all teaching will be suspended in schools until a world convention of teachers agrees about what it is to teach, pupils could joyfully envisage an exceedingly long vacation. The words of a philosopher can bring about no such visible effects; they are the words of a soul quietly talking to itself, but they can be heard by other souls, and invisible effects may attend the silent realization of their meaning.

Let us therefore start from common sense in order to go beyond it. To teach, the dictionary says, is by instruction to enable or to cause a person to do something. And indeed, all teachers know that they are causes. I would even suggest that, the simpler their teaching is, the better they know this. At the end of the year a professor of metaphysics may well wonder what he has caused his pupils to do that they could not already do on the very first day they entered his classroom. But there is no place for such doubt in the mind of the primary-school teacher. At the beginning of the school year he has been given a batch of boys and girls, none of whom could read a line, and, marvel of marvels, at the end of the same year they all can read. By both instruction and training, the teacher has caused them to read, and his reward is not in his salary, for quite a few other jobs would enable him to keep soul and body together, which is about all he does; his true reward is the joy he has taken, despite his hours of discouragement, in seeing his efforts progressively rewarded first by his best pupils, then by all the others. There was something they could not do, and now they all can do it, and he is the cause that they can. Here we are at once stumbling upon a truly metaphysical question. So long as we quietly enjoy teaching, no problem arises; but as soon as we begin to wonder why we enjoy it, we must ask the next question: Why is there pleasure in exercising this kind of causality?

Were we left to ourselves, we might have to wait a long time before finding an answer. We might even despair of ever finding one and quit bothering about the question. Such failures to find an answer can always be blamed on the question; we simply conclude: It does not make sense. But, precisely, this one does, and we can apply for an answer to those who asked it before us. If we believe in teaching, we should also feel willing to be taught.

The first remark to make on this point is that, properly speaking, to learn by being taught is not to invent. Improperly speaking, to invent is to teach oneself. Grown-up people are doing it constantly, and children begin to do so much earlier than we think. As soon as a human being knows something, he begins to enlarge the amount of his knowledge by a personal effort. But unless we use words in a loose way, we cannot say that this process of personal reflection, however fruitful it may be, constitutes a real teaching. When we are learning from a book, the problem becomes different; the book and its author are our teachers. There is teaching here because there is a teacher who is another than the pupil. This personal relation between two distinct human beings is essential to teaching; no man is to himself his own teacher in any department of human life, and we all know this even from common language. When a man says, "I am my own master," he merely means that he has no master. So also in the order of teaching: to be oneself one's own teacher does not mean not to learn, but it certainly means to have no teacher at all.

Now what is this precise relation which we find between teacher and pupil? I have just been using the word "master," and although there is some tendency to shun it in our day, or at least not to use it with the fullness of its implications, it still retains some of them. Besides, it is not used only in the language of schools. The master of the house or the master of a merchantman is supposed to have control over the house or the ship. In medieval universities a master was the holder of a degree giving authority to teach. Today, as in the thirteenth century, a master's control extends not only to his pupils but often to their masters. In all such cases, the notion of master implies that of authority. By its very nature it is not a democratic notion. Assuredly, we are doing our very best to make teaching as democratic as possible. Modern teachers are urged not to boss their pupils and, in point of fact, we sometimes meekly suggest to them that, did they accept to listen to us, we might perhaps teach them something. Yet, when all is said and done, the very act of teaching implies the admission of a certain inequality, not indeed in nature, nor even in intellectual ability, but at least in knowledge. A man knows something, others do not know it, there is no way for the teachers to cause it to become known without putting it, willy-nilly, in the heads of his pupils. There can be no equality between a cause and its effect. To cause is to act upon; to be caused is to be acted upon, and no pedagogy will ever do anything about this.

In the case of teaching, however, this is not the whole story. When we light a wood fire, all that the wood has to do is to be burned. Wood is completely passive with respect to burning, but children are not so with respect to learning. When they enter a school, however young they may be, they have already exercised, practically at every waking moment of their lives, the extraordinary operation called cognition. Mysterious as it is, knowledge is a natural function of man. Children walk because they have legs, they breathe because they have lungs, they see because they have eyes, and they know because they have an intellect. Not only do they know, but they love knowing, just as they love breathing and walking. Let us rather say that they cannot help doing these things because no organ can help performing its natural operations.

Yet we all know that it takes them an effort to learn what they are taught in schools. The reason is that teaching in school confronts the child with a kind of knowing operation he is not yet used to performing. However simple we may try to make it, what we teach in schools always remains a typically adult learning. Left to himself, provided only he is out of early infancy, a child performs marvelous intellectual operations. The first time he says "dog," he has already seen things, perceived analogies between them, formed the abstract concept of a class, and attached a name to it. Any normal child achieves this feat without even being aware of it, and he repeats it endlessly without effort. On the contrary, as soon as we teach him to read, to write, or to count, we ask him to perform operations that are not natural to his intellect, because they are about symbols and no longer about things. The recognition of this fact accounts for the multiplication of images and pictures in modern schoolbooks; and we all know their danger as well as their usefulness. By putting pictures under the eyes of the child, we are inviting him to exercise natural cognition, which he loves to do, but, by the same token, we are postponing the time when he will have to make the very effort we must cause him to make if he is to be trained to think in an adult way. There is no natural relation between the letters of the alphabet and the sounds they are supposed to represent, nor between the words and the things they point out, nor yet between numbers and the possible concrete objects whose substitutes they are. Now these are precisely what we consider the simplest things to teach: reading, writing, and arithmetic; but they are indeed the least natural things to learn. This is the reason why learning them requires from the child such an effort, the very same kind of effort he will be asked to furnish throughout the whole course of his studies. If we think of it, most of what we are teaching consists of techniques, either scientific or linguistic, whose practical usefulness, supposing it exists, the young student cannot see. Since he cannot see it, the effort required for the mastering of such techniques is made doubly hard because, in his mind, it has no justification.

This is precisely the point at which the teacher not only has a part to perform but becomes a necessity. We should not imagine that school children know nothing more than what they are taught in schools. In fact, what we teach them is but an infinitesimal part of their knowledge, but it is precisely made up of what, without us, they would never learn. No wonder, then, that in the good old days teachers were so commonly called masters. Where an effort is required, to obtain it by persuasion is by far the best thing to do, when it can be done; otherwise, there is no other recourse than to authority, unless, of course, we renounce obtaining it.

Now, to obtain from the pupil this effort upon himself, which he can see no reason to give, except the words we say, is the highest and noblest part in the work of the teacher. It also is by far the most difficult one; so much so that we are all trying to ease the difficulty. The present tendency to make everything as easy to learn as possible is perfectly justified so long as it is a question of teaching those elementary techniques which are part and parcel of the mental equipment of a civilized man. The three Rs need not be made more difficult than they naturally are, but beyond the level of elementary education, while there is still no reason to make things harder than they actually are, we should not wish to rid our pupils of the effort necessary to learn them. First of all, the thing cannot be done; where the pupil has no personal effort to make, he needs no help and consequently no teacher. Next, if the difficulties are inherent in the teaching matter at stake, they usually can be simplified up to a point, but we cannot eliminate them without eliminating the matter itself. Hence the sometimes bitter disappointment of so many grown men and women when they remember their school years. How is it, they sometimes say, that I have had three or four years of this and that, and yet I don't know it? The reason often is that, when a subject is made easy to the point of ceasing to be what it is, it is simply not being taught.

This first way of avoiding the difficulty is a question of programs, schoolbooks, and teaching methods. If mistakes are made there, the teachers are in no way responsible for them. But there is a mistake for which some teachers are responsible, and I myself have made it so often that I feel entitled to say something about it. I beg to symbolize it by the well-known aside which escapes us after a strenuous effort to explain a difficult point: "I hope I am making myself clear." Now of course we must try to make ourselves clear; this certainly is one of the most important results to achieve for any master interested in his work, but we should not consider it *the* most important one. There is no use in displaying evidence before eyes that make no effort to see it; when they do see it, the reason is not that we made it so clear that we understood it for our pupils; sooner or later they have to understand it by themselves, and their own effort to understand it is for them the only way there is to learn it. The most scientifically pedagogical methods are bound to fail if they go against the facts of nature. In this case, the fundamental fact of nature is that no man can understand anything for another one. No master can take his own knowledge out of his own mind and put it in the heads of his pupils. The only thing he can do is to help them to put it themselves into their own minds. To the extent that he has achieved this result, a teacher can justly feel conscious of having attained the proper end of his professional activity.

Abstract as it may sound, this general conclusion can help to clear up certain pedagogical controversies. For instance, if what precedes is true, there is no fundamental difference between the classical method, which proceeds by professorial expositions and lectures, and the so-called Socratic method, which proceeds by questions and answers; that is, by mode of dialogue. However you may choose to teach them, your pupils have the same kind of intellect that you have, they use the same principles of natural reason that you yourself are using; the only difference is that, in your own mind, a certain number of consequences are related to these principles and follow from them according to a certain order which you know but which your pupils do not know. What you achieve in teaching is precisely the communication of this order. Whether you do this by continuous exposition or by questions and answers does not make any difference. If you are lecturing, you know the order beforehand; if you are asking questions, these must needs be leading questions and their order is precisely your own lead. The teacher is equally active in both cases and he is so in the same way; and the learner is equally passive in both cases, in the sense that his mind has to follow the order already present in the mind of the teacher. But there again the learner's passivity comes to an end, for indeed, for him to reproduce this order is to produce it. Having to answer the objection of those who precisely denied that a master could put into the heads of pupils something that was not already there, Thomas observed that "if questions be put in orderly fashion, they proceed from universal self-evident principles to what is particular. Now by such a process knowledge is produced in the soul of the learner." So the master really causes knowledge to be in the mind of the pupil; but, Thomas goes on to say, when the learner answers the truth, "this is not because he had knowledge previously, but because *he then acquires knowledge for the first time*."[1] And indeed, there is no other choice. The proper effect of the act of teaching is to cause a personal discovery in the mind of the pupil.

Thomas Aquinas has several times considered this remarkable problem, and apart from minor variations in the expression of his thought, he has always answered it in the same way. One of the favorite examples he uses in such cases is a comparison between the art of teaching and the art of healing. In both cases, a certain acquired learning is at the origin of the process. The physician knows what he has to do in order to heal the patient, just as the teacher knows what he has to say in order to instruct the pupil, but the physician can no more give to the patient his own health than the teacher can give his own learning to the pupil; last, not the least, the physician can do little more than to cause nature to recover health in the body of the patient, just as the teacher does nothing more than to cause the intellect to acquire knowledge in the soul of the pupil. Only—and I hope you will remember this in view of the conclusion of this lecture—the relation of master to pupil is a still more intimate one than that of physician to patient, because it does not obtain between a mind and a body, but between two minds. What is the term of the teacher's action, Thomas has just told us, is that the pupil acquires knowledge for the first time; and this is true, but it has its counterpart on the side of the teacher. In order to cause his pupil to invent learning, he himself must invent again what he is teaching, or, rather, he must go again, before his pupils, through the whole process, now familiar to him, of the invention of each and every truth. The teacher, Thomas says, begins to teach in the same way as the inventor begins to invent.[2] In other words, unless he is actually thinking aloud and engaging his own intellectual activity in his lecture, the teacher does not really teach. Incidentally, this is one reason why it is doubtful that any mechanical device will ever replace the actual presence of the real teacher. Only a living intellect, patiently preceding us on the way to truth, can effectively teach us how to think.

Although I am mostly using modern words, what I am now telling you is a very old truth, or, rather, a standing one. It can easily be found in one of the disputed questions of Thomas Aquinas *On Truth:*[3] "When they say that a teacher transfuses his learning to his pupil, this does not mean that the learning that is in the master is to be found afterward, numerically the same, in the pupil; it means that a learning similar to that of the master is caused in the pupil by the fact of his being taught." In other words, there is no transfusion of learning in the sense that there are transfusions of blood. We can give our own blood to others; we cannot give them our own learning.

And yet, see what an extraordinary thing teaching is! St. Thomas Aquinas died in 1274—that is, nearly seven hundred years ago—and on the very moment he died, his own learning died together with him. From the new life he was then beginning to live, he could no longer communicate with us by means of words. But today, men unknown to him ask themselves the question: What is it to teach? And remembering that he himself spent his whole life teaching or being taught, these men turn to him for an answer. All that is left of him in this world is paper covered with ink and sentences written in a dead language that is not even our own. We read his words, however, and suddenly what was alive in his mind seven centuries ago begins a new life in our own understanding. How is this possible? Simply because, while reading the dead signs symbolizing his thought, our own minds have themselves formed the same notions that were in the mind of Thomas Aquinas at the time when he wrote those lines. In saying the same notions, I naturally mean to say not the very same notions which once lived in his mind but, rather, similar ones. His learning has become the cause of our learning, and still this learning is truly our own, not his. In short, Thomas Aquinas has been our teacher, and we have been his pupils, because he has caused us to produce in our own minds a learning similar to his own learning.

Here is precisely the point where the eminent dignity of teaching appears in full. Without attempting a philosophical definition of man, this at least can be said, that he is the only known species of speaking animal, and the reason why he has an articulate speech is that he has an articulate thought. The thinking power of man, which we call his intellect, is what makes him different from all the other kinds of living beings. If to teach is what we said it is, it implies the meeting of two human intellects—that is, of two human beings taken precisely in that which makes them to be men; namely, their understandings. Every other kind of job has its usefulness; consequently, it has its own dignity; but this particular one does not consist in producing material goods, in exchanging them, or in selling professional advice, or in taking care of the bodies of our fellow men. In point of fact, it is like nothing else. The relationship that obtains between the master and his pupils is that of an intellect which has already actualized its own potentialities, with another intellect whose potentialities are still to be actualized by the teaching of the master.

From this point of view, the reason for this ancient appellation should become clear. Whether or not we give him the title, the teacher is indeed a master because, owing to his intellectual maturity and his own learning, he alone is the prime cause of the whole teaching process. But the nobility of his work arises as much from its end as from its cause. What his intellect is acting upon is another human intellect, endowed with the same natural light as his own, just as noble and irreducibly personal as his own intellect is, and which, if his pedagogy is sound, he can cause to think, but for which he cannot think. It is true that in comparison with the understanding of the master, that of the pupil is in a state of receptivity or, to use the technical term familiar to philosophers, of potentiality. But, if I may be permitted to borrow once more from Thomas Aquinas one of his more felicitous expressions, I shall say that the understanding of the pupil is in a state of "active potentiality."[4] Without this active receptivity, Thomas Aquinas goes on to say, man could never learn anything by himself, which he certainly can do. In short, man does not have two distinct intellectual powers, the one by which to learn by himself, the other by which to learn from his teacher. The intellect by which the pupil can learn from his teacher is the very same intellect by which he can learn by himself. For indeed he has no other one. This is the true reason why the ultimate end of our pedagogy should be to teach children to learn by themselves, because, in fact, there is nothing else we can teach.

How impractical all this probably sounds! And yet how practical it is! However heavily we load our programs, and however widely we may diversify them in order to answer the future needs of all our pupils, many of them will feel later on that they have been taught many things they did not need to know, whereas what they did need to know has never been taught to them in school. There is a safe way for us to protect ourselves against this otherwise inevitable reproach, and it is to teach our pupils to learn by themselves instead of trying to impart to them an always larger amount of learning.

Should we consider it possible to do this still more than we are already doing it, no pupil would ever regret having spent so many years in school and no master would ever wonder if he has not been wrong in his choice of a career. For we now know the answer to one of the first questions we asked at the beginning of this lecture: Why do good teachers love to teach? Why do they take pleasure in exercising this particular type of causality? The answer is that since to be is to act, all beings like to exercise causality for the same reason that they like to be. Now causality is the very act by which a being gives something of itself to another being, and this is the reason why effects naturally resemble their causes. The good teacher then loves to teach because he loves to impart to his pupils the very best thing there is in him; namely, intellectual life, knowledge, truth. The generosity inherent in the very act of being finds here its highest manifestation, and the purest kind of pleasure should naturally attend its exercise. The highest reward of teaching is the joy of making other minds similar, not indeed to ourselves, but to the truth which is in us.

To cause, Thomas Aquinas says, is to produce something which resembles its cause, and this is a universal law of nature; but if we think of it, this is a law of nature only because it is first the divine law. Before being a cause, the teacher himself is an effect of God; as such, he resembles his cause, and all his actions and operations, when properly directed, have for their own end to make him more and more similar to the sovereign cause whose effect he is. This is true not only of man but of each and every thing that is, moves, acts, and operates. In Thomas' own words: "The last end of all things is to become like God."[5] This is what a stone does when it falls, what an animal does when it lives, and what a man does when he thinks. Only, because thought is the highest and most noble known form of activity in nature, man is the highest and noblest among the known images of God. If to teach is to cause others to think, it is to help them in becoming not only like unto their masters but unto the Master of their masters, God.

In concluding, and since I myself am an old teacher, I had better remind myself that I have not spoken about the eminent dignity of teachers but about the eminent dignity of teaching. A true teacher is what, as I hope, we all are, at least up to a point, but the ideal notion of what teaching truly is should not be considered a description of what we are; it is the yardstick that measures what we ought to be. Just as few men measure up to the eminent dignity of man, few teachers are fully equal to the eminent dignity of teaching. This is so true that when one of them is, the Church, in her truly divine wisdom, proclaims to the whole world that he is a saint: St. John Baptist de la Salle, for his infinite love of the little ones and a whole life devoted to turning them into better images of God; St. Albert the Great, on account of his unquenchable thirst for scholarship, which consists in knowing all that is knowable to man just as God knows all that is knowable to God; and Thomas Aquinas, who preceded them both on the altars for the very remarkable reason that he had dedicated his whole life to the pursuing of truth for the pure love of truth.

Now, since he himself was a professor, Thomas Aquinas once asked himself if he had not better spend his life speculating about truth, which is contemplation, rather than teaching it to others, which is action. In doing this, he was asking himself a rather embarrassing question. Not that he ever took any pride in being a professor. As he liked to say: *To be a master is not an honor, it is a task.* But like all good masters, despite some occasional grumbling, Thomas loved to teach. On the other hand, he had read in the Gospel the well-known story of Martha and Mary, and since Mary had chosen the better part, how could he doubt that contemplation was better than action? Of course he did not doubt it, but he had spent his whole life teaching the truth; he still wanted to do so and he could not persuade himself that his life would have been a better one if he had kept to himself his own accumulated learning instead of sharing it with so many disciples. So he found this remarkable way out of the difficulty: to act is not as noble as to contemplate, and it is true that to teach is to act, but to act in view of imparting to others the fruit of contemplation is more noble than contemplation alone.[6]

Majus est contemplata aliis tradere quam solum contemplari: it is a greater thing to distribute to others what one has contemplated than only to contemplate. What life, then, could be more noble than that of a teacher, if it achieves in its perfection the unity of action and of contemplation? Yes, some will say, but Thomas Aquinas was a teacher, and his answer was very clever; only the teaching of the Gospel remains what it is, and when all is said and done, Mary has still chosen the better part. Who would deny this? Certainly not Thomas Aquinas, for he was not trying to be clever; as usual, he was simply trying to say the truth. And the truth is that if there has been a teaching of the Gospel, there also must have been a teacher. Not this time St. John Baptist de la Salle, nor St. Albert the Great, nor St. Thomas Aquinas, but He better than whom no man can ever pretend to do: the teacher and the divine model of all teachers; namely, Christ.

NOTES

1. *Summa Theologiae,* I, 84, 3, ad 3; transl. A. C. Pegis, *Introduction to St. Thomas Aquinas* (New York: Random House, 1948), p. 385.
2. *Summa Contra Gentiles,* II, chap. 75.
3. *De Veritate,* q. XI, a. 1, ad 6.
4. *Op. cit.,* q. XI, a. 1.
5. *Summa Contra Gentiles,* III, chap. 20; ed. cit., p. 439.
6. *Summa Theologiae,* II–II, q. 186, a. 6.

19. Education and Higher Learning

The aim and purpose of this address* will be to describe the proper relationship that obtains, or should obtain, between education and higher learning. By the word "education" I intend to signify the system of schools now existing in most American and European countries, from primary schools up to universities, together with the programs and the general spirit that inspire their teaching methods. Naturally, since there is a great deal of variety within this system, my remarks will be of a general nature. They will deal with tendencies rather than with concrete facts. If and where exceptions are to be found, it should be understood beforehand that my remarks simply do not apply. If there is any truth in what I am about to say, it can be a global truth only. As to "higher learning," it will always signify that part of any complete school system that deals with liberal learning and, in consequence, with creative learning. We may have to use one or two concrete examples; yet, thus considered in its entire abstraction and generality, our problem will not be discussed in terms of any local, national, or continental situation. Even the political notions it may have to touch upon will not be borrowed from practical politics, but from political philosophy. I trust, however, that the main consequences of these reflections will not appear irrelevant to practical life. For education is a field of human activity in which it is most necessary that speculation go before action.

Let us first consider teaching as it is commonly understood in European as well as in American public schools, or even high schools, below the university level. Its object is an immediately practical one. A civilized country is made up of citizens who can read and write, perform elementary arithmetical operations, say something about the place of their

* This selection was given as a lecture in Convocation Hall of the University of Toronto as part of the centennial celebrations of St. Michael's College in 1952.

own country in both space and time; last, not the least, it is made up of citizens who know enough in order to discharge one of the many functions necessary to the welfare of the community. Incidentally, this is what justifies the right of intervention by the State in matters of education, and this right extends much farther than some of us would feel willing to concede. In his encyclical letter *Repraesentanti in terra*, December 31, 1929, Pope Pius XI expressly says: "The State can demand, and therefore see to it, that all citizens be endowed with the necessary knowledge of their civic and national duties, nay, with a certain amount of intellectual, moral, and physical culture which, given the conditions prevailing in our own times, is necessarily required for the common good." Education, then, has become a public service to the full extent to which it has become a public necessity. At the same time, and to the same extent, education is tending to become more and more practical in nature, because, for the State, the common good of the body politic is a practical end. Such is the reason why our schools are progressively tending either to become vocational schools or, at least, to prepare children in view of such schools, wherein they will ultimately qualify for some specialized job.

The same remark applies even to colleges and universities. From a mere glance at their programs, it appears that their proper function is to turn out, year in, year out, the right number of trained engineers, physicians, lawyers, farmers, and businessmen necessary to the welfare of a civilized country. Professors and teachers of all types are no exceptions to the rule. Our students express themselves correctly when they say that they are looking for a teaching *job*. To teach is not to speculate, an avocation for which nobody ever was paid. To teach is to act. What do we require from future teachers at all levels? Simply that they know what they will have to teach. In many cases we content ourselves with making sure that they will be able to learn it a week ahead of their pupils. Indeed, there would be no sense in protesting against the generalized tendency that now prevails to assign useful ends to our modern system of education.

Here, however, a distinction should be made between the two notions of "practicality" and of "usefulness." Were these identical, there would be for us no problem to discuss. We could then quote with unqualified approval the forceful remarks of A. N. Whitehead on the subject.[1] "Pedants," Whitehead says, "sneer at an education which is useful. But if education is not useful, what is it? Is it a talent, to be hidden away in a napkin? Of course education should be useful, whatever your aim in life. It was useful to St. Augustine and it was useful to Napoleon. It is useful, because understanding is useful." To this, which is undoubtedly true, we nevertheless beg to add that understanding is not always useful in the same way. What Napoleon learned at the artillery school of Brienne was the art of handling guns; a useful art in its own way, to be sure, but a very practically useful one. As to what St. Augustine had learned from St. Ambrose and from Plotinus, it was infinitely more useful still, since it was the way to achieve salvation, than which nothing can be more useful to man; yet, at the same time, he had also learned that salvation was beatitude; that is, the love of truth for its own sake, than which nothing less practical and more speculative can possibly be conceived. Understanding is always useful indeed, but when he himself wrote about the "divine beauty" of Lagrange's equations, Whitehead would have been much better understood by St. Augustine than by Napoleon. *Gaudium de veritate*, the joy born in us from the mere sight of truth: is it useful? Of course it is. But because it is an end in itself, not a means to any other end, it is not at all practical.

Seen from this precise point of view, the practical trend now prevailing in modern education raises a difficult problem. Does it provide boys and girls, students in all fields, with the proper feeling for the supreme importance of that type of knowledge which, precisely because it is not practical, might well be the most useful of all? In protesting against those who believe in the possibility of useless knowledge, Whitehead probably had in mind the distinction drawn by Cardinal Newman, whose works he knew so well, between a "liberal" education and a "useful" education. But a more careful examination of his text clearly shows that where he was writing "useful," what the Cardinal had in mind was "practical." In his Fifth Discourse, *On the Scope and Nature of University Education*, Newman has lovingly described what he used to call "liberal knowledge" as a knowledge "sufficient for itself, apart from every external and ulterior object."[2] To which he added that to educate for such knowledge is the true scope of a university. Even after granting to Whitehead that this knowledge is eminently useful, the fact remains that its own type of usefulness has nothing to do with practicality. How is it, then, that instead of keeping faith with Newman's ideal, the general trend of our modern school system is to stress the kind of knowledge that is not sufficient for itself, but always aims at some external and ulterior object?

Let us honestly face the difficulty. "Liberal knowledge" is not a new formula. Originally it pointed out the knowledge of the so-called "liberal arts"; that is to say, according to Cicero's own commentary, the knowledge of those arts which it is befitting for a free man to know: *artes libero dignae*. As to the other arts—namely, the mechanical ones—they were good for hand workers or, to say it more bluntly, for slaves. Of course legal slaves have long ceased to exist, yet, unless I am mistaken, more than a shade of this ancient meaning is still hovering over the language of Cardinal Newman[3] especially where he identifies "liberal knowledge" with "a gentleman's knowledge."[4] Not being myself an Englishman, I cannot pretend to know what it is to be a "gentleman." Yet I will make bold to say that, in Cardinal Newman's own mind, to study in view of becoming a skilled carpenter, a bricklayer, or even a trained mechanic would not have answered his definition of a gentleman's knowledge. When, to his own dismay, a true gentleman finds himself afflicted with a natural gift for such mechanical avocations, to resort to the British category of "hobby" is for him the only way to indulge his taste without losing his social dignity. Whatever else he may have been, the student described by Newman as a gentleman could certainly afford a university training free from immediate professional preoccupations. A truly Oxonian ideal indeed, at least as Oxford used to be in the good old times, but one which, in most parts of the world today, looks more like a dream than a reality. This gentlemanly type of education presupposes a measure of those worldly possessions which only wealthy men can afford to despise. Without in the least denying that modern universities are still successfully engaged in the task of turning out gentlemen, one may at least observe that the meaning of the word no longer is exactly what it used to be. In our own day, just as all women are ladies, all men are gentlemen.

The reason for this change is a political one. A democratic type of society has progressively replaced the aristocratic social order of Newman's England. This is not a question of political regimes, but rather a change in social structures, coming in the wake of political revolutions. There is no other choice than between aristocracy, which stands for inequality, and democracy, which stands for equality. Whether it calls itself a kingdom, an empire, a republic, or even a democratic republic, a society remains an aristocracy to the full extent that it maintains a privileged class, be it only that of those who "have" as against those who "have not." In modern democracies, this measure is steadily becoming an always smaller and smaller one, and this fact is not without deeply affecting the nature and the spirit of their systems of education, especially with respect to their attitude toward liberal knowledge and higher learning.

From the time of its very origins, which, for Western civilization, is that of ancient Greece, free and liberal speculation has always been made possible by the existence of a leisured class whose members, if they felt so inclined, could dedicate themselves to speculative research and to contemplation. For this reason, Aristotle says, the first men to philosophize were priests. The remark clearly applies to the middle ages, when nobody could become a scholar unless he was a cleric.[5] When both in Greece and in modern societies laymen became interested in learning, the existence of lay philosophers, scientists, and scholars of any sort was made possible either because they themselves belonged to the aristocracy of their time, which was the case for Francis Bacon and for Descartes, or else because some enlightened members of that aristocracy provided them with the intellectual leisure necessary for disinterested speculation. The Florence of the Medici, Elizabethan England, the France of Louis XIV, where writers, artists, and scientists of all countries stood a fair chance of being supported by the King or by the nobility, are so many outstanding examples of what aristocratic societies can do for liberal knowledge. This type of culture was truly liberal, because it was not expected to bring about any practical results either for those who paid for it or for those who were being paid to produce it. Princes would then find it natural to favor the development of the arts and the sciences simply because they knew that beauty and truth were good things to be enjoyed for their own sake. Artists and scientists had no idea of making a fortune out of their work. So long as their protectors gave them enough to live, they considered themselves highly privileged, as indeed they were, since they were free to live a wholly unpractical life, the only one in which they were interested.

The kind of education that befits such a type of aristocratic culture is easy to define: it is the education of the elite, by an elite, and for an elite. In such circumstances, education is the received method whereby an aristocracy recruits its future members or, at least, the competent body of citizens who, sharing in the benefits of the prevailing social system, are interested in insuring its survival. No wonder, then, that at the very times when it gave birth to a Dante, a Shakespeare, or a Descartes, Europe had practically no system of public schools; so much so, that by far the larger number of its inhabitants were illiterate. Aristocracy is a great producer of higher learning and of liberal knowledge, only it keeps it to itself; it is a spring rather than a stream.

Not so in democratic societies, whose systems of education naturally follow the rule of their political life. What they want is an education of the whole people, given by men who themselves belong among the people and, consequently, intended for the greater benefit of the people in its entirety. This time we find ourselves confronted with a powerful system of intellectual irrigation whose streams are visible everywhere; the only questions are: Where is the spring? Where are the sources? Can there still be sources in a society whose natural tendency is to universalize education and, consequently, to equalize it?

This is a genuine issue, which we must have the courage to face, not in any spirit of criticism, and still less of hostility, toward democracy, but with the sincere desire to understand its educational problems and thus throw some light on its difficulties. There are several interrelated reasons why, whereas aristocracies were more interested in creating intellectual culture than in spreading it, democracies seem to be more eager to distribute higher learning than to create it. Among these reasons there is a particularly obvious one. If our school system exists, not in view of a chosen minority, but in view of all, its average level should answer the average level of the population as a whole. Hence the unavoidable consequence that the best gifted among the pupils will be discriminated against. Nor should we imagine that creative minds will multiply in direct proportion to the growth of the school population. The reverse is much more likely to happen. In aristocratic societies, genius has often found access to higher culture, even under adverse circumstances; in democratic societies, it will have no higher culture to which to gain access. Since equality in ignorance is easier to achieve than equality in learning, each and every teacher will have to equalize his class at the bottom level rather than at the top one, and the whole school system will spontaneously obey the same law. It is anti-democratic to teach all children what only some of them are able to learn. Nay, it is anti-democratic to teach what all children can learn by means of methods which only a minority of pupils are able to follow. Since, as has been said, democracy stands for equality, democratic societies have a duty to teach only what is accessible to all and to see to it that it be made accessible to all. The overwhelming weight of their school population is therefore bound to lower the center of gravity in their school systems. The first peril for democracies, therefore, is to consider it their duty, in order to educate all citizens, to teach each of them less and less and in a less and less intelligent way.

It is not easy to say such things without sounding satirical, which I have no intention of being. I myself am an old teacher, and I would not let it be thought either that I am pining for a return of our countries to some aristocratic type of society, or that, when I remember what schools used to be around 1890, I see things deteriorating from bad to worse. Much progress has been achieved; the only point I am stressing is: Has there been progress all along the line? We are teaching more and more, but are we teaching better and better? And, if not, is it not because, confronted as they are with the legitimate task of providing learning for all their citizens, modern democracies have to cope with entirely new problems for which they are not prepared? The task of turning learning into a commodity and education into a public service is something both necessary and unheard of, for which there is no historical precedent. We should not feel too surprised to see the democratic State handling education like coal, hydroelectric power, or public means of transportation. The State must control everything in order to insure the equal distribution of all necessary goods among all citizens, including even education. We do not want this progress to stop, we simply do not want it to defeat its own purpose; and this is what the democratic State is going to do if it does not handle learning according to its own nature, which, because it is born of the mind, is wholly unlike any other kind of commodity.

We have reached such a pass that pedagogical authorities are beginning to think that learning is there in view of the schools, not the schools in view of learning.[6] This very year some schoolteachers made once more the time-honored discovery that the spelling of their mother tongue stood in need of being simplified. I need not quote the name of the country, because there is not a single language in the world whose spelling could not be made simpler than it is. The only trouble is that, in order to be perfectly simple, spelling has to be purely phonetic, in which case nobody can understand what he reads. This, however, is not my point. What I am interested in is the main rule set up by the committee on the simplification of spelling in that country. According to the school inspector who wrote the report, the committee decided either to accept, or else to reject, all suggested changes "according as they could, or could not, facilitate the teaching of the language." This curious pedagogical imperialism implies that the proper function of spelling is to be taught. Such teachers do not consider themselves the servants of learning, but its owners; so they have a full right to change it in order to facilitate their work. And indeed, why not? If all citizens have an equal right to know spelling, spelling should be made foolproof and equally available to all citizens. I am sorry to say, without any trace of irony, that this is the principle which we now apply to practically all disciplines, from spelling to metaphysics. We do not impart learning such as it is, but such as it ought to be in order to be teachable to the millions. From time to time, some simple-minded professor attempts to make his pupils understand, not himself, but that which he teaches. The rumor soon begins to spread that the poor man cannot make himself understood. So he is a bad teacher, and we turn *him* out of his class, not the pupils.

Besides the general lowering of its level, another consequence follows from this democratic treatment of education at the hands of the State; namely, its predominately practical character. Nothing is more logical; and this time, since all citizens are part and parcel of the democratic State, all we have to do is to consult ourselves in order to know its will. Time and again, we have heard fathers say with solemn gravity: "I want my son to have an education." In point of fact, we all have said it ourselves, but what we really have meant is: "I want my son to get a job." A perfectly legitimate desire indeed. At the end of their studies, good students should get jobs that will turn them into citizens equally useful to themselves, to their future families, and to their country. Since such is the wish of the vast majority of its citizens, the democratic State will naturally tend to give them what they want; that is, a sound, practical education with no frills. This is what all teaching States are now doing, and they do it pretty well. Once more, I am not criticizing; I am merely trying to observe facts, and the outstanding fact, in this case, is that what we agreed to call "liberal knowledge," precisely because it has no practical usefulness, is bound to be eliminated together with the frills. The steady decline of classical studies, in Europe as well as in America, is a clear instance of what I have in mind. Even their strongest supporters cannot pretend that classical humanities are practically useful in everyday life; those among us who try to defend them on this ground are simply betraying their cause. Even if classical humanities may be put to practical use, this cannot be the reason why they should be taught. Such an aristocratic type of education simply cannot be universalized. As a consequence, no room can be made for it in the programs of schools which must cater to all citizens. So we teach them too little, or too late, which is little better than not to teach them at all. Why complain? Liberal knowledge, Newman says, is to itself its own end; in our industrial age, contemplation is a luxury which very few States can afford to subsidize. The cold truth is that the practical uselessness which recommended liberal education to Cardinal Newman's mind today justifies its exclusion from the curriculum of our democratic schools. Even societies cannot have their cake and eat it.

Yet there should be somebody to make the cake, and it is to be feared that, unless they re-examine their own educational problem, democracies will soon find themselves with nothing to eat. First of all, democratic education rests upon the principle of equality applied to the human understanding. But this application is a fallacy of the well-known type, which consists in applying to two different orders what is true of only one of them. The notion of democracy is a social one; it expresses the common will of a people to deal with its own members as if all men were born free and equal. On the contrary, human understanding is a fact of nature, and whether we like it or not, facts of nature are not equal. Nature is not democratic. Physical and intellectual inequalities can be corrected, or compensated; the democratic State can see to it that even the less gifted among its citizens be given a fair chance to learn and to know something; it can narrow the gap that separates creative genius from merely normal intellects, and even from abnormally backward ones; above all, democracy can prevent natural inequalities from begetting social privileges sometimes worse than the natural ones; yet, when all is said and done, nature can be corrected, not suppressed. Understanding is not equal in men. Intellectual life is just what it is, not what society would like it to be. Unless democracies accept its laws just as they are, they may well turn out an always larger number of teachers, they will have less and less to teach.

We are simply forgetting that intellectual superiority and fitness for speculative knowledge are one and the same thing. In this sense, liberal knowledge is the only source of all practically useful knowledge, without any exception. Classical humanities are not the only relevant example. As a token of the general nature of the problem, I beg to quote the growing misconception of what science itself actually is. On June 16,

1952, the continental edition of the British *Daily Mail* announced to its readers that the United States had their first atom submarine "nearly ready." To this the same newspaper added the following personal comment of the President of the United States: "The day that the propellers of this new submarine first bite into the water will be the most momentous day in the field of atomic science, since the first flash of light down in the desert seven years ago." A typically democratic statement indeed, in which "science" merely means "engineering." The first flash of light in the field of atomic science did not shine in any desert seven years ago, but in the minds of Einstein and of other scientists who were speculating about the structure of matter and not looking for atom bombs or for atom submarines. True science is liberal knowledge; scientists seek after it for its own sake; engineers put it to practical use; they do not want to know in order to know, but in order to make. Yet it is a positive and well-established fact that the more speculative and liberal it is, the more fruitful scientific knowledge proves to be in its practical applications. Pasteur saved millions of human lives although he himself was not a physician. Nearer home, I do not think that Dr. Banting, who was a physician, ever intended to find a specific for diabetes; yet when he first isolated insulin, the specific was found. Science found it; medicine applied it.

If this be true, our democratic system of education now finds itself at a crossroad. It has done wonders in the past and we do not want it to undo them. There must be an education for the millions; the learning included in this type of mass education should be both practical and simple, that is to say, adapted to the general needs and to the average intellectual aptitudes of its pupils; yet, at the same time, even a thoroughly democratic system of education should not allow its ceaselessly growing body to lead its head. Unless they themselves provide, not a new aristocratic social class, but their own intellectual elite, which is something different, the social and technical progress of which our modern democratic States are so justly proud will soon come to an end. In peace and war, the powerful industrial equipment of the greatest among modern nations can be rendered obsolete at any time by the abstract speculation of some unknown scientist using a few sheets of paper and a pencil in the solitude of his own study. Nor should we forget that the times of the greatest national perils are also those when foreign scientists are no longer an available commodity.[7] This is not for democracies a matter of choice. None of them can hope indefinitely to consume the products of natural aristocracy without adding its own contribution to the common good. What we now need, within our present system of universal education, is another system, this time of selection, whose proper object will be not to thwart the best gifted intellects which it is our task to educate. Unless it follows such a policy, no nation can hope to prosper for a very long time. True democracy in education certainly consists in insuring the intellectual survival of even the unfit; it cannot possibly consist in preventing the natural superiority of the fittest from bearing their fruits to the greater benefit of all.

This obvious truth should not be so hard to understand. There is nothing less democratic, in the usual sense of the word, than sports and games. Championship is the triumph of carefully cultivated natural inequalities. There is no point in pretending that, in a democracy, every citizen should be able to beat Olympic records. We simply could not do it, however hard we might try, but we do not resent the fact. We do not ask our directors of athletics to prevent some students from running as fast as they can because if they did they would run faster than the others. We do not consider it democratic to set athletic standards as low as possible. On the contrary, we fully realize the fact that the exceptional performances of a few world champions act as a fruitful challenge whose effects are actually felt in all stadiums and on all athletic fields. What is democratic, here as everywhere else, is to keep both competition and selection as widely open as possible, and then to set up the highest conceivable standard as a standing invitation to all. In short, the only sound policy for any democracy is to raise the average level of its people by cultivating the excellency of the best among its citizens.[8]

What we understand so well concerning the education of the body, could we not understand it concerning the education of the mind? Unless we do, we shall go on drifting along the same way which has already led us to make pedagogy the judge of learning. It can be concisely described in Shakespeare's terse words: "My foot my tutor." High school programs adapted to the kind of pupils they receive; university programs adapted to the kind of pupils that high schools are permitted by law to provide; and no provision made for the free development of liberal knowledge under all its forms, whose creative activity is the life and blood of any system of education! Things have gone so far that I might cite several countries in which, despairing as it were of saving higher learning, their governments have erected, outside universities, new institutions specialized in research work, where scholars seek but do not teach, while university professors teach but do not seek. I beg to say that, in so far as public education is concerned, wholly to surrender to this new tendency would be nothing less than the beginning of the end. The remedy we need should not consist in killing the patient. Since it is the course of nature that education derives its substance from the creative activity of a few speculative minds, let us rather help nature to follow its course. Where there is no higher learning, the presence of creative minds becomes less probable, intellectual light ceases to shine, routine and pedantry set in, and living truths shrivel into desiccated formulas. Then we begin complaining about the general decay of studies, as if students could still take an interest in matters which, even for those who teach them, have already lost their meaning. The situation needs attention, but it is not desperate. All we have to do in order to mend it is to refuse to allow our educational body to grow too big for its soul, and to remember that its soul is liberal knowledge, itself the source of higher learning.

NOTES

1. A. N. Whitehead, *The Aims of Education* (Mentor Books, 1949), p. 14.
2. Newman was well aware of this derivation as well as of its ideological implications. Speaking of the word "liberal," Newman says: "Now, first, in its grammatical sense it is opposed to *servile*; and by 'servile work' is understood, as our catechisms inform us, bodily labour, mechanical employment, and the like, in which the mind has little or no part." (*The Idea of a*

University, London: Longman's, Green and Co., 1912, p. 106.) Liberal knowledge, Newman has just observed, is "the especial property of a University and a gentleman" (p. 106). When such expressions are used in their literal meaning, "we contrast a liberal education with a commercial education or a professional" (p. 107).

3. Newman, *The Idea of a University*, pp. 107–108.
4. Newman, *The Idea of a University*, p. 111.
5. One of the most revolutionary effects of Christianity was to call *all* men, slaves or not, ignorant or learned, to the most liberal type of knowledge, which is that of truth embraced for its own sake. Faith made it accessible to all. This is the deep-seated reason why the Catholic Church has always favored liberal studies. In as much as they are truly liberal, studies aim to lead human minds to truth enjoyed for its own sake; that is, to contemplation. And what is eternal life, if not the eternal enjoyment of absolute Truth?
6. A striking symptom of this disease, and one that deserves special study, is the present tendency of pedagogy to become an independent discipline. There are pedagogues whose ambition it is to teach how to teach. As often as not, such teachers undertake to teach disciplines which they themselves do not know, or know imperfectly, to those who know them. Their attitude implies that the divorce of teaching from learning is now complete. Moreover, this also turns teaching itself into a "servile work." What is more, the divorce of teaching from learning threatens our whole educational system with failure; for the only effective pedagogical methods are those that proceed from learning itself, through the person of the teacher, to the person of the pupil.
7. Even this very practical point is not always understood. In the Toronto *Globe and Mail*, Sept. 12, 1952, Sir Eric Rideal, a distinguished British scientist then visiting Ottawa, issued the timely warning: "You cannot trade on the originality of another country forever." If there is an obvious truth, this is one. Yet the next issue of the same paper (Sept. 13) summed up the consensus of a group of leading Canadian industrialists in this terse sentence: "Sir Eric is all wet." Their main objection was that, to carry out his suggestion "would definitely not be good for the Canadian pocketbook," the more so as "the importation of ideas is easy and there is no tax on them." This statement deserves to endure as an outstanding specimen in the history of mental parasitology. At any rate, the complete failure of Sir Eric to convey an exceedingly simple idea is enough to show that the task of importing them is not as easy as it might seem.
8. Many professors and college presidents bitterly complain about the fact that students exhibit a much more marked taste for athletics than for academic studies. I beg to suggest that the students are right on this point. To the extent that they are not "professional," sports and athletics are enjoyed for their

own sake and are to themselves their own end. From this point of view, which has not escaped the perspicacity of Cardinal Newman (*op. cit.*, pp. 107–108), "manly games, or games of skill, or military prowess, though bodily, are, it seems, accounted liberal." And rightly so. But if this is true, then athletics is now the only part of our school programs which is, officially and unrestrictedly, animated by a liberal spirit. Instead of asking for less athletics, we should rather bring back to the classroom the liberal spirit which once inspired it and still inspires athletics. Our only choice, therefore, is either to eliminate from our programs everything whose practical usefulness is not perceptible to students themselves, or else to say to them frankly that practical usefulness should not be the end of their education. Where the liberal spirit still prevails, students derive as much pleasure from the classroom as from the athletic field.

PART SIX

Summing Up

Beyond all human expressions of Christian doctrine, the living reality of divine truth, on earth and in the world of time, resides for Gilson within the Church. That is why Christianity is not for him an abstract doctrine embodied in a book; it is the eternal God present in the Church. If Christian doctrine is expressed in human words, Gilson also believes that the faith of the Church in divine truth transcends the merely human and therefore changeable expressions of that truth. And Gilson, himself a wandering scholar in the service of Christian truth, has come to know the Church the world over and to know as well, with moving sensitiveness and humility, when he is on Christian soil anywhere in the world.

20. Wisdom and Time

One of the most noteworthy characteristics of present-day Catholicism is the desire of Catholic believers to be better instructed in their faith. The fact is not absolutely new. In a sense, it is as old as the Church herself. For not only has baptism always implied a profession of faith from which was born the Apostles' Creed, but we can scarcely read the sermons preached by St. Augustine to his people without envying the faithful to whom the Bishop of Hippo set forth, with moving eloquence, the most profound knowledge of God and of the economy of salvation. Today it is no longer only the faithful of Hippo or of France that are in question; it is the whole body of the Church taught that is seeking instruction from the teaching Church. The Christendom of today, like that of the distant and more recent past, believes and knows what it believes, but it has never experienced so strong a desire to know why and how it believes.

This desire is born of a need. From the time of her birth, and by the express injunction of Jesus Christ Himself, the Church has taught "all" nations. For one who reads attentively the writings of the Apologists—Justin, Tatian, Minucius Felix, and so many others—nothing is more remarkable than their sharp awareness of the new character and (if one may venture to adopt today an epithet so cheapened by current usage) the truly revolutionary nature of the Christian enterprise. Before the time of the Gospel, the truth concerning man and the world had remained the privilege of a single social class, and even of the intellectual elite of a chosen people, the Greek people. Chosen in another sense, the Jewish people themselves hesitated to believe their own prophets when they invited them to recognize the sublime truth that God was not their God alone but the God of all men. Contrariwise, from the time of the preaching of Christ and the teaching of St. Paul, it became clear that all men, learned or ignorant,

Greeks or barbarians, rich or poor, free or slave, were called by God to know the very same truth concerning the universe, man and his destiny. In the whole history of humanity one has never seen the abolition of privilege comparable in depth or universality to the preaching of the Gospel offering to all men without distinction a saving faith. Indeed, it was even because this faith was offered to all men without exception, as well as by a God Who transcended both the world and man, that its truth had to be a truth of faith.

It is still a truth of faith. It will always remain such, and this is what we must understand before anything else in entering upon the salutary and even indispensable work of instructing ourselves in our religion. Twenty centuries of philosophy, of science, and even of theology have not added or taken away an iota from the substance of hope and faith that all Christians have in the word of God. One need not at all be a learned theologian to understand the main points of this divine teaching. The Christian understands that the universal history of the world is a "sacred history" whose decisive moments are creation, the fall of man, the Incarnation and the Redemption, and including the return to God, through His grace, of a nature at length restored by justice and by love. Open at random any of the voluminous thirteenth- or fourteenth-century commentaries on the *Sentences* of Peter Lombard, for example, those of St. Bonaventure or Duns Scotus; open any of the learned theological *summae* that have come down to us from Albert the Great, Alexander of Hales, or Thomas Aquinas; pile these mountains of theology one on the other; add to them all the speculations of the Fathers throughout the first twelve centuries of the Church, all the speculations of the masters of theology who commented on them and developed and enriched them, including the writings of Cardinal Newman and of so many others as well—you will not find there anything more or anything other than what every Christian can understand of his catechism, anything that is not implied in the Apostles' Creed, any truth that is not first received from the word of God.

Under the first and most striking of its aspects, therefore, the substance of faith presents itself to the Christian, even in the very letter that expresses it, as possessing a stability that is impervious to the passage of time. Only, it is of the first importance to understand a certain point if we wish to avoid illusions that can be fatal as well as rich in misleading problems. This stability of the substance of faith is not part of the order of time; this immobility is not an exemption from movement that is possible; this immutability is not the privilege of a reality which, of itself mutable, would be placed under a divine injunction not to change. Divine by its essence, the substance of the Christian faith is not motionless but eternal. This is indeed why the countless problems that torment the mind of so many unbelievers as well as believers, and sometimes even theologians, concerning the manifold relations of the Christian faith to history must be set aside because they are, first and foremost, tricks of the imagination. For the believer, the deposit conserved by the Church is something divine. It is therefore neither in time nor part of time, and hence the problem is groundless. For the unbeliever, there is nothing divine or eternal present in history, and the problem is therefore equally groundless. Faith alone, stark and unadorned, is worth infinitely more to us than any so-called theological speculation that is saddled with an illusion of this kind. There is no becoming of the eternal. God has no history, and neither does faith have a history, since, even in time, faith is the grasping of a substance that is eternal.

But if faith does not have a history, the believer and his world do have one. They are history in their very essence, since, with the exception of Him Who is, everything is a creature; that is to say, that mixture of being and non-being which is called "becoming." The universe has a history, and physics is today trying to decipher its origins, to calculate its probable duration, and to visualize its course. Life has a history, which includes within its course the appearance of man, but which forms as a whole a "universal history" that includes all living things. Human events form a history, including that of Revelation, whose moments are registered in time, and that of the Church, with her theologians and their theologies following after one another according to dates that we know and under diverse circumstances, of which each doctor and each doctrine bears the recognizable imprint. There is no formula or word to designate correctly this co-presence of faith to time which it enriches but which it transcends. Since becoming does not involve faith, faith is not truly "engaged" in time. Having neither a past nor a future, faith is not present to time as one instant of time would be present to another. Indeed, it is only by a metaphor that we can situate "in" time this participation in the divine, which, being That Which is, escapes becoming. Hence, without abandoning a language that is necessarily deficient in such questions, we must be on our guard against the tricks of imagination to which language gives rise. Faith, which does not change, sheds its abiding light on a world that is ceaselessly changing; or, to adopt a more generalized statement of the problem, the redemptive grace of Christ dwells abidingly in a nature that is in continual change.

This relationship is a fundamental one. That is why every Christian who wishes to understand the place in the world that his faith has established for him must begin by trying to understand the meaning of the relationship. Some opponents of Christianity follow the line of denouncing its sterility, and sometimes even its harmfulness, in order to fight against it. The Church, they say, has brought forth nothing new, it has created nothing in any domain whatever. Coming to terms with all political and social regimes, the Church accepted the slavery of the ancient world without denouncing its immorality; she accepted the absolutism of kings and emperors, just as she has siphoned off her part of the benefits resulting from the profits of capitalism; she has used science without having done anything to aid in its birth, if indeed she did not oppose it; she has exploited for her own strictly theological purposes philosophies which, like those of Plotinus and Aristotle, she had no part whatever in creating. Briefly, in all orders of human activity, all the great revolutions and all the decisive steps of progress were taken without her, if not against her; and one may conclude that, far from serving as the guide of the human caravan, the Church has never done anything else than to misdirect or retard the march of that caravan. Contrariwise, some Christian apologists continually exalt the genius of Christianity whose enriching and endlessly creative activity in the course of history they have no difficulty in showing. What a change in morals since the coming of the Gospel! A society of beings free and equal in their rights, in which woman has progressively acquired a place of honor alongside man; the revelation of the high dignity of the human person, who can never be used as a means but must always be treated as an end; everywhere, in the arts and letters and even in philosophy itself, such an unprecedented blossoming of discoveries, forms and ideas unknown in antiquity, that it would be impossible to write the history of human progress for the last twenty centuries without revealing at every step of the way the enriching influence of the Church. In this controversy, which has a new birth in the course of centuries under a new form, and in which every Voltaire finds a Chateaubriand to answer him, every Condorcet a Bonald or a de Maîstre, who is wrong, and who is right?

We cannot reply that one or the other is, or even that both are, since the formulation of the problem is common to both parties and presents the same deformity in both. The adversaries of the Church and the apologists who pursue them both commit the error of reasoning as though the deposit of faith were a temporal reality; that is to say, a reality engaged in time and working together with the other forces of nature to bring about, like them, effects that are strictly natural. Hence the indignation of those who speak as though Christianity has produced everything. But the problem does not lie here. For faith is a grace whose work does not consist in producing nature but in sanctifying and saving nature.

Those who neglect this distinction open themselves to inexplicable confusions, and they blame or praise the Church for having accomplished or not accomplished that which she did not have the mission to accomplish. At one and the same time, they either oppose the Church or count on her to accomplish that which she will never accomplish. The Church has no *Christian* solution to the problem of government; she is neither monarchist nor republican nor even democratic. There is not, let us say it in so many words, there is not any political regime that takes its origin in Sacred Scripture; but Christians can learn from Sacred Scripture how to make Christian any political regime in which they may take part, under particular circumstances, in the course of time. No more than she is in charge of the political organization of peoples, which is a task belonging to the temporal order, the Church has no

"Christian" solution to economic or social problems. She is neither capitalist nor Socialist, neither for nor against free trade, neither for nor against free enterprise. Neither the Gospel nor the Christian faith has any opinion on bimetallism and on the question of knowing whether a money system can dispense with the gold standard. All this belongs to Caesar, and it belongs to men to find working solutions to such problems. The Church knows very well that, in a temporal order subject to constant change, every solution of any given problem is provisional. She neither can nor wishes to bestow her own eternity on any of these solutions, since they cannot be the vessels of such an eternity. But the Church has Christian rules—that is to say, immutable and divine rules—to which every solution of a temporal problem must defer in order to be right. When Isaias declares that a king rules through justice and that princes exercise their power through the right, it matters little whether the prince is a king, one of those so-called democratic majorities whose tyranny is no less terrifying than the tyranny vested in one person, or some supreme soviet enslaving the people in the name of the rights of the people: the Church has no human formula by which to assure political, economic, or social justice; but she knows that every solution of the problem in question which does not aim to let justice prevail is in principle false and evil. Everything that takes place in time, and does so even for ends and through means that belong to nature, is directed, set straight, and judged by the Church in a light that is eternal.

The relations of faith to reason and to philosophy are of the same sort. Many persons—indeed many Christians and even Catholic theologians—deny that there can exist a "Christian philosophy"—and, in a sense, they are right. Sacred Scripture is not a treatise in philosophy: there is not a single proposition in it formulated by any author under philosophical inspiration, even though there are not wanting propositions in Scripture from which a philosopher can profit. Everything in Scripture is true because God Who says it is infallible. Faith in God precedes the acquiescence of the Christian to the truth of Scripture. Inversely, neither Plato nor Aristotle nor Plotinus, who created philosophy, owes anything to the Judeo-Christian revelation. Using, within the domain of time, the sole light of the natural reason in order to find a meaning for the destiny of man and to give man his proper place in the world, these philosophers have formulated answers to the problem, in part contradictory and in part coherent among themselves, which will never be final and which other philosophers will constantly take up, criticize, and complete. Philosophy is something temporal in the same sense, though not to the same degree, as is politics or sociology. In one sense, of course, the problems of philosophy likewise transcend time, but, in point of fact, it is not philosophy but the philosophers who pose these problems—the very same philosophers who live and follow after one another in time, who ask themselves the same questions in a variety of languages, and who discuss these questions on the basis of data that are perpetually changing. Scientifically, politically, economically, and socially we are no longer living in the same world as that of Aristotle, of St. Thomas Aquinas, of Descartes, of Kant, or even, in spite of the pretensions of his disciples, of Karl Marx. Repeatedly undertaken in the past with varying outcomes, the work of philosophy will always be there to be undertaken again, and those who will undertake it will again be philosophers, whether Christians or not, seeking within time what can be learned on the destiny of man and of the world from the natural light of reason.

The extreme complexity of the problem raised by the relations of philosophy to the Christian faith is due precisely to this fact. On this very morning, Monday, June 11, 1950, I returned to the writing of this article after reading in a current Parisian daily the following words: "The Church possesses a philosophical doctrine that is proper to her; to make Christians that are subject to her teaching, this is what the Church requires before anything else." No, the Church does not have a "philosophical" doctrine that is proper to her, but she has a faith that is proper to her; and since this faith implies a general view of the universe and of man, almost from the very beginning the Christian faith entered into a dialogue with rival views that the philosophers owed to the light of the natural reason unaided by any religious faith. This was inevitable. More than any other part of nature involved in time, metaphysics had to be assumed by the word of God and by the eternal truth that this revealed word made known to men. This is the origin of the progressive elaboration of what is today called "theology," whose peak is to be located in the twelfth, thirteenth, and fourteenth centuries, when, in the words of one of them, the Scholastics understood the necessity of "mixing" philosophy with sacred teaching; that is, without interruption or division, to help theology through the resources of metaphysics to reach a certain understanding of faith and likewise to help philosophy through the transcendent illuminations of faith, by directing the natural reason—"*sicut stella rectrix*"—toward truths of which it did not as yet know that it was capable. The only "philosophy" proper to the Church is linked to the *intellectus fidei:* the understanding of the revealable and, to some extent, the understanding of what has been revealed.

This situation of theology, conceived as a science of the word of God received by faith, exposes the student of theology to two contrary illusions, against both of which he must be on guard with equal diligence. These are the identifying of theology with faith, or, contrariwise, the identifying of the word of God with his own natural understanding in philosophical terms. A simple remark, left to the reflection of the reader, will perhaps best clarify the delicate point at issue. Since her beginnings, the Church has had only one and the same faith, but she has known and she continues to permit several theologies. In fact, to use philosophy as an auxiliary science of theology, which indeed uses many others as well, is to place at the service of the word of God a type of knowledge that is in itself more perfect than the knowledge of faith—since to know is better than to believe—but one whose certitude, being purely human, is not infallible as is the certitude of the word of God. Every Christian believes unshakably that God is Being, because God has said so Himself and He cannot deceive either Himself or us. This certitude of faith is, for every Christian, one, necessary, and universal. But what is "being"? To this philosophical question Scripture does not give an answer. A theologian such as St. Augustine who, as St. Thomas Aquinas has aptly remarked, "was filled with the teaching of the Platonists," did not understand being as did St. Thomas himself, whose own personal genius directed itself rather to the data furnished by the teaching of Aristotle. The absolute transcendence of faith is precisely what permits the theologian to call that which is weaker to the aid of that which is stronger without in any way compromising the strength of the latter. The eternity of faith equally permits the theologian to seek his understanding in doctrines known to the theologian either at the time when they appear or at the time when he is living. Had he lived at the time of Augustine, Thomas Aquinas would not have known Aristotle; and Augustine would not have been filled with the Neo-Platonism of Plotinus if Marius Victorinus had not translated the writings of Plotinus, just as William of Moerbeke was later to translate the writings of Aristotle to the profit of St. Thomas Aquinas. Inferior in certitude to the divine word, involved in the becoming of history through the philosophy that it is using, the theological understanding of faith cannot have either the necessity or the immutability of its object.

By a contrary illusion, some imagine that theology is necessarily caught within the ceaseless becoming of the philosophy whose services it needs. It seems to them that since philosophy is constantly changing, theology must constantly change along with it. This is to confuse two disciplines that everyone distinguishes by their objects, their methods, and their ends. It is not yet clear that the latest philosophy is necessarily the best. Science alone progresses in time with an irreversible movement. When science approaches those general theories that border on metaphysical speculation—for example, in dealing with the origin of life or with the continuous or discontinuous structure of matter—it is then seen to hesitate at different times and even sometimes to retrace its steps. On the contrary, when it does not mistake itself for an appendix to positive science, metaphysics is or can be entirely present to itself at any moment in time when it is brought together in the thought of a philosopher. It is possible that a given metaphysician, coming after another one, sees the truth better than his predecessor, but the contrary has often happened and is happening every day. Any schoolboy knows more science than Plato did, but not one of our contemporaries is Plato's equal as a philosopher. That is also why one can be a scientist without knowing the history of the sciences, whereas one cannot be a philosopher without knowing the history of philosophy. As for theology, it is strictly true to say that the adventures of metaphysics do not concern it. Its object is not the meaning of the world, but the meaning of the word of God; its proper light is not reason but faith; its method does not lead it from understanding to understanding: *non intelligo ut credam, sed credo ut intelligam.* We are at this point outside time and the becoming that belong to philosophy; we are involved in the impenetrability of a faith whose substance is as eternal as its object.

That is why the evolution of theology in no way resembles the evolution of science or of the philosophies that derive from it. True, it admits of progress, and this progress is irreversible, as is that of science; but this is true for another reason, in a different sense, and according to a different rhythm. It is not necessary that every change in the face of the world brought about by science and metaphysics carry with it a corresponding change in our understanding of God and His word. A recent example will best express the point. When Bergson, in his criticism of the naïve mechanism of the scientism of his day, brought to light the aspect of becoming in reality, excellent minds immediately concluded from this, and some still think, that Catholic theology had therefore to be reformed and to be endowed with a modern God Who likewise was becoming. Today other thinkers are disturbed at a theology that does not quickly set about to remake itself to the image of contemporary existentialism. This is to be mistaken concerning the science of theology and its object. Theology undertakes to say what we can know about God, not by beginning with the philosophies of Heidegger, of Bergson, of Descartes, or even of Aristotle, but by beginning with the word of God, which does not pass away.

We are now led to certain important consequences. In the first place, no theologian worthy of the name has ever adapted the Christian faith to any philosophy, even when he made use of the language of that philosophy. This would have been to reduce theology to being nothing more than a metaphysics. That philosophy has surpassed Aristotle is therefore not a sufficient ground for thinking that Thomistic theology has itself been surpassed. In fact, to surpass Thomistic theology, one would have to surpass the Thomistic understanding of *Ego sum qui sum*, which lies well beyond Aristotle and the opposition between being and becoming proper to the finite being of the philosophers. Secondly, the irreversibility of theological progress does not rest on its irrevocable advances but on its definitive acquisitions. Since faith does not change, there are some understandings of its object which it was once permissible to discuss but which are withdrawn from discussion as soon as their definitive formula has been found. Theology contains definitive gains, and those who are disturbed by this fact simply do not know what theology is. What they are seeking is a philosophy, and that is also why—as one can see from the tragically moving instance of Father Laberthonnière harshly criticizing St. Thomas Aquinas—they reduce to a philosophy the theology they are attacking and are astonished that it does not satisfy them either as theology or as philosophy. Finally, because the steps of progress made by theology are the result of the deepening of its object, they are slow and far apart in time, even though a continuing and collective effort of reflection joins and prepares them. One can say of these steps that they are the grasping of a tradition, internal to that tradition itself. Theology must thus be learned. Nothing is more dangerous or, alas, more common than a theologian who chafes under his own ignorance, who is impatient to surpass a limit that he himself has not reached, and who is determined to replace by a new construction the old one whose order and significance escape him. Among all the sciences, there is none in which docility is more imperatively needed on the part of the student. The worst enemy of discovery in theology is the impatience to innovate.

What is the measure and the norm of theological progress? The Church, which is Christ Himself, keeper and sole interpreter of His thought. She alone can know and decide whether what was in doubt ought to have been said or not said, ought henceforth to be said or not said. By all that it includes of the human, the work of the theologian is fallible. It is not a cause of scandal, nor is it even something necessarily blameworthy, if an error should find its way within the most scrupulous effort of a finite mind striving toward the understanding of its faith. Indeed, it is hard to see how there could be theological progress without running the risk that accompanies all research, even though there is a radical difference that at this point separates theology from the other sciences. There is no orthodoxy in the sciences of nature, but there is an orthodoxy in the science of God. This is demanded by the nature of theology itself, as well as by the nature of its object. The rule of faith and the rule of the Church are absolutely one, and that is why the Church is the only authorized interpreter of faith, the only competent and supreme judge of that understanding of faith that constitutes theology. The Church's definitions, decisions, and even recommendations fix the true positions of faith wherever these are known and direct the effort of theologians toward the acquisition of new positions. The history of theology is the history of theologians who have dedicated themselves and who are still dedicated to advance, under the teaching authority of the Church, within the understanding of one and the same faith.

This simple truth is not always understood by historians, even by some historians who are Catholics. God, Who is the object of theology, transcends theology; all the more does He transcend philosophy, science, and history. And just as the methods of philosophy are no longer adequate when we turn to the consideration of God, the methods of history are found to be inadequate and even misleading when they are applied to the word of God and to the truth that this word expresses. There is no philosophy or exegesis of history adequate to the task of determining completely and once for all that literally supernatural reality that is the "meaning of the word of God." Since it refused the authority of the Church, which is Christ Himself, interpreting for us His own word, Protestant theology had to take refuge in philology, as though the teaching of our Savior, having died with Him, was reduced to the meaning of certain words pronounced once upon a time and definable with the aid of grammars and dictionaries. The outcome of this undertaking is well known, and the work of the learned Adolf Harnack is its permanent model: beginning with the Gospels, Christianity is thought of as forming a departure from the teaching of Christ, the whole theology of the Fathers is a contamination of that teaching at the hands of the Hellenic spirit, and the Scholasticism of the middle ages is its final corruption. A strange historical method, surely, whose last word is that the history it is recounting is devoid of meaning and strictly without object!

But even greater is the illusion of a Catholic historian measuring by this criterion alone a reality that for him completely transcends it! No more than philosophy, and indeed less so, will philology exhaust the meaning of the word of God. It is a profound truth, grasped from the beginning of Christian speculation, that the literal sense of Scripture, while always true in itself, is pregnant with other truths of which it is the sign. Up to a point, philology can certainly establish the probable meaning of the sacred text for a man of a certain historical period expressed in words taken from his mother tongue; but to accept by faith that a text is inspired is at the same time to believe that God is speaking to man in that text—and God is not in time. Protestant exegesis proves nothing at all in establishing that a certain Catholic dogma, defined in the twentieth century, is not found in so many words in the text of Scripture; but Catholic exegesis has equally no need to prove that it is found there identically in this form. Certain that the word of the Church is the word of the living God, the Catholic theologian knows very well that the unfolding of the divine deposit of faith of which the Church is the guardian will come to an end only when time does, and even then the infinite richness of this deposit will not be exhausted. But the Catholic theologian likewise knows that this work of developing, which does not belong to any one man of whatever holiness or genius, belongs in fact to the Church, of which Christ is the head and he is a member. The teaching voice of the Church is alone the judge of the understanding of faith.

Words of this sort seem harsh, and especially to those for whom theology is nothing more than a kind of pious reflection in which each one ought to remain free to make his own way. But for anyone who understands and accepts them, such words are a source of liberation. And this they are for philosophy no less than for theology, since they are an invitation to both to fill themselves at the spring of wisdom instead of abandoning it to follow the course of the stream. Assuredly philosophy is wisdom in its own order, and theology is wisdom in a still higher order, but which yet is not the highest of all. It is St. Thomas Aquinas himself who recalls this fact from the very first lines of his Commentary on the *Sentences*. Among so many definitions of Wisdom that have been proposed, the best is that of St. Paul: Wisdom is Jesus Christ. Wisdom is therefore the Word, the cause of that which takes place in time, not at all as Himself involved in time, but as eternity.

21. Where Is Christendom?

Where have I known Christendom?

I have known it in books, to be sure, since it is impossible to write or teach the history of the middle ages without at every turn meeting this reality, so living, so manifold, so difficult to define. Yet I believe that I have also known the reality in itself and, so to speak, that I have experienced it in many an encounter during a life that was not much less wandering than that of a thirteenth-century teacher. Where, then, have I known this reality Christendom?

The name begins by raising in my memory the vision of a multitude of churches, great and small, that welcomed me and sometimes harbored me, for an hour, a few weeks, even months, as I went from city to city teaching like a wandering scholar of bygone days. How can I name them all? They are too many to remember, and there are some I no longer remember by name, although their images still bring back to me, after so many years, the very same emotion that I once experienced on entering them.

What was the name of that church in Chicago, not far from the station, to the right and near the entrance to Michigan Avenue? I no longer know. But how good it was to be there, and what peace of mind awaited me there as I entered from the streets of the great city! Nothing in it disturbed the silence, save for a thin trickle of water from Lake Michigan that fell drop by drop in a grotto of Lourdes. Where was I? Neither in America nor in France, nor at any geographical point on earth. Yet I had surely reached a journey's end, since I was at home: I was in Christendom. And you, St. Agnes of New York, that every year celebrates Midnight Mass but two steps from Grand Central Station; you, Church of St. Paul, my Cambridge parish while I was at Harvard, where there are so many communions that they begin at the elevation; you, St. Basil's Church, my Toronto parish, not to call you my family;

you, Notre Dame of the Assumption, enthroned over Rio de Janeiro, amidst banana gardens, between the most beautiful sky and the most beautiful sea in the world—are you not all my parishes when I am away from my own? The same Mass, the same priests, the same communion in the same God given by the same priests to the faithful of the same faith—all this creates, at every moment and in every place, an immense spiritual society which knows neither geographic barriers nor political boundaries and in which the Christian always feels that he is at home. How, how shall I forget that humble church in Bloomington that was my parish during the week in 1940 when I was teaching at Indiana University?

It was my very first Mass at this church. All of us—or almost all—had received communion, when a choirboy left the sanctuary, walked the length of the church to the last row of pews where, as a stranger, I had taken my place. With folded hands he bowed slightly and whispered the following words with a perfectly straight face: "The pastor wishes to inform you that if you do not take breakfast with him in the rectory you will be excommunicated!" Thus did I become a member of that parish, and also learned on that very day that, wherever he may be, *the Christian is not a stranger in any parish, for whereever there is a parish he stands on Christian soil*. But, once again, where have I known Christendom?

Let me go back twenty years, all of them crowded with so many such memories, and let me stop a moment in August of 1926 at Charlottesville, near that charming University of Virginia where the double colonnade of Jefferson so gracefully encircles lawns that are always green. How can I speak of the peculiar charm of that part of the United States where the South begins, with its ever-present old-world civilization and that refined courtliness of manners that lived once upon a time, so it seems, in France? I find it again in my colleagues, my students, and, as it seems to me, among the colored people, whom you will meet everywhere and who are engaged in the humblest occupations of social life. Shall I admit that the mystery of their smile and the sweetness of their singing speech have drawn and intrigued me since my arrival? Yet I have been forestalled. Between these men and myself the difference in color raises an insuperable barrier. Even if he has only one drop of black blood in his veins, not one of these men can be enrolled among my students. The truth that I teach to others I cannot teach to such a person. I could not without public scandal invite him to take lunch with me, and, as happened to me early in my stay, I would be guilty of an error if I sat near him in a streetcar; the conductor would then invite me firmly to take another seat, since the seats for the whites are for whites and those for blacks are for blacks. But let us not judge. These are complex problems whose essential factors no doubt escape me. Instead, let us enter the Catholic church at Charlottesville when Mass is being celebrated. I shall not say that the blacks do not tend to group together, but this is without doubt a matter of habit, since the groups mingle with one another and it is perfectly clear that no pew is specifically set aside for them. But there is especially one moment during Mass when even the social decree that separates them seems to disappear: it is the moment of communion. United in the same faith, all proceed together to kneel side by side at the same table of the same Father, to Whom they are all equally sons. Shall I admit that I expected to find my Church there? Yes, it was she, and I knew her by this sign. But at the same time I learned that, *wherever the love of God breaks the barriers of race and class, there also Christendom is to be found.*

But, finally, where have I known Christendom?

Let us journey even farther into the past. In September 1922, I was in Moscow, in a Russia convulsed by revolution and ravaged by famine. I was welcomed by portraits of Lenin and Trotsky in the stations and by busts of Karl Marx on the squares. Perhaps a Catholic church still remained somewhere in Moscow, but I doubted it and, whatever may have been the case, no one was able to point it out to me. On the other hand, wandering alone up and down the streets, I came upon a chapel at the meeting point of Krasnaia Place and the Kremlin walls. A glance at my Baedeker informed me that I was in the presence of one of the most celebrated shrines of Russia, the Iverskaïa Tchassovnia, or Iberian Chapel of the Mother of God. The Baedeker adds this prosaic remark: "The chapel is regularly full; be careful of pickpockets." It was in fact so full that many of the faithful, being unable to enter, knelt on the steps to pray, out in the street and against the walls behind which Lenin himself and the supreme government of the Soviets sat on guard. I shall never know whether this or that Christian was a pickpocket. But I do know this. Seeing a prisoner coming toward us on the same side of the street between two guards, one Christian present rose, walked toward the prisoner, and gave him the kiss of peace. On that day, before the Iverskaïa Tchassovnia, I am sure that I saw Christ Himself console an afflicted man. This time we were not in a church and this man was not a Catholic, but he taught me that *wherever my neighbor is Christ, there also Christendom is to be found.*

To these varied experiences each one of us could add many others that are probably still more varied. So much so, that it is a question to know how to bring them together into a unity. Nothing would be more convenient than to reduce them all to some simple notion. But perhaps this is not possible, and it is certainly noteworthy that theologians have never tried to do it. For centuries people have used the term *Christendom*, or its Latin equivalent *Christianitas*, to designate something other than *Christianity*, but it is not apparent that any effort has been made to define a precise concept corresponding to it.

It is enough to speak to a few theologians about Christendom and to observe their spontaneous reactions to it in order to understand how it has come about that we do not as yet have a theology of Christendom. As soon as they are asked for a definition, they reduce it to the notion of the *Church*, without which in fact *Christendom* is incomprehensible. The notion of the Church alone can enable us to establish Christendom on a firm foundation, but there is reason to think that on certain points Christendom is distinguished from the Church. No doubt the notion of the Church, conceived as a society spiritual in essence, necessarily includes something temporal within it. This is to be seen more clearly in Vatican City than anywhere else. Moreover, to be assured on the point, one has only to think of the immense organization of the "Ecclesiastical Hierarchy"—a prolongation on earth of the "Celestial Hierarchy"—to have some realization of the many temporal embodiments with which the Church has covered the whole earth. Let us realize, however, that this temporal embodiment of the Church is the one that she herself has given to herself as Church, and that it is therefore wholly spiritualized. This hierarchy that proceeds from the Pope down to the humblest believers; these churches, missions, and parishes, with all their Christian members; these convents without number with their religious men and women; finally, all those institutions, whether of corporal mercy or instruction, that form as it were the flowering and the growth of the Christian life of grace in the temporal order—all these manifestations are nothing other than the soul of the Church herself in her sensible incarnation and thereby rendered visible before all eyes. Created by the Church and for her ends, the temporal body of the Church is consequently an integral part of the Church herself; and this is precisely why it is not exactly the temporal of Christendom. As subject to the State, we Christians are all members of a society of which the State is seeking the common temporal end; as subject to the Church, we are all members of a society of which the Church is seeking the common spiritual end, and the very temporal part of the Church is integrally directed to this end; as members of Christendom, we are part of a third social group, one that is neither quite the State nor quite the Church, but one that is formed by the various members of various states in so far as they are aware of belonging to the same Church and of being all disciples of Christ.

PART VII

The Writings of Etienne Gilson

Etienne Gilson has been a writer for over fifty years. From among his many writings the present listing includes the titles of his books, the titles of books translated into English, and the titles of a few well-known articles. I have left out all translations of Gilson's books into other modern languages. With few exceptions, I likewise have not mentioned any of the several hundred articles and reviews that Gilson has written between 1908 and the present. Thus, articles in *Sept* (1934, 1935), in *Vie intellectuelle* (1945), and in *Le Monde* (1945–1950), not to mention purely professional periodicals, are missing from the present bibliography. Such as it is, this bibliography has a very modest purpose; namely, not to meet the technical needs of the research student, but rather to serve the general needs of anyone interested in the fundamental writings of Gilson as a historian and philosopher.

The Writings of Etienne Gilson

1. *Index Scolastico-cartésien* (Paris: F. Alcan, 1912, 1913).
2. *La liberté chez Descartes et la théologie* (Paris: F. Alcan, 1913).
3. "Art et métaphysique" (*Revue de métaphysique et de morale*, vol. XXIII, 1916, pp. 243–267).
4. *Le Thomisme, Introduction au système de saint Thomas d'Aquin* (Strasbourg: Vix, 1919).
   ——Second edition, Paris: J. Vrin, 1922.
   ——Third edition, Paris: J. Vrin, 1927. English translation, from the manuscript of the third edition, by Edward Bullough, entitled *The Philosophy of Saint Thomas Aquinas* (Cambridge, England: Heffer & Sons, 1924).
   ——Fourth edition, Paris: J. Vrin, 1942.
   ——Fifth edition, Paris: J. Vrin, 1944. English translation by L. K. Shook, C.S.B., under the title *The Christian Philosophy of Saint Thomas Aquinas* (New York: Random House, 1956).
5. *Études de philosophie médiévale* (Strasbourg: Université de Strasbourg, 1921).
6. *La philosophie au moyen age* (2 vols. Paris: Librairie Payot, 1922. Reprinted in one volume, 1925, 1930).
   ——Second edition, Paris: Librairie Payot, 1944.
7. *La philosophie de saint Bonaventure* (Paris: J. Vrin, 1924). English translation by Dom Illtyd Trethowan and F. J. Sheed, under the title, *The Philosophy of Saint Bonaventure* (New York and London: Sheed and Ward, 1938, with later reprintings).
   ——Second edition, Paris: J. Vrin, 1942.
8. "Descartes et la métaphysique scolastique" (*Revue de l'Université de Bruxelles*, vol. XXIX, 1923–24, pp. 105–139).
9. *René Descartes, Discours de la methode, Texte et commentaire* (Paris: J. Vrin, 1925, with later reprintings).

10. *Saint Thomas d'Aquin* (Paris: Gabalda, 1925, with later reprintings).
——English translation by Leo R. Ward, under the title, *Moral Values and the Moral Life* (St. Louis: Herder and Co., 1931).
11. "Pourquoi saint Thomas a critiqué saint Augustin" (*Archives d'histoire doctrinale et littéraire du moyen âge*, vol. I, pp. 5–127).
12. "Avicenne et le point de départ de Duns Scot" (*Archives d'HDLMA*, vol. II, 1927, pp. 89–149).
13. "Les sources gréco-arabes de l'augustinisme avicennisant" (*Archives d'HDLMA*, vol. IV, 1929, pp. 5–149).
14. *Introduction à l'étude de saint Augustin* (Paris: J. Vrin, 1929).
——Second edition, Paris: J. Vrin, 1942.
15. *Études sur le rôle de la pensée médiévale dans la formation du système cartésien* (Paris: J. Vrin, 1930).
16. *L'Ésprit de la philosophie médiévale* (Gifford Lectures, University of Aberdeen. 2 vols. Paris: J. Vrin, 1932).
——English translation by A. H. C. Downes, under the title, *The Spirit of Mediaeval Philosophy* (London: Sheed and Ward, 1934; New York: Charles Scribner's Sons, 1934; with many later reprintings).
17. *Les idées et les lettres* (Paris: J. Vrin, 1932; reprinted, 1955).
18. "*La specificité de l'ordre philosophique*" (*Vie intellectuelle*, no. 21, pp. 404–424).
19. *Pour un ordre catholique* (Paris: Desclée de Brouwer, 1934).
20. *La théologie mystique de saint Bernard* (Paris: J. Vrin, 1934).
——English translation by A. H. C. Downes, under the title, *The Mystical Theology of Saint Bernard* (New York and London: Sheed and Ward, 1940).
21. *Le réalisme methodique* (Paris: Tequi, n.d. [1935]).
22. "Saint Thomas Aquinas" (Master Mind Lecture. *Proceedings of the British Academy*, vol. XXI, pp. 29–45; also separately printed).
23. *Christianisme et philosophie* (Paris: J. Vrin, 1936).
——English translation by Ralph McDonald, C.S.B., un-

der the title, *Christianity and Philosophy* (New York and London: Sheed and Ward, 1939).

24. *The Unity of Philosophical Experience* (The William James Lectures, Harvard University. New York: Charles Scribner's Sons, 1937).
25. "Mediaeval Universalism and Its Present Value" (given as a lecture at the Harvard Tercentenary Conference, September, 1936. For the text, see the Conference proceedings, *Independence, Convergence and Borrowing in Institutions, Thought and Art*, Cambridge, Mass.: Harvard University Press, 1937, pp. 194–215). There are several reprintings.
26. *Heloise et Abélard* (Paris: J. Vrin, 1938).
    ——English translation by L. K. Shook, C.S.B., under the title, *Heloise and Abelard* (Chicago: Henry Regnery Co., 1951).
27. *Reason and Revelation in the Middle Ages* (The Richard Lectures, University of Virginia. New York: Charles Scribner's Sons, 1938; with later reprintings).
28. "Les seize premiers theoremata de Duns Scot" (*Archives d'HDLMA*, vol. XI, 1938, pp. 5–86).
29. *Dante et la philosophie* (Paris: J. Vrin, 1939).
    ——English translation by D. Moore, under the title, *Dante the Philosopher* (New York and London: Sheed and Ward, 1948).
30. *Realisme thomiste et critique de la connaissance* (Paris: J. Vrin, 1939).
31. *God and Philosophy* (The Mahlon Powell Lectures, Indiana University. New Haven: Yale University Press, 1941; with many reprintings).
32. *Philosophie et incarnation selon saint Augustin* (Conférence Albert le Grand. Montreal: Institut Albert le Grand, 1947).
33. *L'être et l'essence* (Paris: J. Vrin, 1948).
34. *History of Philosophy and Philosophical Education* (Aquinas Lecture, Marquette University. Milwaukee: Marquette University Press, 1948).
35. *Being and Some Philosophers* (Toronto: Pontifical Institute of Mediaeval Studies, 1949).
    ——Second edition, Toronto: PIMS, 1952.

36. *Saint Bernard, Textes choisis et présentés* (Paris: Librairie Plon, 1949).
37. *L'École des muses* (Paris: J. Vrin, 1951).
———English translation by M. Ward, under the title, *The Choir of Muses* (London: Sheed and Ward, 1953).
38. *Wisdom and Love in Saint Thomas Aquinas* (Aquinas Lecture, Marquette University. Milwaukee: Marquette University Press, 1951).
39. *Jean Duns Scot, Introduction à ses positions fondamentales* (Paris: J. Vrin, 1952).
40. *Les métamorphoses de la cité de dieu* (Chaire Cardinal Mercier, 1952. Louvain: Publications Universitaires de Louvain, 1952).
41. *The Church Speaks to the Modern World, The Social Teachings of Pope Leo XIII* (An Image Book, New York: Doubleday & Company, 1954).
42. *History of Christian Philosophy in the Middle Ages* (New York: Random House, 1955).
43. *Painting and Reality* (The Mellon Lectures, National Gallery, Washington, D. C. New York: The Bollingen Foundation, 1957).

INDEX